# Dickens and the Sentimental Tradition

## Anthem Nineteenth-Century Series

The **Anthem Nineteenth-Century Series** incorporates a broad range of titles within the fields of literature and culture, comprising an excellent collection of interdisciplinary academic texts. The series aims to promote the most challenging and original work being undertaken in the field, and encourages an approach that fosters connections between areas including history, science, religion and literary theory. Our titles have earned an excellent reputation for the originality and rigour of their scholarship, and our commitment to high quality production.

### Series Editor

Robert Douglas-Fairhurst – Oxford University, UK

### Editorial Board

Seamus Perry – Oxford University, UK
Archie Burnett – Boston University, USA
Michael O'Neill – Durham University, UK
Dinah Birch – University of Liverpool, UK
Clare Pettitt – King's College London, UK
Linda K. Hughes – Texas Christian University, USA
Jo McDonagh – King's College London, UK
Simon J. James – Durham University, UK
Kirstie Blair – University of Stirling, UK
Adrian Poole – University of Cambridge, UK
Jan-Melissa Schramm – University of Cambridge, UK
Heather Glen – University of Cambridge, UK
Angela Leighton – University of Cambridge, UK
Christopher Decker – University of Nevada, USA

# Dickens and the Sentimental Tradition

*Fielding, Richardson, Sterne, Goldsmith, Sheridan, Lamb*

Valerie Purton

ANTHEM PRESS
LONDON · NEW YORK · DELHI

Anthem Press
An imprint of Wimbledon Publishing Company
*www.anthempress.com*

This edition first published in UK and USA 2014
by ANTHEM PRESS
75–76 Blackfriars Road, London SE1 8HA, UK
or PO Box 9779, London SW19 7ZG, UK
and
244 Madison Ave. #116, New York, NY 10016, USA

First published in hardback by Anthem Press in 2012

Copyright © Valerie Purton 2014

The author asserts the moral right to be identified as the author of this work.

Cover image © Christie's Images Limited 2012

All rights reserved. Without limiting the rights under copyright reserved above, no part of this publication may be reproduced, stored or introduced into a retrieval system, or transmitted, in any form or by any means (electronic, mechanical, photocopying, recording or otherwise), without the prior written permission of both the copyright owner and the above publisher of this book.

*British Library Cataloguing-in-Publication Data*
A catalogue record for this book is available from the British Library.

*Library of Congress Cataloging-in-Publication Data*
The Library of Congress catalogued the hardcover edition as follows:
Purton, Valerie.
Dickens and the sentimental tradition : Fielding, Richardson, Sterne, Goldsmith, Sheridan, Lamb / Valerie Purton.
  p. cm.
Includes bibliographical references and index.
ISBN 978-0-85728-418-1 (hardback : alk. paper)
1. Dickens, Charles, 1812–1870–Criticism and interpretation. 2. English literature–18th century–History and criticism. 3. Sentimentalism in literature. I. Title.
PR4592.S44.P87 2012
823'.8–dc23
2012021806

ISBN-13: 978 1 78308 309 1 (Pbk)
ISBN-10: 1 78308 309 3 (Pbk)

This title is also available as an ebook.

For Harry, Ford and Kisa

# CONTENTS

*Acknowledgements*   ix

*A Note on the Text*   xi

Introduction   xiii

Chapter 1   Dickens and the Sentimentalist Tradition   1

Chapter 2   Sentimentalism and its Discontents in the Eighteenth-Century Novel: Fielding, Richardson and Sterne   19
*'There was more of pleasantry in the conceit, of seeing how an ass would eat a macaroon – than of benevolence in giving him one.'*

Chapter 3   Sentimentalism and its Discontents in Eighteenth-Century Drama: Goldsmith and Sheridan   45
*'Humanity, Sir, is a jewel. I love humanity.'*

Chapter 4   Dickens and Nineteenth-Century Drama   69
*'We would indict our very dreams.'*

Chapter 5   The Early Novels and *The Vicar of Wakefield*   91
*'Everything in our lives, whether of good or evil, affects us most by contrast.'*

Chapter 6   The Later Novels   121
*'What the Waves were always saying'*

Conclusion   The Afterlife of Sentimentalism   151
*'Who will write the history of tears?'*

*Notes*   161

*Bibliography*   179

*Index*   185

# ACKNOWLEDGEMENTS

My work on Dickens and sentimentalism began when I was an undergraduate at Newnham College, Cambridge and continued under the guidance of Norman Page at the University of Alberta, Canada. I completed my PhD on the subject under the supervision of Angus Wilson, Lorna Sage and Victor Sage at the University of East Anglia. To all of my teachers I owe a great debt of gratitude. A readership at Anglia Ruskin University, Cambridge has given me the opportunity to bring my work up-to-date. I am indebted to Michael Slater for commissioning me to edit *Dombey and Son* for the Everyman series. I would also like to thank my sister Joan Williams for proofreading and copyediting, far beyond the call of sisterly duty; Jane and Bill Barry for translating German secondary sources; my Anglia Ruskin University students, especially Kathy Rees, Juliet Binns and Anne-Louise Russell, for many helpful discussions; and most of all my family, Campbell Purton, Dinah, James, Ford and Kisa Robertshaw, Harry Neale and Tom Purton for making it all worthwhile.

The Dickensian and Orion Press, publishers of the *Everyman Dickens*, have kindly given permission for the reproduction of sections of Chapters 4 and 6 which originally appeared in their pages; I am grateful to Christie's for allowing me to use a reproduction of 'What Are the Wild Waves Saying?' by Charles Nicholls (1831–1903) as part of the cover design.

# A NOTE ON THE TEXT

Unless otherwise stated, references to Dickens's novels are to the Clarendon Edition (Oxford: Clarendon Press 1966–); references to Dickens's letters are to the Pilgrim edition, ed. Madeline House and Graham Storey, 12 vols (Oxford: Clarendon Press, 1965–2002). Page references are given in the text, as are other references throughout this book, when this seems possible and useful.

## Cover Illustration

The cover illustration is a detail from 'What Are the Wild Waves Saying?' by Charles Nicholls (1831–1903), reproduced by kind permission of Christie's Images Limited, who own the copyright.

# INTRODUCTION

A colleague here asked if I didn't find the whole thing [a television documentary about the Munich Air Crash] just too relentlessly sentimental. Well, as it happens, I did, and I liked that. I don't think there's enough sentiment around. Sentimentality is a maligned emotion…I'm particularly fond of it because it's kryptonite to irony and cynicism…

—A. A. Gill, 2011[1]

Oh my dear, dear Dickens! What a No. 5 you have now given us! I have so cried and sobbed over it last night, and again this morning; and felt my heart purified by those tears, and blessed and loved you for making me shed them; and I can never bless and love you enough.

—Francis Lord Jeffrey, 1847[2]

Men ought not to be laughed at for weeping until we come to a more clear Notion of what is to be imputed to the Hardness of the Head, and the Softness of the Heart.

—Richard Steele, 1722[3]

This book began over two decades ago with my desire to achieve a fuller and fairer reading of Dickens. It seemed to me then that critics dismissing great swathes of Dickens's novels as 'sentimental', felt that they had thereby satisfactorily settled a critical question, whereas in fact they had merely raised several new ones. Dickens's sentimental scenes and characters were to me as crucial to the overall power of the novels as his darker or comic figures and scenes. Oscar Wilde, who famously could not read the death of Little Nell in *The Old Curiosity Shop* without laughing, was, on this view, as misguided as Edward FitzGerald, who edited himself a 'Nelly-ad' from the sentimental sections of the same novel. My original aim quickly expanded as the wider cultural implications became apparent: condemnation of Dickens's 'sentimentality', though it was amply present in his own time, developed further in the twentieth century into a manifestation of modernist elitism, became linked with a more general fear of emotional expression and a preference for irony, and persisted from the 1920s into the late twentieth century as an increasing and socially debilitating distrust of the expression of 'tender' emotion in general. In Gabriel Pearson's words in 1962, 'Everyone today is of the devil's party, and knows it.'[4] These wider implications seem to have become even more intrusive and more urgently in need of exploration in the twenty-first century. The central argument of this book (no longer nearly as outrageous as it seemed when I first made it) is, therefore, that we now need to rehabilitate the adjective 'sentimental' as a useful critical concept rather than as a casual term of condemnation or dismissal. Until we do, we will remain ill-equipped to understand not only Dickens, but persistent aspects of our own culture, from our addiction to soap operas to our inadequacy in finding words for coping with death.

Sentimentality is almost always described by its critics as 'mawkish'. The slippery choice of adjective may be suggestive of cultural unease, even in the compilers of the *Oxford English Dictionary*.[5] The *OED* reveals that a 'mawk' once meant a maggot and describes 'mawkish' as meaning 'inclined to sickness, having a nauseating taste; imbued with sickly or false sentiment; lacking in robustness' (1702). This, however, untypically for the *OED*, ducks the issue, merely substituting another unexplained metaphor, 'sickly' for 'mawkish' and seeming to elide 'sickliness' and 'falsehood'. It does suggest the possibility that there might be such a thing as unsickly, *healthy*, true expressions of 'sentiment', though it gives no suggestion as to what these might be. To define what is involved in the concept of 'sentimentality' critically rather than merely pejoratively, I soon found it necessary to abandon that hopelessly compromised word and to use instead the more neutral 'sentimentalism'. This made it easier for me to make a link between the eighteenth- and the nineteenth-century literary traditions, to explore the similarities and differences between them, and to approach a key question, as important in the twenty-first century as when it was formulated in 1963:

> Criticism so far has not defined the basic relationship between sentimentalism and virtue or morality; nor has it explained why the term, if occupied with man's noblest ideals, carries a generally unfavourable connotation.[6]

\*\*\*

Before academic discussion of Dickens and the eighteenth- and nineteenth-century literary contexts can begin, some popular objections to 'sentimentalism' need to be addressed. Sentimental values have been variously dismissed as irrelevant, inappropriate, excessive, insincere, simplistic and unrealistic in the twenty-first century. The implication is that we can no longer share such values. This last is a statement never made about, for example, gothic literature. Much attention was and still is being paid to the gothic, where the question of 'shared values' (the exaltation of fear and terror, perhaps?) never seems to arise. The reason these values are now irrelevant, another argument runs, is because they are so patently unrealistic after the twentieth century's experience of two world wars and egregious examples of human inhumanity. Audiences in Dickens's own day, however, had their own egregious examples of inhumanity, no further away than in the streets of London where pauper children were 'dying thus around us every day', to challenge the sentimental worldview. The 'unrealistic' accusation is mysterious: most literature is blatantly and uncontroversially 'unrealistic'. Comedy, tragedy and farce go unchallenged. Why should sentimentalism be singled out for such opprobrium? Its use within the 'realist' novel is part of the answer: it is, the argument goes, an affront to realism. This does not explain why 'unreal' bizarre comedy within the same novels is regarded (certainly in the case of Dickens) as an unmitigated strength. Of course literary sentimentalism is 'unrealistic'. It is a highly stylised mode. The final, linked accusation of 'insincerity' seems otiose in a postmodernist world, which values the playful, the self-reflexive, the consciously artificial. Ironically, though, the possibility of hypocrisy behind the sentimental mask was a constant source of anxiety to both eighteenth- and nineteenth-century sentimental writers and is a theme in Goldsmith, Sheridan and (through Mr Pecksniff) in Dickens himself – though the anxiety seems dated now. Juliet John's comment on melodrama could surely apply equally well to sentimentalism: that its 'stylized mode of representation can be seen as pre-empting postmodernism in its telegraphing of its own artificiality'.[7]

An attack very often levelled at Dickens's sentimental style is that it is characterised by the production of an 'inappropriate' response, usually involving excess (hence the 'spilling over' into tears). This is temptingly explanatory and was the accusation most often made in Dickens's lifetime. It can be countered, however, by asking, what can possibly be 'excessive' in the response to a dying child? Something other than excess must surely be involved. Another characteristic, over-simplification, might be a stronger objection and would best account for the modernists' contempt for sentimental writing: it is not intellectual. Indeed, in its nineteenth-century form, it works effortlessly to evade or to numb intellectual analysis in order to produce the characteristic rush of tears which marks its successful climax. Nineteenth-century sentimentalism, following the Romantics, values heart over head, and privileging the former involves consciously suppressing the latter. Dickens works hard to achieve the effects of simplicity, intensity and excess and, my argument goes, to do so he crafts a complex rhetoric which merits careful analysis. In what follows

I argue that literary sentimentalism, rather than being dismissed out of hand as a defect of style, should be neutrally examined as simply a mode, a literary convention, with its own rules, register and vocabulary. If it is 'unrealistic' or 'simplifying', perhaps it is so for a precise rhetorical and cultural purpose: perhaps these are features, shared with the gothic, which might, for example, suggest opposition to eighteenth-century rationalism.

***

Alison Case and Harry E. Shaw provide a useful summary of the current critical understanding of sentimentalism, though they struggle to distinguish between 'feelings' and 'sentiment':

> With their philosophical roots in Adam Smith's 'Theory of the Moral Sentiments,' sentimental scenes in novels are supposed to work roughly like this: sympathetic identification with the suffering object produces a gush of feeling – ideally signalled by a gush of tears – that affirms and strengthens the reader's innate capacity for good – his or her 'moral sentiments.' Fictional sentimentality, the theory goes, promotes real benevolence by heightening and reinforcing our sensitivity to claims, via our feelings, on our benevolence: they help, in other words, to cultivate the right kind of feeling.[8]

Sentimentalism in this account involves both an ethical and physical dimension – but other disciplines can be used and other approaches are possible. Wolfgang Herrlinger, in his treatment of *Sentimentalismus und Postsentimentalismus* (1987),[9] therefore begins by rehearsing the range of possible aims and approaches. Like me, he hopes to 'define such imprecise attributes as "melodramatic" and "sentimental" in a new and tighter way.' However, he deliberately eschews mere etymology: 'In this book I shall not be interested in the history of words, but rather will focus on the functional changes in… concepts and structures'.[10] Herrlinger takes key terms in what he calls the 'grid of ideas' of sentimentalism, such as benevolence, sympathy, reason, self-denial and innocence and examines the shift in the ways in which these terms were used by the eighteenth-century and then by nineteenth-century English novelists. He aims to show 'how and why, around the turn of the eighteenth/nineteenth centuries, sentimental elements were the object of fierce criticism only to find their way back into the novel towards the middle of the nineteenth century'. His study, he says, 'will point to the differences in motivation between the "weeping readers" of the eighteenth century and the readers of the nineteenth century.'[11] This functionalist approach is close to my own, though my concerns are more overtly about the features of sentimentalist *rhetoric*. Like Herrlinger, I address the move from the eighteenth to the nineteenth century and the issue of readership – particularly important in the case of Dickens.

Both defining my central term and finding an appropriate way of approaching its complexities presented difficulties, but it seemed imperative to address these questions before I turned to Dickens's work itself. I begin, therefore, in this Introduction, by exploring recent academic approaches to sentimentalism in literature. I then summarise very briefly what I take to be the ten literary/cultural issues most often raised in connection with the term. In arguing that Dickens is not uniquely 'guilty of sentimentality', but is rather the inheritor and transmitter of a rich literary and cultural tradition, I need to engage with the question of 'influence', of how Dickens assimilated the work of his predecessors; here I follow Gillian Beer in her account of how Victorian writers read Darwin. Reading, she says, involves a 'difficult flux of excitement, rebuttal, disconfirmation, pursuit, forgetfulness, and analogy-making, which together make up something of the process of assimilation'.[12] My discussions of 'influence', 'debt', 'borrowing', 'misreading' and so on, assume much from Beer's seminal account of the processes of literary and cultural assimilation.

\*\*\*

When I first began my work on sentimentalism, the times were inimical to its pursuance. Only Fred Kaplan in *Sacred Tears* (1987) seemed to be working on similar lines and, though his book was praised by Michael Goldberg of the University of British Columbia as 'a radically new and interesting approach', Kaplan was also recognised by Goldberg as being 'untrendy'.[13] Things are very different now. Interest in 'affect' has increased in recent years, with the work of Gilles Deleuze and Félix Guattari in philosophy and of Patricia Ticineto Clough and others in the social sciences and in cultural theory.[14] This has led to a new interest in affective theories of the body, in the physical manifestations of emotion. In 2010, a one-day conference at the University of London was entirely devoted to 'Mr Popular Sentiment: Dickens and Feeling' and included recent work by Isobel Armstrong, Nicola Bown and Catherine Waters, among others, on Dickens and affect.[15] The very public nature of Dickens's sentimentality and its physical manifestation in tears links it with such books as Dylan Evans's *Emotion: The Science of Sentiment* (2001) and Elspeth Probyn's *Blush: Faces of Shame* (2005). Gesa Stedman, in *Stemming the Torrent* (2002) analyses *Hard Times* and *Great Expectations* in terms of Pierre Bourdieu's (very Dickensian) concept of habitus which 'implies an embodied emotional ideal' in which 'conscious or unconscious mental notions and processes 'are linked to 'bodily action'.[16] Kirstie Blair's *Victorian Poetry and the Culture of the Heart*

(2006) considers the cultural shifts in Dickens's time between the metaphysical and the physical.[17] Roy Porter in 'The History of the Body' refers to the 'body as the crossroads between self and society'.[18] Emotional expression has an implicit political dimension, linked with the 'expression-and-control' paradigm which Stedman identifies. The physical display of emotion is inevitably public, affective, and as a result potentially politically dangerous.

Another approach, therefore, might be through the politics of sentimentalism. Juliet John's *Dickens's Villains* (2001) and Sally Ledger's *Dickens and the Popular Radical Tradition* (2008) reclaim melodrama for serious study by revealing its radical roots. The present book seeks to make a similar argument for at least some examples of sentimentalism. In championing 'the good heart' Dickens was often striking a blow against Benthamism and mechanism. Fred Kaplan argues that sentimentalism has always been 'an oppositional mode', a 'protest'[19] and it is true that Dickens very often employs sentimental techniques subversively and with the aim of reforming society – most notably in Jo's death in *Bleak House*. The motives behind Dickens's sentimental writing, however, are very varied and it is certainly not *always* subversive nor invariably progressive, as the conclusion to *Nicholas Nickleby* reveals. Frank H. Ellis, extolling sentimentalism, concludes that 'the evolution of a species mentality [involving] "pity for all humanity" may be man's last chance on this ravaged planet'.[20] Ellis chooses to ignore the fact that the Nazis were notoriously 'sentimental', and that the sentimental response can often be simply pleasurable, an indulgence in emotions which makes the indulger feel better (see Jeffrey, above) without necessarily prompting him to reform anything, or indeed to think beyond his own gratification. Following on from this is the often heavily disguised erotic element in sentimentalism – particularly in the presentation of the sufferings of the sentimental heroine, which made Dickens many enemies among twentieth-century feminists who saw his sentimentalism as rooted in misogyny. Dickens's rhetoric often seems to work to disable the intellect – to aim through intensification for a climactic (a 'gushing') emotional response. John sees this as a deliberate and democratic effort at inclusivity, an admirable populism; this is a powerful argument, but I argue in what follows that there may be personal reasons too behind Dickens's impulse to make his audience cry. Political and psychoanalytical approaches may both be useful, and are not mutually exclusive.

Sentimentalism's eighteenth-century philosophical base has been amply discussed as a utopian philosophy based on Rousseau and on the assumption that human nature is basically good; it embodies an unfashionable optimism which needs once again to be given its due, alongside our many twenty-first century dystopian fantasies. In recent critical rereadings by Monika Fludernik and others, Dickens's use of the sentimental mode is examined positively.[21] Sentimentalism can even be regarded as a recurrent psychological impulse, evident early in literature in the medieval mystery plays. I shall return to this early tradition in the next chapter. It could therefore be read through the psychology of the audience rather than the politics of the audience, as being based (according to Ellis in *Sentimental Comedy*) on each audience member's memory of being mothered.[22] Sentimentalism can, finally, be examined as a set of rhetorical practices, making up a schema which can be set beside other rhetorics, of violence, for example, which are equally powerful today. This notion of 'the sentimental' as one of many available discourses is an important corrective to the attacks of philosophers such as Mary Midgeley and Mark Jefferson, who treat it as uniquely dishonest, a way of making people 'unable to deal with the real world'.[23] The present work operates under the assumption that we live in a society made up of many discourses, none of which can be unproblematically privileged as 'real'. Every popular discourse, of sex, of violence, of mystery, is simply a discourse – a reconstruction of the world. 'Realism' itself is yet another discourse, not itself 'real'. This final notion of examining 'sentimentalism' through its rhetorical techniques is a manageable proposition, the most obvious one to use in the case of Dickens and the approach I shall most frequently employ. At the same time, I intend to keep a cluster of definitions in play in the course of this book, so as to be able to refer to some of the many literary and extra-literary manifestations of sentimentalism.

In what follows, then, I shall raise and attempt to address the following cluster of questions:

What was the sentimental tradition that Dickens inherited and how did it change from the eighteenth to the nineteenth centuries? In particular, to what extent was the integration of sentimentalism and humour, which Sheridan, Goldsmith, Fielding and Sterne all achieved, made impossible for Dickens by the intervention of Romanticism? Whereas in the eighteenth century, 'heart' and 'head' were equally valued, Dickens inherited from the Romantics the assumption that the heart was superior and should be privileged. This meant that he often kept his 'serious' characters insulated from his humorous ones. Does this vitiate his achievement, or is the energy required to keep the two apart precisely where the power of his novels lies? Did Dickens's approach change during his career – was he in any way less sentimental or more effectively sentimental in his later novels? Finally, what might change in our reading of Dickens (and of Victorian literature and culture generally) if we develop a set of analytic tools to examine sentimental writing?

✻✻✻

## Sentimentalism: Some Issues in Brief

### 1) Sentimentalism as philosophical optimism

With its background in eighteenth-century optimism and the secular humanism of Lord Shaftesbury, philosophical sentimentalism was transmitted to Dickens's generation through Adam Smith's *Theory of Moral Sentiments* (1759) and through the essays of Joseph Addison and Richard Steele. Dickens's own use of the term in *Household Words* (June 1856) suggests his recognition of its eighteenth-century roots. Describing the demeanour in the dock of William Palmer, the Rugeley poisoner, he asks 'Can anyone…suppose it possible…that in the breast of this Poisoner there were surviving, in the day of his trial, any lingering traces of sensibility, or any wrecked fragments of the quality we call sentiment?'[24] Therefore 'sentiment' to Dickens is a civilised and civilising form of emotion, one which distinguishes the human from the animal. It is the prop of what John calls his 'ethically framed universe' (77) and, as such, militated against the rise of the empiricism of the realist novel. Fred Kaplan argues persuasively that what he calls 'sentimentality' was 'central to the attempt of British literature and philosophy in the first half of the nineteenth century to defend the value of the ideal against the increasingly powerful forces of philosophical realism'.

### 2) The vocabulary of sentimentalism: The heart and the head

Sentimentalism seems to depend upon this binary opposition which, philosophically, might be said to have begun in European culture with Descartes although, as Chapter 1 will suggest, the sentimental impulse is already evident in medieval literature. It is arguably inappropriate to use the term of works predating the medieval. *Beowulf*, for example, deals with the themes of maternal love and the death of the mother, but in a way which it would be at best quixotic to call 'sentimental'!

Coleridge's extolling of the imagination, contrasted with mere 'fancy', contributed to the post-Romantic semantic and cultural shift from 'sentiment' as rational to 'sentiment' as emotional.[25] At the centre of this Romantic paradigm shift is the apotheosis of the heart as the seat of sublime emotion. Mid-Victorians from Sarah Stickney Ellis to Dickens himself argued that the 'heart' is just as much in need of training as the 'head', if not more so, because it so powerfully influences human behaviour. The educationalist Charles Bray's *The Education of the Feelings* (1838) examines 'the natural Laws which the Creator has established, by which the feelings are to be trained and cultivated.'[26] Dickens's early novels participate, in their plots, their structure and their rhetoric, in these contemporary discussions. Gesa Stedman's account

of the nineteenth-century use of the heart to describe emotions suggests the
literary habitus within which Dickens wrote:

> The heart can appear as the 'human' or 'universal' heart on the one hand, or, on
> the other, as the more specific 'feminine' or 'woman's heart, but only rarely as an
> explicitly male one. In both these cases, the dominant concept of the heart is that
> of the 'container': the heart can boil, it can be warm, it can be a fountain, ready
> to overflow, it can be full or overcharged, and one can pour out one's heart. By
> extension, feelings are often represented as 'floods of happiness', fountains of love'
> or 'torrents of passion'. A related spatial metaphor sees the heart as a space: the
> 'core' of the heart or the 'inmost' heart is the dwelling place of true religion or true
> feeling, and the 'desert places' of the heart signify the absence of emotion.[27]

### *3) Sentimentalism and Christianity*

Although the eighteenth-century roots of sentimentalism were largely secular,
it was early nineteenth-century Christian apologists who gave Dickens a
detailed template for his sentimental characters:

> True religion is seated in the heart, and sends out from thence a purifying influence
> over the whole character… It aims not at ostentatious display of principles but
> a steady exhibition of fruits. Qualities which it cultivates with especial care are
> humility, and charity, and mercy, – the mortification of every selfish passion, and
> the denial of every selfish indulgence. [Christianity] recognises no distinction of
> persons, but produces similar effects on the poor illiterate man as on the rich and
> educated… [T]he tendency of the Christian religion is to exalt all those faculties
> of mind, and all those moral feelings that elevate character and promote health,
> usefulness and happiness; and to repress those exercises of mind, and those moral
> feelings (or excesses or perversions of feeling), which produce distress, defame the
> character, and impair health.[28]

Popular fiction of the time, according to Gesa Stedman, did 'not intend to teach
its readers specific religious practices or points of doctrine, but…[wanted] to
encourage a certain latitudinarian Christian attitude of submission, humanity,
and benevolence as opposed to selfishness' (135). This is very much the context
for Dickens's own Christian expression. Christian goodness is presented in
his novels as both spiritually and physically beneficial – and it is a notably
Anglican Christianity, as Valentine Cunningham argues:

> Dickens is, of course, a Christian writer. A very English, Protestant, and
> Anglican-inflected one… Dickens's narratives are greatly held, like his people,

in a literal and imaginative landscape charged with the flavour and force of a strongly Christianised *imaginaire*.[29]

### 4) Sentimental tears

Laurence Sterne's parodying of Locke's associationism, which projected a continuum between the bodily and the emotional, is central to the impact of his novels and made its own contribution to the nineteenth century's uneasy physicalising of emotions. Tears in Sterne are equated with all bodily secretions – a sort of seminal fluid giving life to secret sympathies. He sees ideas in similar terms:

> The thought floated into Dr. Slop's mind... millions of which, as your worship knows, are every day swimming quietly in the middle of the juice of a man's understanding, without being carried backwards and forwards, till some little gust of passion or interest drives them to one side.[30]

Tears in eighteenth-century literature were used as signifiers of an emotional arousal which was analogous to (and in Sterne's novels, often identified with) sexual arousal, and was presented as part of a process of 'melting', a softening of the heart, which was both morally and physically beneficial. Richard Steele, however, presents the onrush of tears as an intellectual problem to be solved. He does so in language which very closely anticipates Dickens and the nineteenth-century sentimentalists:

> Men ought not to be laughed at for weeping until we come to a more clear Notion of what is to be imputed to the Hardness of the Head, and the Softness of the Heart.[31]

The tradition of 'sentimental tears' will be discussed more fully in Chapter 1.

### 5) Sentimentalism and the 'Romantic child'

The Romantic child in Wordsworth and his contemporaries emerged from the eighteenth-century philosophy of Rousseau and its development in the early nineteenth century by Friedrich Schiller. Rousseau views the child as endowed from birth with natural tendencies to virtue which can be nourished slowly towards the needs of social existence. 'Love childhood,' he declares, 'promote its games, its pleasures, its amiable instinct.'[32] Friedrich Schiller goes on to show how reason and emotion should come together in the moral elevation of the child:

> The child is therefore a lively representation to us of the ideal, not indeed as it is fulfilled, but as it is enjoined; hence we are in no sense moved by the notion of

its poverty and limitation, but rather by the opposite: the notion of its pure and free strength, its integrity, its eternality. To a moral and sensitive person a child will be a sacred object.[33]

Dickens's version of the 'sentimental child' in *Oliver Twist* is little different in conception, but the sentimental as opposed to the Romantic response is achieved by a new stress on the child as victim. Peter Coveney's seminal study, *The Image of Childhood* tracks this move from the Romantic to the sentimental child.[34] He observes: [t]he victimised condition of the child in early Victorian England did not square with the image of childhood [innocence and frailty] that had been created in the Romantic period' (92) and continues: 'the child became for [Dickens] the symbol of sensitive feelings in a society maddened with the pursuit of material progress [and his novels] are an account of the plight of human sensibility under the cast iron shackles of the Victorian world' (115).

The Romantic child as philosophical ideal acquired extra resonance during the rapid industrial and social changes of the early nineteenth century, and in Dickens became a symbol of resistance to the values of utilitarianism.[35] The child is a major element in Dickens's sentimental rhetoric, first in the allegorical simplicity of Oliver Twist or Little Nell, but in the later novels as a more complex figure. Victimhood is important and 'Little' becomes a signifier of moral worth. Paul Dombey is, however, presented on his deathbed not as a sentimental object for the emotional delectation of the readers, but as an experiencing subject. A moral test throughout the novels is the attitude to childhood. There are sympathetic childlike figures such as Mr Dick or Tom Pinch, but the false assumption of childhood, for example in Mercy Pecksniff or Harold Skimpole, results in withering narratorial condemnation.

## *6) Sentimentalism and eroticism*

> There in the anguish of her soul, her streaming eyes lifted up to my face with supplicating softness, hands folded, dishevelled hair; for her night headdress having fallen off in her struggling, her charming tresses fell down in naturally shining ringlets, as if officious to conceal the dazzling beauties of her neck and shoulders; her lovely bosom too heaving with sighs and broken sobs...
> —Samuel Richardson, *Clarissa*[36]

> Maria, though tall, was nevertheless of the first order of fine forms – affliction had touched her looks with something that was scarcely earthly – still she was feminine – and so much was there about her of all that the heart wishes, or the eye looks for in woman, that... [she] should lay on my bosom and be to me as a daughter.
> —Laurence Sterne, *Tristram Shandy*[37]

The eighteenth-century effulgences of Samuel Richardson and Laurence Sterne over the sentimental heroine suggest a knowing eroticism. Marcus Wood identifies Sterne's 'auto-erotics' of empathy:[38] 'Sterne's narrator' he says, 'pursues painful fantasies up to the point at which "my heart bleeds"; at this point he breaks off and takes a new narrative tack, only for the process to start all over again' (17). In contrast, the mid-Victorian novelists manifest what might be termed an 'enforced innocence'. Thackeray's deep suspicion of Sterne (he referred to his 'evil Satyr's leer') suggests that he recognised but violently rejected the eroticism of *Tristram Shandy*. In Dickens, eroticism is more deeply disguised in the sentimental register, but it is through that register, as I shall discuss in Chapter 6, that Victorian sexual taboos are negotiated.

### *7) Sentimentalism as 'curative'*

The open expression of emotions is linked explicitly by Sterne with good health:

> True Shandeism, think what you will against it, opens the heart and lungs, and like all affections which partake of its nature, it forces the blood and other vital fluids of the body to run freely through its channels, and makes the wheel of life run long and cheerfully round. (333)

Francis Jeffrey's thanks to Dickens for enabling him to cry, quoted at the beginning of this chapter, reveals a similar underlying belief in what seems to be a version of Aristotelian catharsis (but see Probyn, in Chapter 1). Dickens's 'healthy' characters, such as Kit Nubbles, are characteristically able to express their emotions and are presented as crying or laughing readily. Pip in *Great Expectations* eventually allows himself to admit his love of Joe and of home, sheds tears 'and felt the better for having shed them'. The opposite tradition, however, derived from medieval courtly love, is also present: sentimental characters readily pine away and die. Kirstie Blair discusses 'the curative properties of affective literature', arguing that in nineteenth-century culture, '[f]eeling was seen as a performative act that had consequences for the body'.[39] Gesa Stedman argues more negatively that, for Dickens, emotions 'have to be controlled – otherwise the passionate, animal-like mob threatens to swallow the middle classes – but not suppressed, since affection and feeling are necessary to maintain social order'.[40]

### *8) Sentimentalism and death*

Death for Tristram Shandy is a threat to be fled from in a wild and desperate journey. For Richardson's Clarissa, on the other hand, death is an escape, from an unbearable reality to a heavenly apotheosis. The Romantic movement, which separated Dickens from these eighteenth-century forebears, developed a cult of death which could be linked to the erotic, as in Keats's 'I am half in love with easeful Death'.[41] Andrew Sanders in *Charles Dickens Resurrectionist* (1982) explores Dickens's obvious fascination with death but examines the evolution of the Victorian deathbed as part of the wider culture within which Dickens wrote, rather than as his own private obsession.[42]

Though he was scornful of most Victorian funeral customs, many of Dickens's novels centre on death and most establish a grave as a significant place within the novel's structure: Smike's grave in *Nicholas Nickleby* and Pip's parents' graves in *Great Expectations* are two obvious examples, the first affirming continuity with the past, the second helping construct Pip's sense of identity. Little Nell's grave becomes a holy shrine, a place to keep safe the values she embodied in her life. Death is a favourite subject in the sentimental scenes of all Dickens's novels; it is the ultimate test of the sentimental hero or heroine, a guarantor of their moral superiority over the non-sentimental characters.

### *9) Sentimentalism and subversion*

It has been argued, notably by Stanley T. Williams, that sentimentalism's 'belief in virtue' underpinned many of the key social and political reforms of the eighteenth and nineteenth centuries and that 'it is difficult in this twentieth century to comprehend the subversive character of this belief'. Williams goes on to show how much modern Western culture depends on the sentimentalist belief in human goodness:

> Our philosophies of religion, of social reform, of education, of politics, of war, accept as a matter of course the theory that man is at heart good... [As a result of this] we have abolished slavery, established democracies, and in some religions, denied the existence of sin.[43]

Eighteenth-century writers used the resources of sentimentalism consciously to evoke public sympathy in order to attack great social evils, most notably slavery. Harriet Martineau and other reformers, including William Wilberforce, encouraged identification with the slaves – a recognition of a shared humanity, based on Rousseau's 'sentimental' idealism. However, Marcus Wood counters Williams by revealing the solipsistic side of sentimentalism. 'What a feast to a benevolent heart!' writes Ignatius Sancho to Laurence Sterne, hoping to persuade him to write a political piece focusing on the sufferings of the slave. This cannibalistic imagery is, for Wood, significant. 'The empathetic fantasy which attempts to reconfigure the suffering of the slaves, gives the memory of slavery over to the sentimentalist as aesthetic property'[44] he declares. Wood's conclusion is that apparently progressive eighteenth-century sentimental texts, about slavery in particular, actually rely on a self-indulgent solipsism, being more concerned with the feelings of the observer than the observed. The discussion in Chapter 5 of the death of Little Nell returns to this issue of emotional self-indulgence. Dickens's belief in the power of the 'change of heart' is central to his political and ethical thinking, and it is often framed in terms of sentimental 'melting'. The following chapters examine the ways in which sentimentalism, in Dickens's novels, veers between nostalgia and subversion.

## *10) Sentimentalism and drama*

The link between the two is suggested by the powerful tradition of eighteenth-century sentimental comedy, discussed in Chapter 1. The essentially public nature of sentimentalism – the paradox that sentimental tears are felt to be deeply private but are actually part of a shared public response – is evident in the performative nature of character in Dickens's novels. My exploration of Dickens's acting experience in Chapter 4 reveals its contribution to his sentimental writing. His 'sentimental narrator' is in a long tradition of classical acting, going back to Shakespeare and his contemporaries, which was built on a particular view of how emotion works and how it is elicited from an audience.[45] Interiority, on this analysis, has no place in sentimental rhetoric: it was and is conceived in terms of the stage.

***

In the following chapters, I focus successively on the 'sentimental tradition', on Dickens's eighteenth-century predecessors, on nineteenth-century contemporary drama, and, finally, on Dickens's novels themselves. There is no attempt at an exhaustive reading of the major novels: each is considered insofar as it contributes to my overarching argument about the sentimentalist mode. *Dombey and Son*, for me Dickens's greatest triumph in the sentimentalist mode, acts as a 'base text' and focal point throughout, being used illustratively in every chapter before being dealt with at length in Chapter 6. I deliberately employ a variety of critical approaches. I begin in Chapter 1 with a brief review of the semantic background, arguing for the existence of a centuries-old 'sentimental tradition' in English literature, but then move on to something more like Herrlinger's functionalism, exploring how key terms were actually used in different contexts; the main body of my study then examines the 'rhetorical practices' of Dickens's sentimentalism. I employ narrative theory to attempt to unravel the vexed question of irony, arguing that it is the complex cluster of 'implied readers' available to the late eighteenth-century dramatists and novelists which enabled them to achieve more nuanced and open-ended effects than Dickens and his nineteenth-century contemporaries. My aim is to identify the many different, complex and often conflicting ways in which the rhetoric of sentimentalism operates in Dickens's works. Ultimately it may be possible to provide critical tools for dealing with that strange effect, the welling of tears or even the tightening of the throat ('a lump in the throat') which surprises the casual viewer when someone – anyone – weeps in a play or film, or, more specifically, when the mid-Victorian audience read, often aloud and with others, of the death of Little Nell.[46]

## Chapter 1

## DICKENS AND THE SENTIMENTALIST TRADITION

The literary and cultural history of eighteenth-century sentimentalism is a relatively familiar story. Less often identified is a trait of sentimentalism evident in English literature at least since the medieval mystery plays. When in the Chester Cycle, Isaac, thinking himself about to be killed at God's command by his father Abraham, says 'Father, tell my mother for nothing' (that is, 'Don't let my mother know!').[1] The combination of pathos and humour is instantly recognisable. Even more so are the blandishments lavished by the shepherds on the Christ child in the Second Shepherds' Play in the Wakefield Cycle: 'Lo, he laughs, my sweeting!' 'Hail, little tiny mop!... little day star'.[2] This suggests the 'folk' side of the sentimental mode. In the sixteenth and seventeenth centuries, however, it becomes part of the vocabulary of high culture. The family reunion scene in Shakespeare's *The Winter's Tale*, reported, not acted out, is an early configuration of Dickens's Dombey family of jealous father, persecuted mother, ill-fated son and cruelly rejected daughter. Father and daughter are reunited after the death of the son and the (apparent) death of the mother and an onlooker tells the audience: 'their joy waded in tears. There was casting up of eyes, holding up of hands, with countenance of such distraction...[they] did – I would fain say bleed tears; for I'm sure my heart wept blood. Who was most marble there, changed colour; some swooned, all sorrowed' (V.ii.50, 96–7). Shakespeare here exploits the power and persuasiveness of the sentimental effect long before he could turn for support to a popular philosophical system that proclaimed the basic goodness of the human heart. The public expression of emotion, the consciously tableauesque qualities, the stress upon sentimental expression as aesthetically pleasing (the onlooker talks of 'One of the prettiest touches', line 89) – these are all traits of much later sentimentalism. In Thomas Otway's *Venice Preserved* (1682), Belvidera's power over her father anticipates very precisely in action and in metaphor Florence Dombey's final victory:

> Fall at his feet, cling to his reverent knees,
> Speak to him with thine eyes, and with thy tears
> Melt his hard heart, and wake dead nature in him,
> Crush him in thy arms and torture him with thy softness. (IV.iv.532–5)[3]

A full history of literary sentimentalism would reveal many such instances and would entail both cultural and psychological analysis. It is beyond the remit of this narrower study of Dickens, where the conventional place to begin is with the seventeenth-century reaction against Calvinism and its belief in 'fallen man', led in Great Britain by the Earl of Shaftesbury and by Scottish philosophers such as Adam Smith. Smith's *Theory of Moral Sentiments* (1759) is a seminal text, propounding the belief in man's natural goodness and in the beneficial link between innate, spontaneous feeling and the ability to make moral reflections. The early eighteenth-century dramas of Richard Steele and Steele's work with Joseph Addison on the *Tatler* and the *Spectator* all communicated an optimistic belief in the ultimate triumph of sensibility and the supreme importance of human sympathy. Dickens assimilated this early eighteenth-century tradition in his reading – but he also enjoyed the more complex late eighteenth-century reworkings of the tradition in the plays of Oliver Goldsmith and Richard Brinsley Sheridan.

## The Sentimentalist Tradition: Eighteenth-Century Drama

Allardyce Nicoll, in his six volume *A History of English Drama from 1660–1900*,[4] tracked sentimentalist rhetoric back as far as Restoration drama, finding the plays of Colley Cibber 'a mixture of the flagrantly indecent and of the moralistically sentimental', while Thomas Otway in *Venice Preserved* and in *The Orphan* brought (as has been shown) 'true pathos and sentiment to the stage' (I: 263). Nicoll makes other points relevant to Dickens. Early sentimental drama, he reveals, was 'fundamentally opposed to the cynical aristocratic existence of former times. From its inception the middle classes were intimately associated with the development of the type' (II: 181). In discussing later eighteenth-century sentimental drama Nicoll turns to the key element: the audience. Audiences, he says, showed both 'excessive sensibility' and 'extreme political emotions' (III: 15, 17) He also usefully identifies another key feature of sentimental writing: its self-contradiction. (I shall explore this later in relation to the 'double-voiced discourse' of Sterne, Goldsmith and Sheridan.) Frederick Reynolds, he says, 'mingles manners, sentimentalism and satire' (III: 132); George Colman the Elder satirised the sentimental school but himself wrote sentimentally at times (III: 140). The link with melodrama is soon established: Thomas Morton's *Speed the Plough* (1800) is described as a 'sentimental, melodramatic comedy' (III: 143).[5] Sentimentalism, Nicoll concludes, 'can be both sincere and hypocritical; it can be both radical and conservative' (III: 109). It is, in short, a literary sub-genre rather than a single politically identifiable position.

Nicoll narrates the triumph of sentimentalism in the late eighteenth century: 'The whole of the dramatic literature of this time is influenced, directly or indirectly, by sentimentalism' (III: 109) and suggests that three strands of 'sentimentalism' emerged as the theatre moved towards the nineteenth century. These were: Colley Cibber's genteel comedy (the particular target of Goldsmith); the mawkishly pathetic theatre of Richard Cumberland; and the more revolutionary humanitarian drama of Elizabeth Inchbald and Thomas Holcroft (III: 108–10, 124). It is the last-named which Nicoll identifies as inspiring the Romantic poets, though for students of Dickens it is perhaps the Cumberland link which seems the most germane. A rather different, though related, account is given by Charles Whibley in his notes to a volume of William Hazlitt's essays. Whibley supplies an amazingly succinct guide to the whole eighteenth-century sentimentalist tradition, moving from Alexander Pope to Jane Austen in five sentences:

> Sense, sentiment, sensibility were favourite terms in the eighteenth century. Hazlitt (Round Table, p. 44) notes that in Pope's *Essay on Criticism* 'there are no less than half a score couplets rhyming to the word "sense". The period witnessed the development of Reid's philosophy of "common sense". There are numerous thrusts at the play of fulsome sentiment in Sheridan's *School for Scandal*. Mackenzie's *Man of Feeling* and Goethe's *Sorrows of Werther* illustrate the extremes that may be touched by sentimentality. Jane Austen's *Sense and Sensibility* marks the impress of an expiring fashion.[6]

Whibley's view that sentimentalism 'expired' at the beginning of the nineteenth century is contradicted by Mario Praz's belief in *The Hero in Eclipse in Victorian Fiction* (1956),[7] that this is where it began. The present study aims to link what are obviously conceived here as two separate traditions – 'sentiment' as on the one hand, rational and on the other, pathetic – in order to reveal the contradictions inherited by Dickens and his contemporaries, which complicated their own vocabulary and the nature of their achievements.

## The Sentimental Tradition: Etymological and Functionalist Approaches

A popular approach often used in discussing sentimentalism is the etymological, which tracks the semantic shift of 'sensibility' and 'sentiment' from the eighteenth to the nineteenth centuries. I shall briefly sum up what is relevant in this etymological approach but will then turn to a second, more original approach developed by Wolfgang Herrlinger (1987).

Eric Erämetsä, in *A Study of the Word 'Sentimental'* (1951) shows how the word meant for Shaftesbury simply 'the moral reflections of the cultivated man.'[8] The heart was in the early eighteenth century constructed as the seat both of judgement and of right feeling. Lord Kames, says Erämetsä, made the natural next step: 'Every thought is prompted by passion and is termed sentiment'[9] and it is presumably in this sense that Richardson's Clarissa refers to 'such expressions of duty as my heart overflowed with'. Thus the shift from thought to feeling was slight and hardly noticed during the eighteenth century – seemingly too slight to merit a different term. In 1762, Goldsmith is still using 'sentiment' in the older way: in *The Citizen of the World*, he condemns the man who 'separates sensual and sentimental enjoyments, seeking happiness from the Mind alone'.[10] By the end of the century, however, 'sentiment' had expanded to mean both the 'moral reflections' of Shaftesbury and the 'emotional susceptibility' of Sterne. Both meanings continued well into the nineteenth century, though the ideas behind them were increasingly conceived as being directly in opposition to each other.

Wolfgang Herrlinger, examining eighteenth- and nineteenth-century literary sentimentalism in the 1980s, strikes out in a different direction, arguing that 'mere studies in the history of words cannot lead us much further on their own' and proposing instead that 'one will get further through working out of concepts and themes like *benevolence, pity, melancholy* or even *self-denial*'.[11] Herrlinger usefully sums up what he takes to be the common characteristics of the eighteenth-century sentimental novel and the Victorian novel. Although he ignores drama and seems also to ignore Sterne and Fielding, his list still provides a useful schema:

> One can point to a whole row of common elements shared by the sentimental novel and the Victorian novel: in both the heroes often burst into tears, in both, the figure of the guardian appears repeatedly, someone who has the task of protecting a parentless lost child from the dangers around them, in both the virtuous heroes are regenerated in a pastoral setting, in both the heroes find happiness in reading, in both the virtuous heroes are repeatedly overcome by a feeling of melancholy, in both pity, benevolence and self-denial are regarded as genuine virtues, both have heroines and heroes who place intuition ahead of logical operating reason as a source of knowledge. (2)

Isobel Armstrong had adopted a similarly functional approach to 'The Role and the Treatment of Emotion in Victorian Criticism of Poetry' (1977). What she says of Victorian poetry can equally well be applied to Victorian prose and to Dickens's approach to his task as a novelist. Armstrong begins by looking at the Victorians in terms of 'the emotions they liked and the emotions they did not like' arguing that they 'needed to see emotion as the fundamental of poetic experience for poet and reader alike. And yet they had a powerful distrust of emotion'.[12] She goes on to examine the results of this 'divided feeling about emotion' in terms of Victorian expressive theory. John Stuart Mill's enormously influential essays on poetry in the *Monthly Repository* contain the uncompromising dictum that '[t]he object of poetry is confessedly to act upon the emotions'. Science 'addresses itself to the belief', poetry 'to the feelings'.[13] George Henry Lewes followed Mill's lead in the *British and Foreign Review* ten years later, by arguing that 'thoughts do and must abound in all good poetry, but they are not there for their own sake, but for the sake of a feeling… Thought for thought's sake is science – thought for feeling's sake, and feeling for feeling's sake, are poetry.'[14]

Arthur Hallam (not discussed by Armstrong) had gone much further in his 1831 *Englishman's Magazine* essay,[15] in which he prescribed an absolute division between reflective and expressive poetry in his famous formulation: 'It is not true…that the highest species of poetry is the reflective… Whenever the mind of the artist suffers itself to be occupied during its periods of creation, by any other predominant motive than the desire of beauty, the result is false in art' (35). Hallam thus dethrones the intellect in favour of the imagination and recommends an absolute separation of the two. Using vocabulary Dickens later adopts, he talks of 'the powerful tendency of the imagination to a life of immediate sympathy with the external universe'; of 'the sacred ideas of our nature, the idea of good, the idea of perfection, the idea of truth'; he sees as the greatest danger the sinking of the mind 'to the level of a mere notion in the understanding' (37). The mind, the understanding, are significantly less important to Hallam than the imagination then. A recent critic, Jason R. Rudy, describes him as a radical figure who allows 'the brain to take a passive role while sensory experience plays out howsomever it may in the human body'.[16] Hallam declares that it might well be 'morally impossible' to 'attain the author's point of vision', but that 'it is never physically impossible, because nature has placed in man the simple elements, of which art is the sublimation' (39). Dickens was of course, not an aesthete in any sense; nor was he a theorist of prose, let alone of poetry. However, he did adapt the 'reflection versus sensation' distinction in his own work into the rival rhetorics of sentiment, designed to bypass the brain, and humour or wit, designed to stimulate it. He reinvented the eighteenth-century sentimentalist tradition, via Hallam and Mill's post-Romantic expressive theory, into the favourite nineteenth-century formulation of head versus heart. Such terms were usually capitalised. Against sentimentalism were arraigned industrialisation, science, mechanisation, in all their power: it is this polarised system that he develops as he energetically separates his 'feeling' characters such as Nicholas Nickleby, or Sissy Jupe in *Hard Times*, from those who think and reflect (or, in the Dickens's rhetoric, plot, plan and scheme), such as *Hard Times*'s Thomas Gradgrind or Nicholas's uncle and adversary, Ralph Nickleby. Dickens's binary rhetoric thus followed Hallam's in cordoning off imagination and sympathy from the hardness of the industrial world.

## Johann Wolfgang von Goethe, *The Sorrows of Young Werther* (1774)

The early nineteenth-century literary treatment of the passions owes a great deal to the indirect influence on succeeding European literature of that pivotal sentimental/Romantic text, Goethe's *The Sorrows of Young Werther*. The direct influence of this semi-autobiographical epistolary novel must, as he knew no German, have come to Dickens via translations and adaptations. One, called simply *Werther*, is included in Elizabeth Inchbald's *Farces*, which he read and relished as a child and acted in as an adult. He may very well have seen a parody of *Werther* in 1822, starring his favourite Charles Mathews, in a double bill with a farce by Charles Lamb. He may also have seen his friend Macready in the role.[17]

Goldsmith and Sheridan slipped easily between the erotic and the spiritual, using identical registers for scenes of seduction and scenes of conversion. In mid-Victorian literature, however, the hero is obliged to construct his passion for the heroine as 'pure', that is, non-physical. Any trace of physical passion is assumed to be destructive of the sentimental value system. The beginning of the divide may be found in *Werther*, in which the young hero is attracted to Charlotte's goodness but also feels a strong physical attraction. Goethe shows rival discourses at work as Werther's vocabulary of feeling becomes disordered:

> How my heart beats when by accident I touch her finger, or my feet meet hers under the table; I draw back as from a flame; but a secret force impels me forward again, and I become disordered. Her innocent, pure heart never knows what an agony these little familiarities inflict upon me. Sometimes when we are talking she lays her hand upon mine and in the eagerness of conversation comes closer to me, and her divine breath comes to my lips – I feel as if lightning had struck me, and I could sink into the earth. And yet, Wilhelm, with all this heavenly confidence – if I should ever dare – you understand. No! My heart is not so depraved! It is weak, weak enough – but is that not a kind of depravity? She is sacred to me. All passion is subdued in her presence; I do not know what I feel when I am near her. It is as if my soul beat in every nerve of my body.[18]

Physical passion is not yet in itself taboo, but the beginnings of its eventual Victorian condemnation are evident: 'My heart is not so depraved! It is weak, weak enough – but is not that a kind of depravity?' The heart, which during the Enlightenment had been seen as the seat of moral judgement, here becomes the regulator of sexual desire. The introduction of 'soul', a deeply unstable word, adds to the emotional and rhetorical confusion: 'It is as if my soul beat in every nerve of my body.' Eventually rhetoric and metaphor both break down and Werther kisses the forbidden lips – and dies.

In *Werther*, passionate action is almost entirely translated into tears. Even the crude and simplified version in Elizabeth Inchbald's collection is remarkably faithful to the original in the climactic scene in which Charlotte and Werther read *Ossian* together.[19] Through the catharsis of art they can release their own passion, first metonymically through tears and then in an actual embrace. The stage direction in Inchbald's version reads:

> Here Werther throws down the book, seizes Charlotte's hand, and weeps over it – she leans on her other arm, holding a handkerchief to her eyes – They are both in the utmost agitation…the whole world disappears before them – He clasps her in his arms and strains her to his bosom. (308)

Goethe's original states even more explicitly that the merging of tears is the necessary prelude to physical union:

> A torrent of tears which streamed from Charlotte's eyes, and gave relief to her oppressed heart, stopped Werther's reading. He threw down the sheets, seized her hand, and wept bitterly. Charlotte leaned upon her other arm, and buried her face in her handkerchief; both were terribly agitated. They felt their own fate in the misfortunes of Ossian's heroes – felt this together, and merged their tears…they lost sight of everything. The world vanished before them. He clasped her in his arms, and covered the trembling stammering lips with furious kisses. (117)

Dickens's encounter with Goethe through Inchbald shows the contribution of popular culture, and in particular of popular drama, to the construction of his sentimental habitus: it is revealing, however, that the passionate world of Werther seems to lie most obviously behind his melodramatic villains such as Bradley Headstone and John Jasper, rather than behind his innocent heroes.

## Nahum Tate's *King Lear* (1681) and W. C. Macready's *King Lear* (1838)

Nahum Tate's adaptation of Shakespeare's tragedy (the play which Dr Johnson found too painful to watch) held the stage throughout the eighteenth century – in fact, from 1681 until 1838, when Macready revived the original version. Dickens, who was later a friend of Macready and had always been a keen theatregoer, wrote a lively and positive report for Forster's *Examiner* on this production and on the return of the Fool, banished for decades by

Tate. He must therefore have been keenly aware of the earlier version, the controversial nature of the decision and the sentimental issues involved. Tate's *Lear* explains away the darker side of the action, inventing a love affair between Edgar and Cordelia which, Tate says proudly, 'renders Cordelia's Indifference and her Father's Passion in the first Scene, probable'.[20] Along with the banishing of the irrational runs an optimistic presentation of human nature and interpretation of motives and, of course, the happy ending in which Cordelia revives after all and is reunited with her father. Shakespeare's aim seems to be to work through pathos to a complex sense of a tragic world, while Tate's is simply to produce pathos, exercising the audience's human sympathy. The many echoes of *King Lear* in Dickens's novels (notably in *The Old Curiosity Shop*, *Dombey and Son* and *Hard Times*) suggest a lifetime's engagement with the play. Indeed, Alexander Welsh declares that 'Dickens, in fact, cannot be said ever to have completed the study of *King Lear* inspired by Macready's production of 1838.'[21]

## The Sentimental Tradition in Nineteenth-Century Culture

The *Call for Papers* for a November 2011 conference at Queen Mary, University of London, neatly sums up the current academic interest in emotion and the desire to provide a scientific and sociological context for Dickensian sentimentalism: entitled 'Wandering Feelings: The Transmission of Emotion in the Long Nineteenth Century', it declares that in the nineteenth century,

> a new unifying category of "the emotions" replaced earlier notions of passions and sentiments, while scientific and evolutionary accounts sought to define how such emotions develop, and what they are for. The traditional location for "higher" feelings – the soul – was challenged by theories of physiology which posited instead reflex actions and the localization of brain functions. At the same time, literature was pervaded by new anxieties about the consequences of too much feeling, and of feelings insufficiently under control, as political democratisation enfranchised the working class, and mass forms of production helped commercialise sentiment.[22]

Although my approach in later chapters generally favours close reading over cultural analysis, what follows is a brief survey of some of the key texts which contributed to this mid-Victorian debate about the feelings, since they inevitably constructed and constricted Dickens's own literary expression of emotions. It was these non-literary texts which combined with the more obvious literary and theatrical texts to make up his sentimentalist tradition.

## John Keble, *Lectures on Poetry* (1832–41)[23]

Keble's account (translated from the original Latin) of the importance of the expression of emotion contributed signally to the mid-Victorian debate about the feelings. Gesa Stedman calls him an 'ardent advocate of emotional expression'. Keble argues that:

> [W]e are all so framed by nature that we experience great relief, when carried away by any strong current of thought or feeling, if we are at last able, whether by speech or gesture, or in any other way, to find an expression for it. This is most clearly seen in the case of those who, even when alone, mutter and croon to themselves, under the influence of strong emotion. (I: 19)

Keble also speaks of 'the gift of tears' which gives relief from extreme emotional pressure.[24] Keble believes, however, in the necessity of 'order and due control' once the feelings have found their way into speech or gesture. He criticises men for speaking 'unseasonably and inappropriately' of their own inner feelings and instead recommends 'modest reserve – I might even compare it to the modest blush of a country maiden – which is shown by those who write from the heart'. Dickens's sentimental heroines are notable for such modesty and reserve – from Mary Graham in *Martin Chuzzlewit* to *David Copperfield*'s Agnes Wickfield, they are praised by the narrative voice for their ability to contain and control their emotions. The balancing of the sentimental economy between expression and restraint, which is central to each of the novels, is part of the contemporary debate being conducted by writers such as Keble. It was, however, in Stedman's words, important to be 'legible' (54): character should be readable from a face. It is within such a context of expression that we should read the more dangerous inscrutability of characters such as Lady Dedlock in *Bleak House* or Edith Grainger in *Dombey and Son*.

Three nineteenth-century Charleses apart from Dickens worked exhaustively on problems of the nature of and the transmission of emotions. Two were scientists and one an educationalist.

## Charles Bray, *The Education of the Feelings* (1838)

Bray was associated with the Unitarian *Monthly Repository* and writes from a specifically Christian standpoint. His book, as Stedman points out, ran to four English and one unauthorised American edition, the different editions charting not only Bray's but Victorian society's evolution. A reviewer in the *Westminster Review* (1850) praised his 'unaffected simplicity, and…clear, manly, healthfully vigorous moral tone'.[25] The picture that emerges from his most successful book overlaps at so many points with the basic tenets of Dickens's version of sentimentalism that the elision between the two value systems emerges very clearly. Bray's avowed aim is:

> To urge the great importance of MORAL EDUCATION – to show the bearing of a few great truths upon it – to point out the NATURAL LAWS which the Creator has established, by which the feelings are to be trained and cultivated.[26]

This sounds very much like the shape of the standard Dickensian moral plot as described by Valentine Cunningham:

> It is impossible to think of a Dickens plot, a Dickens fabulation, that is not arranged on [a] Christianized model of best behaviour, best ethnicity, and what is thought of as the best kind of learning curve, or *Bildung*, for his fiction's characters.[27]

Cunningham, like so many literary critics, presents this as if it were an approach unique to Dickens. Study of contemporary non-literary texts suggests that here, as in so much else, Dickens is a man of his time, part of a rich sentimental tradition. Here is Bray's account, in his section on 'Moral Feelings', of what sounds very like Dickens's (and Goldsmith's) 'sentimental hero':

> [A]n open, frank, ingenuous disposition is the most lovely of all [in a child] and that to which we can the soonest attach ourselves. (71)

He believes that 'benevolence', defined as 'the desire for universal good', is the 'most important [feeling] we possess' (123). Like Goldsmith, though, he can see the negative side of benevolence: its 'manifestations in man are often simply instinctive. It then forms the character of the good-natured man. He cannot say "No"' (124). Sympathy, 'the law of Kindness' he says, must help develop Benevolence in order 'to increase the sum of happiness'. Train the child, he concludes, until 'he will have no idea of happiness except that associated with the happiness of others' (130).

    Bray thus shows in his own thinking the development from Goldsmith's late eighteenth-century sceptical view of human goodness to Dickens's much more impassioned response. However, he also suggests an overlap, unacknowledged by Dickens (and indeed violently opposed by him in *Hard Times*) between his own views and those of the Utilitarians: anyone who aims to increase benevolence, argues Bray, is aiming for a social end: 'the largest possible sum of enjoyment' (129). Sentimental values for Bray then, though God-given, are social in origin and purpose.

## Charles Bell, *The Anatomy and Philosophy of Expression as Connected with the Fine Arts* [1806] (1844)[28]

Charles Bell's influential book went into seven editions during the century and was even read by Queen Victoria. A Scottish physiologist, he produced a blend of physiology, art criticism and popular science, which established mid-Victorian ways of imagining the human face and undoubtedly influenced Dickens, whether directly or indirectly, as the following quotations show:

> In the human countenance, under the influence of passion, there are characters expressed, and changes of features produced, which it is impossible to explain on the notion of a direct operation of the [individual] mind upon the features…
>
> Since we are dwellers in a material world it is necessary that the spirit should be connected with it by an organised body, without which it could neither feel nor react, nor manifest itself in any way. It is a fundamental law of our nature that the mind shall have its powers developed through the influence of the body… (82f.)
>
> Human sentiments prevailing in the expression of a face, will always make it agreeable or lovely. Expression is even of more consequence than shape: it will light up features otherwise heavy: it will make us forget all but the quality of the mind. (60)

Despite his scientific background, Bell's belief in the universality of human feeling, together with his Christian faith, make him effectively an apologist for sentimentalism. Bell believes that emotional expression is universal, given to us by 'nature' and finds this most clearly evident in the theatre:

> To see every one hushed to the softest breathing of sympathy with the silent expression of the actress, exhibits all mankind held together by one universal feeling: and that feeling, excited by expression, so deeply laid in our nature, as to have influence, without being obvious to reason. (89f.)

## Charles Darwin, *On the Origin of Species* (1859); *The Expression of the Emotions in Man and Animals* (1872)

Dickens adopted one of Darwin's key phrases for the title of *The Battle of Life* and, as Gillian Beer and George Levine have shown, his later novels are very much shaped by the understanding of the world made possible by the *Origin of Species* (1859). Nothing would seem to be more inimical to the sentimental tradition than Darwin's evolutionary narrative. However, as Peter Ackroyd points out:

> [B]ehind Darwin, was the belief that there were fixed laws of the universe which could be discovered and explained – there was no uncertainty, no relativity in their accounts – and it is this certainty, this knowability of the material world and the continuance of all living things, which lends Dickens's own imagined world the same coherence and structure.[29]

Dickens wrote an enthusiastic review of Robert Chambers's *Vestiges of the Natural History of Creation* (1844), using poetic imagery to demonstrate, in Michael Slater's words, 'how the scientific truths that are fast replacing old myths and superstitions are proving to be "at least as full of poetry" as the latter while "always [bearing] testimony to the stupendous workings of Almighty Wisdom"'.[30] Unlike Bray, Bell and Chambers, Darwin is not limited by a Christian worldview and does not need to distinguish absolutely between human and animal expressions of emotion. Dickens died in 1870, before the publication of Darwin's second great work, *The Expression of Emotion on Man and Animals* (1872), steered debates about emotional expression into a more secular and (what would have been to him) a more threatening direction; this work undoubtedly contributed to the decline in the latter years of the century of the sentimentalist tradition.

## Horace Dobell, *On Affections of the Heart* (1872)

What is missing from the mid-twentieth-century dismissal of sentimental tears is any sense of the habitus of the time, the structures of feeling available to a writer and evident in all textual productions, not simply and narrowly in literary texts. Of particular interest in assessing how the body was imagined are contemporary medical documents. Horace Dobell's *On Affections of the Heart* (1872)[31] illustrates the exact parallelism of medical and affective vocabulary – a parallelism which goes a long way towards explaining the dual spiritual/physical status of much of the vocabulary of sentimentalism, in particular 'the heart'. Several interesting insights can be gleaned from this medical handbook, designed to be read by other members of the profession, about the mid-Victorian world view. One which emerges from a series of 'anecdotes' (case histories) is the importance Dobell places on the constriction of the throat as 'the most fatal portent' of heart disease (43). Dobell addresses 'the Interdependence of Affections of the Heart, Brain, Lung and Stomach' and reveals (what seems to be equally true today) that many of his patients confuse dyspeptic symptoms with dangerous heart disease. Most of these early case histories end cheerfully with patients cured after several weeks of dietary treatment. However, this is not the case with patients who present symptoms of the throat: these, without exception in this collection, meet a quick and sudden end from heart attack. Dickens's keen perception of bodily symptoms and behaviour may well be evident here in the 'constriction of the throat' evinced by Magwitch in the first and in later scenes of *Great Expectations*. That 'click in the throat' which he experiences when faced with the kindness of Little Pip is a signifier of his 'good heart' and ultimate redeemability: Victorian medicine, as has been seen, validated Dickens's link between the throat and the heart.

The Victorian semiotic slippage between the physical and the moral is neatly encapsulated in Dobell's conclusion which I shall quote in full in order to illustrate the easy commerce between the two which was part of Dickens's cultural background:

> Steadily increasing disease of the muscular walls of the heart is frequently the result of persistence in sexual indulgence; and if affections of the heart should become more and more common, I fear we must attribute it, in some measure at least, to the sad fact that sexual excesses, and especially self-abuse, have most alarmingly increased in England since the more facile communications with the Continent of Europe have led to the constant interchange of scholars between French and English schools. (127–8)

Physical health and moral health are thus inseparable. Dickens used to be criticised for the 'bodilessness' of his characters, in particular, his heroines. I would like to argue for the opposite case: that the culture, the habitus of the time, made little distinction between the physical and the emotional: debauchery left unmistakeable physical signs. 'Rude health' was a virtue, as in Kit Nubbles or Joe Gargery; on the other hand, saintly children in decline were obviously 'too good for this world'. Therefore, Dickens's declining heroines and innocent child death-beds need not for nineteenth-century readers be explained by specific medical diagnoses: it is sufficient that their bodies allow a moral point to be made – decades before Oscar Wilde made the same point in gothic terms in *The Picture of Dorian Gray*.

The parallelism of the vocabulary of the head and the (medical) heart is there too in the dedication of Dobell's work in which 'affection' becomes 'affectionate' and slips easily from head to heart. Dobell dedicates his work to Dr Burrows, as

> proof that the affectionate remembrance of a considerate and admired teacher has not been obliterated in that "Darwinian struggle for existence" so long and necessarily associated with the scientific work of

Your Sincere Friend
And Former Pupil
HORACE DOBELL, M.D.[32]

## The Sentimental Tradition and Victorian Tears

Tears in eighteenth-century literature were used as signifiers of an emotional arousal which was analogous to (and in Sterne often directly identified with) sexual arousal. Even the taking of a handkerchief from the pocket carried a heavy freight of meaning! Richardson presents a typical scene in *Pamela*:

> '...so God Almighty bless you, and you, Mr Longman – and good Mrs Jervis – and every living soul of the family! And I will pray for you as long as I live.' – And so I rose up, and was forced to lean upon my master's elbow-chair, or I would have sunk down.
> 
> The poor old man wept more than I, and said, 'Ads bobbers, was ever the like heard, 'tis too much, too much, I can't bear it. As I hope to live I am quite melted. – Dear Sir, forgive her, the poor thing prays for you: she prays for us all: she owns her fault; yet won't be forgiven! I profess I know not what to make of it'.
> 
> My master himself, hardened wretch that he was, seemed a little moved, and took his handkerchief out of his pocket, and walked to the window. 'What sort of day is it?' said he.[33]

In *The Frozen Deep* Dickens acted out through the hero, Richard Wardour, a mid-Victorian version of the problem of expressing emotion through tears. Here restraint rather than expression is seen as the problem:

> WARDOUR: You came on deck and found me alone.
> CRAYFORD: And in tears.
> WARDOUR: The last I shall ever shed.
> CRAYFORD: Don't say that. There are times when a man is to be pitied indeed if he can shed no tears.[34]

The gushing of sentimental tears became a concern for nineteenth-century sceptics such as Thomas Carlyle, but for many of Dickens's readers they were regarded as a token of the success of a sentimental scene or novel. One exception to the mid-twentieth century's dismissive reaction is the renewed attention from Roland Barthes in *A Lover's Discourse* (1978). In 'In Praise of Tears' he takes Goethe's *The Sorrows of Young Werther* as his key text.

> The slightest amorous emotion, whether of happiness or of disappointment, brings Werther to tears. Werther weeps often, very often, and in floods. Is it

the lover in Werther who weeps, or is it the romantic?... By releasing his tears without constraint, he follows the orders of the amorous body, which is a body in liquid expansion, a bathed body: to weep together, to flow together: delicious tears finish off the reading of Klopstock which Charlotte and Werther perform together.[35]

Barthes' account of the breaking of boundaries, the 'weeping together' of the lovers seems particularly relevant to a study of nineteenth-century sentimental writing, suggesting as it does a union which is both romantic (that is, spiritual) and implicitly erotic. It might suggest too the merging of a range of significations, political and religious as well as spiritual and erotic, which make weeping together, for Dickens, the culminating moment in several major novels.

Among recent twenty-first century studies of 'affect', Dylan Evans provides a useful summary of the psychological theories surrounding tears,[36] making a valuable distinction between cathartic and sentimental tears. He argues that cultures and eras which value tears are drawing on the 'hydraulic theory of emotion' which 'envisions emotions as forces that seek discharge by any means necessary' (85). This, he says, is commonly held to date back to the ancient Greeks and their concept of 'catharsis' but, he argues, '[n]othing could be further from the truth' (81). Catharsis, he declares, was not about "letting off steam". He cites the philosopher Martha Nussbaum as arguing that 'it was a fairly intellectual activity, in which the relation of emotions to human action was clarified by a process of experience and reflection'. In contrast, the 'hydraulic theory' upon which sentimentalism depends perhaps emerged originally from Descartes's 'view of the nerves as pneumatic pumps' (83). On this view, Dickens and his nineteenth-century audience had moved away from rationality towards a concept of tears as safety valve – actual physical containers of emotion. Hence the cultural value of tears as accurate measurements of emotional arousal and emotional worth.

## Sentimentalism and Nineteenth-Century Psychology

In Dickens's own time, associationism was still the dominant trend in British psychology. Gesa Stedman points out that 'its development can be traced from John Locke via David Hartley, Thomas Reid, Thomas Brown, William Hamilton, James Mill, John Stuart Mill and Alexander Bain to Herbert Spencer and Charles Darwin'.[37] Dickens took a stand against these utilitarian thinkers in general but in his later novels he certainly seems to recognise associationist principles, most notably in *Great Expectations*, where the adult narrator looks back on his younger self and mourns 'What could I become with these surroundings?' (96). Joe Gargery, Estella and Magwitch are all shown to be products of the associations established in their early life. The specificity of associationism, of course, sets it in direct opposition to the absolutism and idealism of sentimentalist thinking. In his earlier novels Dickens presents Oliver Twist and Little Nell as proof against all environmental corruption. The point in the late novels at which the two theories – the sentimental/idealist and the associationist – come most movingly together is at the end of *Little Dorrit*, when Clennam notices, even in Little Dorrit, a 'speck...of the prison atmosphere upon her' which he forgives, attributing it to her upbringing and to the shade of the Marshalsea.[38]

## Sentimentalism and Nineteenth-Century Drama

For most of the twentieth century it was commonplace for criticism to allege that audiences and readers no longer responded to the way emotions were conveyed in the eighteenth and nineteenth centuries. This seems now to be changing. Josephine Miles gives a salutary reminder that our *own* current assumptions are likely to be subject to fashion and to change themselves.[39] Modern critics, she says, simply assume that 'most of the ways of *implying* feeling [are] more effective than statement itself' (15).

> We now tend to measure emotion more by tension than by spread...its weight is not now, as it was then, present in its very name. The oceans of tears, the gusts of sighs, the heaving of bosoms, the fits and faints, [all] represented moods and reactions with a clear meaning and value to the owners, and if they were obvious, so are most fashionable habits of mind as of manner. (87)

Educational, aesthetic, sociological and scientific accounts of the expression of emotion in the nineteenth century come together, as the Miles quotation implies, in accounts of theatrical speech. What Dickens saw when he watched his friend Macready on stage fed into his own characterisations and into his own rhetoric. Bertram Joseph gives an account of the way in which an actor's voice could create its own climax which suggests parallels with Dickens's rhetoric of intensification.[40] Joseph links this with Elizabethan rhetorical figures known as 'figures of words'. These are essentially patterns of sound, such as rhyme, alliteration, assonance and climax: and the voice suitable for them is described as that 'pleasant and delicate tuning of the voice which resembleth the consent and harmony of some well-ordered song'. The mind trained to recognise the figure of climax, and the voice trained to make the figure 'manifest' would have been able to make the audience respond to Claudius's lines:

> And let the kettle to the trumpet speak,
> The trumpet to the cannoneer without,
> The cannons to the heaven, the heaven to earth
> Now the king drinks to Hamlet. (V.ii.267–70)[41]

Allan S. Downer discusses the actors' textbooks which listed very specifically how an emotion was traditionally registered. He quotes Wilkes's *A General View of the Stage*, describing the 'superlative degree of wonder':

> Simple admiration occasions no very remarkable alteration in the countenance; the eye fixes upon the object; the right-hand naturally extends itself with the palm turned outwards; and the left-hand will share in the action, though so as scarcely to be perceived, not venturing far from the body; but when this surprise reaches a superlative degree, which I take to be astonishment, the whole body is activated; it is thrown back, with one leg set before the other, both hands elevated, the eyes larger than usual, the brow drawn up, and the mouth not quite shut.[42]

To understand the posturing of Sterne's characters or the behaviour of Bradley Headstone in *Our Mutual Friend*, one needs to appreciate the force of that 'naturally' ('the right hand *naturally* extends'). The *shapes* the passions took were seen as equivalent to the passions themselves. Joseph cites Thomas Wright in *The Passions of the Mind in General* (1604):

> It cannot be that he which heareth should sorrow, hate, envy or fear anything, that he should be induced to compassion or weeping, except all those motions the orator would stir up in the judge, be first imprinted and marked in the orator himself. And therefore Horace well observed, that he who will make me weep must first weep himself. (1031)

Richard Wollheim's twentieth-century account of expressive theory also stresses the link between artist and spectator:

> The state expressed by the work of art is among those states, conscious or unconscious, to which the artist and spectator stand in some possessive relation.[43]

Dickens's sentimental narrator is, in these terms, a splendid classical actor in the eighteenth-century tradition of Mountford and Betterton. He induces the reader to weep precisely by 'first weeping himself'. He is intimate with the audience, a close and valued friend. The acting out of emotions in the style of Macready does not, in the mid-nineteenth century, preclude sincerity: as in the case of tears, it authenticates emotion, drawing actor/novelist and spectator into a bond at once public and intensely private.

From the foregoing it should be possible to venture some working definitions of the sentimentalism Dickens inherited and which he developed into a vehicle for his own ethical and rhetorical vision. Some sentimental values are: belief in the basic goodness of human nature, belief in right reason linked with right emotions (the heart as the seat of right judgement), secularity (in the sense of demystification), optimism, sympathy for others, the primacy of the social virtues and yet (in some works) the spiritual significance of the physical world. These are embodied in a rhetoric of: idealisation, hyperbole, blurring of meaning through trains of adjectives, religious imagery applied to secular – often erotic – subjects, deliberate discouragement of mental activity. The sentimental register involves the frequent naming of emotions and a limited range of stylised, highly charged metaphors. The rhetoric of intensification Dickens evolved was also one of paradox. Dickensian sentimentalism is a secular mode presented in Christian terms; a sensual mode presented in spiritual terms; a rational mode whose effect is intensely emotional; a public mode glorifying domestic, private virtues; a mode which idealises woman, but relies for its most powerful effect on the victimisation and suffering of the heroine. What unites works as different as *Clarissa* and *The Old Curiosity Shop* are family resemblances such as Wittgenstein describes in his definition of Games.[44] Northrop Frye's comment on comedy could therefore equally well be applied to sentimentalism: it is 'not an essence word but a context word'.[45] What I attempt to establish in what follows is the sentimentalist context within which Dickens's novels need to be read.

## Chapter 2

## SENTIMENTALISM AND ITS DISCONTENTS IN THE EIGHTEENTH-CENTURY NOVEL: FIELDING, RICHARDSON AND STERNE

'There was more of pleasantry in the conceit, of seeing how an ass would eat a macaroon – than of benevolence in giving him one.'[1]

My father had left a small collection of books in a little room upstairs, to which I had access (for it adjoined my own) and which nobody else in our house ever troubled. From that blessed little room, *Roderick Random*, *Peregrine Pickle*, *Humphrey Clinker*, *Tom Jones*, *The Vicar of Wakefield*, *Don Quixote*, *Gil Blas*, and *Robinson Crusoe*, came out, a glorious host, to keep me company. They kept alive my fancy, and my hope of something beyond that place and time, – they, and the *Arabian Nights* and the *Tales of the Genii*, – and did me no harm; for whatever harm was in some of them was not there for me. I knew nothing of it…I have been Tom Jones (a child's Tom Jones, a harmless creature) for a week together. I have sustained my own idea of Roderick Random for a month at a stretch, I verily believe… This was my only and my constant comfort.[2]

Wilhelm Dibelius commented as long ago as 1916 that Dickens was an author who 'das 19. Jahrhundert mit den Augen des 18. betrachtet' (saw the nineteenth century with the eyes of the eighteenth).[3] This is the accepted view, that Dickens's childhood reading of Fielding, Sterne and Smollett helped form his moral vision.[4] However, my argument in this chapter is rather different: it is that it was his peculiarly nineteenth-century (conscious or unconscious) *mis*reading of his favourites which made that vision, and his own achievement, so different from theirs. Dickens's debt to the eighteenth-century novel has recently begun to be reassessed, for example by Monika Fludernik who aims to identify, as she puts it, 'typical features a) that Dickens shares with eighteenth-century novels; b) that Dickens fails to take over from eighteenth-century fiction and c) that are new in Dickens'.[5] She points out under the first heading the combination of 'oddity and a good heart' common to Sterne's Uncle Toby and to a host of Dickens's 'sentimental grotesques' from Pickwick to Mr Dick; under the second heading, she notes the absence of sexual innuendo and under the third, Dickens's development of symbolic structures to carry his social criticism. I shall develop some of these points alongside my own in this chapter, focusing upon the three novelists I take to have been his major sentimental predecessors: Henry Fielding, Samuel Richardson and Laurence Sterne.[6]

## Henry Fielding

In tracking the origins of the nineteenth-century sentimentalist 'divided style', so apparent in Dickens's linguistic insulating of his heroes and heroines from the threat of the language of wit, an obvious place to start is with what twentieth-century critics saw as the binary opposition between Henry Fielding and Samuel Richardson. The former is regularly adduced as a predecessor of Dickens, but Richardson's influence has been less often mooted. Martin Battestin (1961) clearly sets out that supposed opposition, interestingly already construing it in terms of gender:

> In the early 1749s...the English novel came all at once into being as an art form, its two main directions – inward, toward the individual personality, and outward, toward the panorama of society – arising from the conflicting temperaments and literary motives of two very different men, Samuel Richardson and Henry Fielding. It could hardly be called a marriage, but from the rude and often hilarious conjunction of Richardson's feminine sensibilities and Fielding's robust masculinity, the modern novel was born.[7]

Monika Fludernik also asserts that Dickens 'combines the sentimental (Richardson) and the satirical (Fielding)'[8] while Dickens himself mentions both Fielding and Richardson as literary forebears in the preface to *Oliver Twist*, to be discussed later. I shall look briefly at Fielding, whose influence on Dickens has been well documented, before turning to the much less discussed debt to Richardson.

Fielding's 'robust masculinity' often disguises his own place firmly within the sentimentalist tradition. His description of Sophia Western in *Tom Jones* is as ample, as exuberantly artificial, as excessive, as Dickens's description of the death of Little Nell. Both are prepared for as grand set pieces, trumpeted by the narrative voice. Fielding proclaims the literariness of his enterprise ('A short history of what we can do with the sublime, and a description of Miss Sophia Western.')[9] Dickens, though less overtly self-consciously literary, in fact achieves a similar 'sublime' effect, using a different part of the sentimental register, in the death of Nell. In *Tom Jones*, Sophia's external features are enumerated minutely, in Fielding's joyous appropriation and transformation into prose of the Renaissance 'blazon':

> Her shape was not only exact, but extremely delicate; and the nice proportion of her arms promised the truest symmetry in her limbs. Her hair, which was black, was so luxuriant that it reached her middle… Her eyebrows were full, even and arched…her black eyes had a lustre in them. Her cheeks were of the oval kind; and in her right she had a dimple, which the least smile discovered…[10]

Fielding goes on to balance the physical with the 'sentimental' in the eighteenth-century definition of good sense: 'Such was the outside of Sophia…her mind was in every way equal to her person.'[11] Everything about the literary treatment of Sophia depends on a verbal excess borrowed from sentimentalist rhetoric. This is not often critically recognised as such, partly because of the binary thinking exemplified by Battestin (Fielding must be at every point the opposite of Richardson) and partly because of the knowingness of the narrative voice. I would argue that this knowingness is part of the sentimental tradition, not its opposite. James Boswell noted in Fielding's own day that 'He who is as good as Fielding would make him, is an amiable member of society, and may be led on…to a higher state of ethical perfection.'[12] Fielding's intrusive narrative voice is constructed from the sentimental register, a borrowing from the roll call of sentimental character types: his is effectively 'The Good-Natured Man As Narrator'. *Tom Jones* is therefore narrated by a figure not unlike Goldsmith's Mr Honeychurch. Fielding's irony plays around that central viewpoint: it is the narrative voice itself which is gently ironised – ironised but not undermined. The entire novel, including its comedy, its eroticism (very much part of eighteenth-century sentimentalism, as will be suggested later in this chapter in relation to Sterne), even its darker moments, is contained within a sentimental narrator's consciousness and conveyed through a sentimental narrator's voice. This is perhaps most evident in the novel's opening and concluding moments.

Squire Allworthy, as his name suggests, is offered to the reader by the sentimental narrator as a completely admirable character. The wholeness of the eighteenth-century sentimental habitus is nowhere more evident than in the enumeration of his personal qualities. He was given by nature 'an agreeable person, a sound constitution, a solid understanding, and a benevolent heart'.[13] Physical health and mental toughness are essential to that wholeness. Dickens's benefactor figures, from the Cheerybles in *Nicholas Nickleby* to John Jarndyce in *Bleak House*, are similarly gifted. Fielding is at pains to point out that Allworthy is also a tragic figure, having lost both his beloved wife and their family of three children before the story begins. The voice which conveys Allsworthy's stoicism is sentimental, in its efforts to elicit an emotional response from the reader:

> [He] sometimes said that he looked on himself as still married, and considered his wife as only gone a little before him, a journey which he should most certainly, sooner or later, take after her; and that he had not the least doubt that he would meet his wife in heaven again, never to part from her more – sentiments for which his sense was arraigned by one part of his neighbours, his religion by a second, and his sincerity by a third.[14]

The sentimental narrator's voice noticeably does not undermine Allsworthy's belief: what *is* undermined here (in the manner Jane Austen was to go on to develop) is the cynicism of public opinion. A similarly tragic tale is told by Dickens, in his opening chapter, of the Nickleby family. Here, the evocation of sympathetic tears is more blatant but the underlying belief system is in fact a similar sentimental Christianity:

> Mr Nickleby shook his head, and motioning them all out of the room, embraced his wife and children, and having pressed them by turns to his languidly beating heart, sunk exhausted on his pillow. They were concerned to find that his reason went astray after this; for he babbled, for a long time, about the generosity and goodness of his brother and the merry old times when they were at school together. This fit of wandering past, he solemnly commended them to One who never deserted the widow or her fatherless children, and smiling gently on them, turned upon his face, and observed that he thought he could fall asleep.[15]

The sentimental narrator reveals himself even more obviously in the conclusion of *Tom Jones*, in which, at the final wedding feast, Sophia 'was as much distinguished by her modesty and affability as by all other perfections'.[16] The humour here, it must be noted, is not directed at Sophia, but at the 'seeing eye', the sentimental narrator with his partiality and his emotional excesses. Such a figure appeared on the contemporary stage in sentimental comedy as a 'humour' figure whose generosity would be gently mocked, without the underlying benevolent value system being questioned.

The final paragraph of the novel is a model of eighteenth-century sentimentalism, characteristically balancing emotion and understanding:

> To conclude, as there are not to be found a worthier man and woman, than this fond couple, so neither can any be imagined more happy. They preserve the purest and tenderest affection for each other, an affection daily increased and confirmed by mutual endearments and mutual esteem. Nor is their conduct

towards their relations and friends less amiable than towards one another. And such is their condescension, their indulgence, and their beneficence to those below them, that there is not a neighbour, a tenant, or a servant, who doth not most gratefully bless the day when Mr Jones was married to his Sophia.[17]

The ending of *Nicholas Nickleby* could not be more different and suggests that Dickens's sentimentalism had moved a long way from Fielding's optimistic belief in a stable (albeit almost feudal) social interconnectedness, to a nostalgia which contains within it an implicit rejection of nineteenth-century society:

> The grass was green above the dead boy's grave, and trodden by feet so small and light, that not a daisy drooped its head beneath their pressure. Through all the spring and summertime, garlands of fresh flowers, wreathed by infant hands, rested on the stone; and when the children came there to change them lest they should wither and be pleasant to him no longer, their eyes filled with tears and they spoke lowly and softly of their poor dead cousin.[18]

The ending of *Little Dorrit*, however (discussed further in Chapter 6), which is perhaps the most powerful ending in all of Dickens's novels, suggests a return to Fielding's eighteenth-century optimism, heavily re-inflected for an industrial age:

> They went quietly down into the roaring streets, inseparable and blessed; and, as they passed along in sunshine and in shade, the noisy and the eager, and the arrogant and the froward and the vain, fretted and chafed, and made their usual uproar.[19]

Fielding tells, names emotions, rationalises them; Dickens shows, enacts, embodies. The difference, though, is more apparent than real. Fielding's optimism depends on the individual benevolence resulting from a good marriage; Dickens's optimism, in an urban jungle, depends on exactly the same thing. Both, by this reading are, while well aware of the dangers of the social world, sentimental optimists.

Fielding's frequently cited 'masculinity' of style is usually taken as implying a key difference from Dickens: the earlier novelist's sexual knowingness had to be transmuted by the later into the very different register of his own time. Dickens recognises this himself in the account of his childhood reading quoted above, which describes his invention of 'a child's Tom Jones'. It could be argued that he never progressed beyond this figure. The sequence of good-hearted heroes who owe their existence to Fielding's prototype – from Nicholas Nickleby through Martin Chuzzlewit to Pip in *Great Expectations* – are sexless figures, according to many critics, existing in a sexless literary world. Helen Small declares that '[t]he wish to be identified with Fielding is unmistakable in Dickens's numerous references to the novels, plays and other public writings across the course of his career' but that 'acts of reaffirmation' were accompanied by 'firm repudiation on Dickens's part – most obviously when it came to thinking about sex and class'.[20] She goes on to suggest that Dickens used eccentricity as a substitute for the erotic. Fludernik too notes in Dickens 'the absence of an erotic subtext'.[21] This assessment ignores Dickens's own nineteenth-century rhetoric of sentimental eroticism, expressed through the shedding of tears. Here, the influence is not Fielding, but Richardson in *Clarissa*.

## Samuel Richardson

Diderot's judgement that on closing *Clarissa*, 'I felt I had acquired experience'[22] represents the response of most of Richardson's contemporary readers to the novel. Twentieth-century critics, however, concentrated, as they did with Dickens, on cordoning off and dismissing what they saw as the sentimental elements as essentially vitiating. Anthony Kearney's account may stand for all. Of Belford's description of Clarissa in decline, he writes:

> The writing is strained and appallingly unctuous – almost obscene in its sentimentalising over Clarissa's physical qualities...the truth is that Richardson's own sharper response to language, thought and feeling became dulled when he attempted pathetic scenes, and he fell into *feeble sentimentalisms*.[23]

Such a narrow account of the major literary tradition from which this novel sprang is reductive. As in the case of Dickens, the twentieth-century tendency is to separate out the recognisably 'modern' elements and to discard the rest. I will argue that *Clarissa*, like much of Dickens's work, is conceived and structured within the sentimental mode and that what Kearney sees as its defects are inseparable from its strengths.

To establish first the structure of the novel: it is built upon one unifying action, the pursuit and eventual seduction of Clarissa by Lovelace, but this Restoration surface conceals a drama of conversion. As in Richard Steele's *The Tender Husband* (1705) and many other plays of the period, it is not so much the rape as the ultimate victory of Clarissa's values over Lovelace's that is the climax towards which the whole plot moves. The emotional power of the climax is achieved by a simplifying and intensifying of the action, which is typical of sentimental writing in both the eighteenth and nineteenth centuries. Just as Nahum Tate simplified and sentimentalised *King Lear* in the early eighteenth century by concentrating entirely on the love between Cordelia and her father, so Richardson subordinates everything else to the conversion by the heroine (albeit after death) of the (anti-) hero. A unity of action derived from the drama thus contributes to the emotional intensification of the sentimental novel; this was something Dickens learned in his construction of *Dombey and Son* which, for all its panoramic scale, is focused intensely and exclusively in the end on Florence's sentimental pursuit of her father.[24] Made possible by this intensification are two closely related though apparently contradictory expansions of meaning, in one direction into moral didacticism and in the other towards indulgent eroticism. Long before he attempts the seduction, Lovelace expatiates on its spiritual implications. Clarissa's servants, he says,

> are entirely attached to her. Whatever she says is, must be, Gospel… Is not this the hour of her trial – and in her, of the trial of the virtue of her whole sex, so long premeditated, so long threatened?… And will she not want the very crown of glory…if I stopped short of the ultimate trial?[25]

The sentimental heroine thus becomes a Christ-surrogate, and it is this tradition that Dickens draws upon in the presentation of Florence in *Dombey and Son*. What he cannot draw on so blatantly is the erotic concomitant of that tradition, the sexual titillation involved in the assailing of the virtuous female figure:

> I snatched her hand, rising, and pressed it first to my lips and then to my heart, in wild disorder. She might have felt the bounding mischief ready to burst its bars. You shall go – to your own apartment if you please – but, by the Great God of Heaven, I will accompany you thither![26]

The punctuation, the pauses followed by the final outburst, imitates the sexual arousal which is its subject and the link between sublimity ('the Great God in Heaven!') and the erotic is openly made, in an almost Blakean way, with lust identified with divine energy. A century later, Dickens seems to write exclusively within the religious register in presenting the union of Florence and Walter (see Chapter 6), but he achieves thereby a sentimental climax in his audience, analogous to the erotic arousal in this passage. In *Clarissa*, the religious and sexual connotations can be held in suspension, both sets of meanings being simultaneously available to the reader, which releases the power of both registers:

> I saw that it was impossible to conceal myself any longer from her, any more than (from the violent impulses of my passion) to forebear manifesting myself. I unbuttoned therefore my cape, I pulled off my flapped, slouched hat; I threw open my great coat, and like the devil in Milton (an odd comparison though!)

> I started up in mine own form divine,
> …She no sooner saw who it was than she gave three violent screams.[27]

Held in suspension here are various meanings, and the power of the prose depends on them all being recognised. In one sense, Lovelace is here performing the rape in dumb show, Clarissa acknowledging his invasion with 'three violent screams'. The rich ambiguity of such prose depends upon the range of registers available, as well as on the eighteenth-century epistolary mode and the device of the 'unreliable narrator'. This contrasts with the rhetoric available to Dickens when describing a similar scene, between Rosa and Jasper, in *The Mystery of Edwin Drood*:

> His preservation of his easy attitude rendering his working features and his convulsive hands absolutely diabolical, he returns, with a fierce extreme of admiration:
> 'How beautiful you are! You are more beautiful in anger than repose. I don't ask for your love; give me yourself and your hatred; give me yourself and that pretty rage; give me yourself and that enchanting scorn; it will be enough for me.'
> Impatient tears rise to the eyes of the trembling little beauty, and her face flames; but as she again rises to leave him and seek protection within the house, he stretches out his hand towards the porch, as though he invited her to enter it.
> 'I told you, you rare charmer, you sweet witch, that you must stay and hear me…'
> Again Rosa quails before his threatening face…and she remains. Her panting breathing comes and goes as if it would choke her; but with a repressive hand on her bosom, she remains.[28]

This passage works by a simple rather than a complex rhetoric and lacks the richness and ambiguity of the language available to Richardson. Juliet John has suggested that Dickens explores in Jasper 'the self-consumed, performative personality' who represents 'the social causes and effects of repressive deviance'.[29] The scene certainly suggests that Dickens, while using very similar material to Richardson, is forced into working for quite different rhetorical effects, and achieving an intensity based upon the intensification of a single melodramatic register, rather than on the complex power of the parallel religious and erotic registers available to Richardson.

The sentimental moral tableau is a feature of the mode Dickens could and did inherit and exploit, in *Dombey and Son* and elsewhere. Richardson invites the reader's participation in exploring his central figure as if she were a statue rather than a structure of words:

> We behold the lady in a charming attitude. Dressed in virgin white, she was sitting in her elbow chair, Mrs Lovick close by her on another chair, with her left arm round her neck... One faded cheek rested upon the good woman's bosom.[30]

This picturesque approach is a reminder of the public nature of the mode and its links at every point with both the visual arts and with theatre – another anticipation of the nineteenth-century theatrical sentimentalism of Dickens. What animates Richardson's novel is the fruitful tension set up between the characteristic rhetoric of Lovelace – active, articulated, full of verbs and verbal energy – and the characteristic rhetoric of Clarissa – passive, static, rational – and the drama is contained in the breakdown of each one under pressure from the other. It is precisely this that Dickens borrowed and used, notably in *The Old Curiosity Shop*, in which Quilp's demonic linguistic energy is only made possible by Nell's preternatural linguistic passivity. In both cases, language, rather than plot, is the real site of the ethical struggle.

One final sentimental device used by Richardson and developed by Dickens is that of the shedding of tears – that central authentication of the sentimentalist response, which begins in the character and is then communicated, by sympathy, to the reader. The function of tears can in the eighteenth century be both didactic and sensual. Clarissa's weeping is on an heroic scale, acting as a metonym for the grandeur of her emotions. When Lovelace 'rescues' her from the fire, her weeping (already quoted in the Introduction) is described initially in erotic terms and then suddenly, following the break in punctuation, in the register of eighteenth-century rationality – an option no longer available to Dickens in the following century:

> There, in the anguish of her soul, her streaming eyes lifted up to my face with supplicating softness, hands folded, dishevelled hair; for her nightdress having fallen off in her struggling, her charming tresses fell down in naturally shining ringlets, as if officious to conceal the dazzling beauties of her neck and shoulders; her lovely bosom too heaving with sighs and broken sobs, as if to aid her quivering lips in pleading for her – [shift from erotic to rational register] in this manner, and when her grief gave way to her speech, in words pronounced with that emphatical propriety which distinguishes this admirable creature in her elocution from all the women I ever heard speak, did she implore my compassion and my honour. (263)

Other characters are measured by their response to the heroine's tears (as, by implication, are we, the readers). Belford, unlike Lovelace, passes the test:

> By my soul, I could not speak. She had not her Bible before her for nothing. I was forced to turn my head away, and to take out my handkerchief. (376–7)

Sentimental weeping is a highly operatic mode, a virtuoso linguistic performance. Sometimes Clarissa can extend her emotional range beyond tears, like a soprano reaching for a high note:

> I was speechless. Although my heart was ready to burst, yet I could neither weep nor speak. (36)

Richardson's is heroic drama, built on a grand scale and emotionally pulling no punches. Yet in assessing the relation of Fielding and Richardson to the eighteenth-century sentimental tradition, critics are always tempted to simplify. A notable example of a recent rather counter-intuitive judgement is that of Frank H. Ellis: his assessment needs to be quoted in full for its divergence from the norm to be apparent:

> It seems that the major English writers who deal in 'sentimentals' (Garrick's phrase), Fielding, Sterne, Goldsmith, Sheridan, Jane Austen, without exception satirise sentimentality. It is only the lesser figures, Steele, Cumberland, Henry Mackenzie, Henry Brooke, who take it seriously or play it straight. Samuel Richardson is 'the glory, jest and riddle' of eighteenth-century sentimental writing because one does not know what to make of him... he must be the exception that proves the rule.[31]

Ellis's problems with Richardson suggest the inadequacy of the traditional simplistic reading. The 'Fielding's masculine robustness/Richardson's feminine sensibility' binary with which the chapter began has already been shown to deconstruct at every turn, and with it collapses the clichéd and reductive definitions of sentimentalism. One further twist is that, when Dickens listed his predecessors in the preface to *Oliver Twist* referred to earlier, he was in fact not seeking and describing a *sentimental* tradition, but rather looking for precedents in a tradition of social realism, in order to find literary justification for the heavily criticised Sikes and Nancy:

> If I look for examples, and for precedents, I find them in the noblest range of English literature. Fielding, DeFoe, Smollett, Richardson, Mackenzie – all these

for wise purposes, and especially the two first, brought upon the scene the very scum and refuse of the land.[32]

The fact that he includes Mackenzie and Richardson in this list of eighteenth-century 'social realists' shows just how complicated the question of literary sentimentalism is. Dickens values Richardson not for his sentimental heroines but for his ability to show the darker side of society – presumably the pimps and prostitutes who also inhabit *Clarissa*. The flinging of Clarissa into the depths of social degradation anticipates Dickens's technique with *Oliver Twist*. In each case, the emotional impact comes from the extreme juxtaposition of dark and light and from the extreme vulnerability of the protagonist, just as when Clarissa is thrown into a brothel:

> A horrid hole of a house, in an alley they call a court; stairs wretchedly narrow, even to the first-floor rooms: and into a den they led me, with broken walls, which had been papered, as I saw by a multitude of tacks, and some torn bits held by the rusty heads…
>
> A bed at one corner, with coarse curtains tacked up at the feet to the ceiling. The windows dark and double-barred; and only a little four-paned eyelet-hole of a casement to let in air; more, however, coming in at broken panes than could come in at that. (372)

Fielding and Richardson are not, it turns out, the binary opposites of literary legend. On this evidence, although Dickens does learn from Richardson how to develop the sentimental heroine, he learns from him too the emotional power of presenting social degradation; though he does learn from Fielding how to present farcical scenes and wild comedy, he also learns from him how to contain everything, comedy and seriousness, within an overarching sentimental vision, through the sentimental narrator. Dickens inherited and adapted from Fielding not simply the energy and inventiveness of his prose, the comic afflatus of *Shamela*, but also precisely that underlying belief in benevolence, that amplitude of vision which overarches eighteenth-century 'sentimentalism'. One might therefore invert and collapse the accepted hierarchy and produce 'Fielding the sentimentalist' and 'Richardson the knowing man of the world', as contributors to Dickens's own 'divided style'.

## Laurence Sterne

Charles Dickens revelled in the works of Sterne, and *Tristram Shandy* has a particular role in the inception of *Dombey and Son*. Famously, looking for a prompt to embark on the novel, Dickens took down a copy of Sterne's work from his shelves, opened it at random and came upon the line, 'What a work it is likely to turn out! Let us begin it!'[33] Since Tristram's own conception is itself the problematic theme of Sterne's novel and since *Dombey* is so centrally concerned with fatherhood, this is a nice instance of what Harold Bloom has called 'the Anxiety of Influence'.[34] The opening scene of *Dombey*, with Dr Parker Peps's watch loudly ticking as little Paul enters life and his mother leaves it, reads rather more poignantly in the context of Tristram's parents' concern about winding up the clock at the moment of his conception. The earlier novel seems uncannily to 'father' the later one. Later in the writing of *Dombey*, Dickens wrote to Macready from Geneva, 'Here I am running away from a bad headache, as Tristram Shandy ran away from Death.'[35] This suggests the close link between Tristram's flight from death and Carker's in the later novel, as a stylistic comparison in Chapter 6 will reveal.

Dickens's reading and arguably his *mis*reading of Sterne is thus of major importance in understanding the construction of his own nineteenth-century sentimentalist rhetoric. There are obvious similarities and even more obvious differences between the two writers. The observation that every critic of Dickens is really writing about him/herself surely applies with even greater force to every critic of Sterne. Sterne openly acknowledges the importance of the reader in a well-known letter:

> [A] true feeler always brings half the entertainment along with him. His own ideas are only call'd forth by what he reads, and the vibrations within so entirely correspond with those excited, 'tis like reading Himself and not the book.[36]

The reader of Dickens has no such latitude. Bound in a strong emotional bond to Dickens's narrator, his/her experience is intense albeit narrow, and it is this combination of intensity over a restricted range of emotions that gives the later novels their particular form of affect. In exploring the constraints imposed upon Dickens by the sentimental mode, I shall pursue the theme here by contrasting them with the comparative freedoms enjoyed by Sterne.

Sterne always seems to have aroused strong, apparently contradictory responses in his readers, extremes epitomised by Richard Cumberland in his own time and by W. M. Thackeray in the following century:

> [Sterne] comes at once upon the heart, refines, amends it, softens it; beats down each selfish barrier from about it, and opens every sluice of pity and benevolence.[37]
>
> There is not a page of Sterne's writing but has something that were better away, a latent corruption – a hint, as of an impure presence.[38]

These partial and diametrically opposed views suggest the intensely personal responses Sterne evokes but also hint at the different moral and aesthetic frames of reference of eighteenth- and nineteenth-century readers. Certainly there is circumstantial evidence to support both points of view. When Thomas Jefferson, responding in the same period much as Cumberland did, declared that 'the writings of Sterne...form the best course of morality that ever was written'[39] he was thinking probably of passages like the death of Le Fever, in which Uncle Toby's benevolence is extolled. Thackeray, in contrast, may have had in mind such scenes as Trim's nursing by the nun or Tristram's lubricious disquisitions on chambermaids or old hats. Certainly the central problem of *Tristram Shandy* is one of narrative voice. To put it crudely (as Sterne so often does), when is the author being 'serious' and when is he having a joke at the reader's expense? In tackling that question one is bound to raise some of the basic issues connected with the sentimental mode: what is authorial sincerity? How does it differ from artistic sincerity? Why should two such 'light' works, each ending in a cheap joke, be subjected to such a weight of critical attention? And does all writing, whether humorous or serious, involve a degree of complicity between author and reader, a tacit agreement *not* to entertain certain possibilities in relation to the fictional action?

The answer to the last question is, in most works of literature, yes. If the reader breaks the tacit contract, that act of rebellion is enough to throw the whole relationship of fiction into chaos. It is obviously important to accept genre conventions, the author's 'donnée', and not to ask for something that the author has not contracted to provide. But what if it is the author who breaks the tacit contract? What sort of relationship can possibly be established between an earnest readership and an author who flouts the convention which is the only bond between them? There could, of course, be a relationship based on complete misunderstanding. The importance of *mis*reading, whether wilful or unconscious, in the evolution of literary tradition has been explored in various ways, for example, by John Bayley and Frank Kermode, by Harold Bloom and by Roland Barthes.[40] For the last-named, 'the author' is in any case a chimerical figure. For him and, even more significantly, for Mikhail Bakhtin,[41] meanings are endlessly negotiated and renegotiated between reader and text. The sentimental tradition is particularly open to Bakhtinian readings, as a later chapter will reveal.

In the early nineteenth century, a volume of extracts entitled *The Beauties of Sterne* was published, and it was this extremely selective and narrow approach which helped form Dickens's own reading.[42] Dickens, unlike Thackeray, shared his age's sentimental reading of Sterne. This contributed to – and was a symptom of – his own generally rigid separation of the sentimental and the comic registers. The problem is that, to frame the question of how to read

Sterne in Hegelian terms of him being *either* a humorist or a sentimentalist, is to react as if Sterne were a nineteenth-century rather than an eighteenth-century writer, as my choice of adverbial phrase suggests. The model for Sterne is undoubtedly the Lockean associative one. Although *Tristram Shandy* began, as A. D. Nuttall argues, as an *attack* on Locke's thought, it emerges as 'not a destroyer of the fashionable world-picture, but, with its chaotic determinism, its biological psychology and its microscopic characterisation, its one adequate literary monument'.[43] Nuttall's own mid-twentieth-century reading, however, itself misses much of Sterne's irony and concludes that Sterne's morality is merely 'sentiment, issuing in eccentricity, symbolised by sexual incapacity'.

Certainly Sterne's emotional empiricism produces, for nineteenth- and mid-twentieth-century readers particularly, a rhetoric of bewilderment. Le Fever dies, and the effect seems to be one of pathos:

> Nature instantly ebb'd again – the film returned to its place, – the pulse fluttered – stopped – went on – throb'd – stopp'd again – moved – stopped shall I go on? No.[44]

Bobby dies, and the event is treated satirically:

> 'My young master in London is dead!' said Obadiah. A green satin nightgown of my mother's which had been twice scoured, was the first idea which Obadiah's explanation brought into Susannah's head... 'O! 'twill be the death of my poor mistress!' cried Susannah. My mother's whole wardrobe followed – What a procession! Her red damask – her orange tawny...not a rag left behind. 'No, she will never look up again!' said Susannah.[45]

At times, as in the second extract, what is going on seems a parody of Locke. At others, as in the earlier extract, Sterne seems to be taking Locke straight. What he achieves, in the shifts of response and in the very instability of his approach is, as Nuttall suggests, an enactment of the association of ideas – which might seem to twenty-first century readers to anticipate postmodernism.

What Dickens could and could not take from Sterne emerges if one sets beside the reaction of the servants to Bobby's death, the reaction to Mr Dombey's servants to *his* fall. In the later novel, the narrative voice intrudes to keep the reader's attention firmly on the satirical intent:

> 'How are the mighty fallen!' remarks Cook.
> 'Pride shall have a fall, and it always was and will be so!' observes the housemaid.

> It is wonderful how good they feel in making these reflections; and what a Christian unanimity they are sensible of, in bearing the common shock with resignation.[46]

Humour here reinforces the seriousness of Dombey's fate, the satire highlighting the gulf between his tragic status and the cruel voices of society. Sterne's humour operates quite differently, imitating the anarchic and inappropriate occurrence of incongruity in life. It is the incidental irrelevances, the ludicrousness which emerges in the incapacities of serious mental or physical illness, the impulse to release tension in laughter even at a deathbed, the physical grotesqueness or the irrelevant thoughts which emerge at moments of passion or danger: it is the principle of misrule, of contingency, which governs the natural world and which nineteenth-century writers, faced with the terrors of Darwinism, sought to suppress, in the interests of coherence, of rationality or in sheer panic, and to channel off harmlessly into specially created reservoirs labelled 'humour'. To face the wholeness of the world as Sterne so uncompromisingly does requires courage from the reader – a courage no less than that required to confront the 'blank wall of tragedy' in *King Lear* or in Dostoevsky. It subsumes into itself, but does not negate, all notions of benevolence and compassion. Uncle Toby is in a way both Fool and Lear, both compassionate and tragic. Dickens's strengths very obviously lie elsewhere – in the intensity with which he presents both sentimentalism and humour and sometimes in the very tension involved in keeping them apart. In the *Dombey* extract above, humour is used to highlight Dombey's human dignity and tragic importance. Unlike Sterne's humour, Dickens's satire is intended ultimately to restate the significance of humanity in an increasingly inhuman world.

The linguistic equivalent of Sterne's Lockean philosophy is the easy movement of meaning between the physical and spiritual. This makes his work peculiarly relevant to recent studies of the construction of the body in literature, as in Kirstie Blair's *Victorian Poetry and the Culture of the Heart*.[47] In Sterne's rhetoric, sex, the unspeakable at the physical level, becomes a metaphor for the human relationship with God, the ineffable at the spiritual level. But, at the same time, the reverse is also true: events announced as spiritual become metaphors for sex. Double entendres, as it were, work in both directions. Tristram makes this double relation abundantly clear, for example, in his early assertion that 'a man's body and his mind, with the utmost reverence to both I speak it – are exactly like a jerkin and a jerkin's lining: rumple the one – you rumple the other'.[48] The 'utmost reverence to both' is what makes Sterne's work so important. He is seriously concerned with describing neither jerkin nor lining, but with the actual process of 'rumpling' – the ways in which human emotions are moved and the extent of that movement. Structurally, he achieves this both through the interweaving of heart and head involved in the parallelism of Uncle Toby and Walter Shandy, and through the shifting consciousness of his narrator. A closer examination of what Sterne could achieve in the mid-eighteenth century should reveal more precisely the very different cultural and linguistic resources which were available to Dickens a century later and which so drastically shifted his horizon of expectation. The very different achievement of *The Pickwick Papers* is more clearly recognised in the light of a reading of its illustrious predecessors. Pickwick's enthusiasm for experience is modelled fairly exactly on Tristram's, but the final effect is tellingly different: Pickwick's relationship with the sentimental narrator, though quietly ironised, is consistent. His benevolence is clearly supported, even while his naivety is questioned.

Tristram and Yorick have no sentimental narrator to give a single perspective on their fragmented and centrifugal selves, though there could be, on the surface, no more obviously 'sentimental' narrators in the mid-eighteenth-century sense than Tristram in his eponymous novel and Yorick in *A Sentimental Journey*. Both make a profession of emotionalism and can be moved by a fly, a goat, even a donkey eating macaroons. They are moved, however, along the emotional scale from tears to laughter at dizzying speed and the reader, accustomed to the nineteenth-century novel's omniscient and consistent narrator, is easily bewildered. Both Sterne's major works are closer to the contemporary epistolary novel than to their later nineteenth-century descendants, despite their form, which *seems* to anticipate the later bildungsroman. Sterne is interested in the movement of mind rather than in characterisation. He deliberately unsettles the reader by continuing the 'Yorick' figure from one novel to the next. The earlier 'Yorick-as-object' in *Tristram Shandy*, Tristram declares,

> had an invincible dislike and opposition in his nature to gravity; not to gravity as such – for where gravity was wanted, he would be the most grave or serious of mortal men for days and weeks together: but he was an enemy of the affectation of it, and declared open war against it, only as it appeared a cloak for ignorance or folly.[49]

The Yorick of *A Sentimental Journey* is quite different – a delighted explorer and exploiter of gravity as an emotion enjoyable in itself:

> 'Base passion!' said I, turning myself about, as a man naturally does upon a sudden reversal of sentiment – 'base, ungentle passion! Thy hand is against every man: and every man's hand is against thee–'[50]

The tempting identification of Sterne with Yorick is extremely misleading, though useful to those nineteenth-century readers (including Dickens?) who wished to see him as a simple sentimentalist. Tristram, with his grotesque whimsicality, his impotence and his inadequacies, seems much closer to what is known of Sterne himself. It was Tristram who uttered what might well be Sterne's most astute comment on the nature of his own writing: 'There was more of pleasantry in the conceit, of seeing *how* an ass would eat a macaroon – than of benevolence in giving him one.'[51] Sterne is ultimately motivated, not by benevolence, but by curiosity. He is less a sentimentalist than a scientific – or Lockean – observer of emotions.

The simplest way to reveal Sterne's interest in the movement of emotion, the process of feeling, is to look at one complete episode in each novel. In both *Tristram Shandy* and *A Sentimental Journey*, the visit to Maria of Moulines is set up by the narrator as a sentimental test for the protagonist, a crucial trial of 'the feeling heart'. In the *Tristram Shandy* account when Tristram eventually reaches the heroine, she is presented as an object picturesquely draped to prompt appropriate emotion:

> We had got up by this time almost to the bank where Maria was sitting: she was in a thin white jacket with her hair, all but two tresses, drawn up into a silk net, with a few olive leaves twisted a little fantastically on one side – she was beautiful.[52]

The progress towards this icon, though, has involved the analysis of a range of emotional responses. Tristram's initial eagerness to sample the Maria story 'as knowing it to be the choicest morsel of what I have to offer to the world' is bound to prepare the reader for humour.[53] Tristram's taste so far in 'choice morsels' has certainly proved fallible – in fact, the humour of the situation often hinges on our seeing it as such, as in his chapters on whiskers, chambermaids and buttonholes. We have been continually prompted to laugh at Tristram. The Maria episode seems no different from earlier, overtly humorous ones. The often forgotten invocation to the novel is to the 'Gentle Spirit of Sweetest Humour'. 'Humour' is one of a series of several complex words in this episode, upon the interpretation of which depends the nature of each reading. The *Oxford Dictionary* describes it as 'exciting amusement…less purely intellectual than wit, and often allied to pathos' and gives an example from 1854: 'The happy compound of pathos and playfulness, which we style…humour.' This neatly suggests Sterne's mixed intentions.

The Maria episode continues with some ribaldry on the loss of shirt-fronts, still even less designed to prepare the readers for an elevating experience; then comes a paragraph on being satisfied with one's lot on foreign soil (a jibe at Smollett?). However, the seriousness of even that apparently satirical line is undercut by the revelation that Tristram intended to obtain, as a reward for his uncomplaining attitude, 'a sisterly kiss' from the hostess and the maids. Sterne thus reminds the reader of Tristram's notorious unreliability on sexual matters: we are surely meant to laugh wryly at the use of 'sisterly' and to be forewarned that Tristram's treatment of his 'choicest morsels' is not likely to be purely spiritual. The next paragraph recalls Locke:

> My Uncle Toby's amours running all the way in my head, they had the same effect upon me as if they had been my own – I was in the most perfect state of bounty and good-will.[54]

Sterne pursues the exploration of the Lockean notion of associationism with one of those Shandean 'vibrations' which are manifestly as physical as they are spiritual, and come 'with every oscillation of the chaise alike'. Tristram himself seems very unclear about their provenance. The spring which created his euphoric mood, he hazards, is 'either of sentiment or rapture'. One of the lynchpins of Sterne's complex effect is his narrator's touching uncertainty as to the nature of the 'sentiment' he is at pains to propagate. The 'fine, careless rapture' of Browning's thrush in the mid-nineteenth century epitomised innocent nature. 'Rapture' in the eighteenth century, in contrast, could certainly mean a physical state. Dr Johnson defines 'raptured' as 'ravished, transported' and adds that it is a 'bad word'[55] – which suggests that Tristram's transportations of delight are sexual arousals which he confuses with spiritual elevation. Unlike his nineteenth-century descendants, however, Sterne is not *choosing* between the relative merits of the physical and the spiritual. He is delightedly exploiting all the possible responses to the situation as they move through Tristram's consciousness.

The following postillion's tale of Maria is a deliberate set piece of fine writing, self-consciously announcing:

> Poor Maria...is sitting upon a bank, playing her vespers upon her pipe, with her little goat beside her.[56]

The intention to begin a purple passage is announced as patently as in Fielding, so that Sterne can remind us again of the inadequacy and incongruity of his narrator's responses. The postillion's look is 'so perfectly in tune to a feeling heart, that I instantly made a vow, I would give him a 4X20 sous piece, when I got to Moulines'. (Yorick's responses in *A Sentimental Journey* are much the same: he measures the development of his own 'feeling heart' by the amount of money he is prompted to give to beggars.) The postillion's language is highly stylised, a literary reworking of an already familiar story:

> It is but three years ago, that the sun did not shine upon so fair, so quick-witted and amiable a maid; and better fate did Maria deserve, than to have her Banns forbid, by the intrigues of the curate of the parish who published them...she has

never once had the pipe out of her hand, but plays the service upon it almost night and day.

What exactly Maria does with the pipe later in the chapter, and whether the other meanings of 'service' should be kept in mind – these are questions which Sterne's web of double entendres forces us to set against the rural idyll, producing a sense of mounting hysteria in the reader – an anarchic rather than a sentimental response. The 'goat' quip is the moment of climax, heralded by another 'physical transport':

> I sprung out of the chaise to help her, and found myself sitting betwixt her and her goat before I relapsed from my enthusiasm.

Physical and spiritual are interchangeable, hinged on the keyword 'enthusiasm' – literally, 'taken over by a god' – but still another word in the eighteenth century with dangerous connotations of (usually religious) extremism. Then comes the actual climax – hilarious, obscene or deeply touching, according to changing 'interpretive communities':

> Maria looked wistfully for some time at me, and then at her goat – and then at me – and then at her goat again, and so on, alternately – 'Well, Maria,' I said softly 'What resemblance do you find?'

Tristram's embarrassed withdrawal immediately afterwards merely adds to the delight of that carefully prepared moment:

> I do entreat the candid reader to believe me, that...I would not have let fallen an unseasonable pleasantry in the venerable presence of Misery, to be entitled to all the wit that ever Rabelais scattered.

Rabelais bursts into the text like a revelation. Sterne's achievement is to destabilise all moral codes even in the act of allegedly reasserting them.

Many critics in the nineteenth and twentieth centuries have 'policed' this passage and imposed the sentimental reading, notably Gardner D. Stout, the American editor of *A Sentimental Journey*:

> In describing his [Tristram's] meeting with Maria, he strikes almost as delicate a balance between humour and pathos as Yorick does in his 'sentimental commerce' with her.[57]

Though Stout recognises the co-existence of different responses, words like 'delicacy' and 'balance' suggest very inadequately Sterne's amoral exuberance. Why should he lead up so carefully to the goat debacle, dwell on it for slower-witted readers, even bring up the name of Rabelais – if it not to reveal the wildly humorous potential of the scene? What is important to realise, though – and what seems to have been impossible for Dickens's generation to grasp – is that Sterne is not inhibiting the sentimental response in encouraging the humorous one. Cumberland's 'sluice' metaphor is useful here: what Sterne does is open every emotional sluice in the reader, so that pity, benevolence and laughter join forces in a powerful access of emotion – the Bakhtinian carnivalesque. He is not so much, as Stout thinks, 'striking a delicate balance' between opposing responses, as pouring all the responses together in anarchic overflow. In the final paragraph all these possible responses are even more obviously unstable:

> Adieu! Maria! – adieu, poor, hapless damsel! – Some time, but not *now*, I may hear thy sorrows from thine own lips – but I was deceived: for the moment she took her pipe and told me such a tale of woe with it, that I rose up, and with broken and irregular steps walked softly to my chaise. – What an excellent inn at Moulines!

That final sentence was omitted, naturally, from later selections of *The Beauties of Sterne* as it spoiled the simple tone of the rest of the episode, but it seems to me crucial in suggesting the range of possible readings. Maria's actions with her pipe are left to the imagination, but for some reason this time they send Tristram off 'with broken and irregular steps' back to the chaise. Why should a further account of Maria's woes (which he had been so eager to learn) suddenly send Tristram away? Could he be carrying Maria off to the 'excellent inn at Moulines'? Again, all the implications are meant to be present. We have Sterne's word that he deliberately left in his work 'so many openings for equivocal structures'. The sentimental reading here is, of course, that Tristram is too moved to bear any more details of Maria's plight; the cynical, that Tristram's shallowness is exposed in his rapid reversion to considerations of creature comforts; the practical, that this purging of emotion has done him a power of good, and made him healthily sanguine. It is the presence in suspension of all these possibilities that gives this novel its own complex and 'vibrating' quality – and it is precisely the absence of such complexity, the greater 'policing' of nineteenth-century reading, that makes Dickens's sentimental effects so different, and which necessitated in his writing the development of quite other forms of sentimental rhetoric to achieve an affective response.

The last-mentioned response to the Maria story – the purging of emotion as physically and spiritually beneficial – is the one which predominates in the treatment of the Maria episode in *A Sentimental Journey*. The gulf between the reader's likely response and Sterne's own is openly acknowledged in a letter to 'Hannah' in which he speaks of 'my journey, which will make you cry as much as ever it made me laugh – or I'll give up the business of Sentimental writing and write to the Body'.[58] There is a delicious ludicrousness about the way in which Yorick sets off to enjoy a bout of emotional indulgence to rouse his flagging spirit, much as he might set off to 'take the waters' at a spa for his physical well-being. 'Taking the waters' is an appropriate metaphor here, since the whole episode relies on the importance of tears, a crucial element – in every sense – in the literary presentation of emotion. Yorick's unholy relish in Maria's plight strongly anticipates Mrs Skewton's delight in *Dombey and Son* (with the same soulful improvement in mind) in those 'delicious fortresses, and their dear old dungeons, and their delightful places of torture', which for her sum up the Middle Ages.[59] Yorick finds Maria tastefully arranged, as she had been for Tristram, 'sitting under a poplar – she was sitting with her elbow in her lap, and her head was leaning on one side within her hand – a small brook ran at the foot of the tree'.[60] The essential watery element is thus available. There follows a centrally important passage in understanding Sterne and both eighteenth- and nineteenth-century sentimentalism:

> I sat down beside her: Maria let me wipe [her tears] away as they fell with my handkerchief – I then steeped it in my own – and then again hers – and then in mine – and then I wiped hers again – and as I did it, I felt such indescribable emotions within me, as I am sure could not be accounted for from any combination of matter and motion.
> 
> I am positive I have a soul; nor can all the books with which materialists have pestered the world ever convince me of the contrary.[61]

There is for twenty-first century readers a wildly farcical element in this handkerchief-swapping scene – but the anti-materialist argument being presented, presumably, represents Sterne's own deeply held beliefs, albeit in an exaggerated form. Even his contemporary readers had trouble with this scene and often failed to suspend their disbelief – while continuing to misunderstand and diminish Sterne as so often:

> …a feeling heart is certainly a right heart, nobody will contest that: but when a man chooses to walk about the world with a cambrick handkerchief always in his hand, that he may always be ready to weep, either with man or beast – he only turns me sick.[62]

There is certainly nothing as straightforward as irony in this scene, which Dickens might well have turned into the indictment of one of his monstrous hypocrites as he does with Mrs Skewton in *Dombey and Son*. Instead, there is a restless self-reflexiveness, an awareness both of the ludicrousness of human behaviour and of the possibility that such ludicrousness lies even behind our deepest-held beliefs.

The echoes of Tristram and the goat grow stronger in the following chapter, which Sterne evidently sets up as a parallel to the former occasion:

> Nature melted within me as I uttered this and Maria observing, as I took out my handkerchief, that it was steeped too much already to be of much use, would needs go wash it in the stream – And where will you dry it, Maria? said I – I'll dry it in my bosom said she – 'twill do me good. And is your heart still so warm, Maria? said I. O I touch'd upon the string on which hung all her sorrows – she look'd with wilful disorder for some time in my face; and then, without saying anything, took up her pipe and played her service to the Virgin. – The string I had touched ceased to vibrate – in a moment Maria returned to herself – let her pipe fall – and rose up.[63]

The text contrives to suggest the sexual implications of the scene (comparable to the equivalent account of the physical stimulation in the tale of Trim and the nun) while continuing to validate the sentimental response. A similar glissando along the physical/spiritual scale occurs in the following chapter, also on the subject of Maria. Sterne's register here is more overtly lyrical but his conclusions are just as morally unsettling:

> Maria, though tall, was nevertheless of the first order of fine forms – affliction had touched her looks with something that was scarcely earthly – still she was feminine – and so much was there about her of all that the heart wishes, or the eye looks for in woman, that could the traces be ever worn out of her brain, and those of Eliza out of mine, she should not only eat of my bread and drink out of my cup, but Maria should lay in my bosom and be unto me as a daughter.[64]

The glaring inappropriateness of the 'daughter' role after such a declaration of sexual attraction is perhaps only evident to a post-Freudian readership. Certainly from Richard Steele ('There is no kind of Affection so pure and angelick as that of a Father to a Daughter') through Sterne, who in his *Letters* describes his love of Eliza as 'so like that I bear to my own dear daughter…that I [can] scarce distinguish the difference betwixt it' to Dickens declaring Ellen Ternan to be 'as innocent and pure and as good as my own dear daughters',[65] a central rhetorical technique of the sentimental mode is the idealisation of physical affection by the complete excision of the (implicitly selfish) impulse of lust, so that it can be seen as totally selfless and easily translatable into Christian terms.[66] Nineteenth-century Christianity in particular authenticated sentimental rhetoric by reinforcing the distinction between the physical and the spiritual which in Sterne had been left fluid. What is involved in both eighteenth- and nineteenth-century sentimental writing is, in psychoanalytic terms, a massive act of displacement, emerging in rhetorical terms as the creation of a suitable metaphor: bodily fluids associated with sex, representing individuality, lust, action, are encoded as that central symbol of selflessness, weakness and passivity, the (often shared) flood of tears. Freud's account of dream displacement sums the process up neatly:

> The secretions of the human body – mucus, tears, urine, semen etc. – can replace one another in dreams…what in fact happens is that significant secretions, such as semen, are replaced by indifferent ones.[67]

In Sterne there is no such thing as the 'purely sentimental' register. The language operates at different levels simultaneously, producing kaleidoscopic effects. In the description of Le Fever's death (quoted above) rhetoric is more complex than it appears, conveying both the pathos of what is happening and the inadequacy of the narrator to deal with it: 'Nature instantly ebb'd again, – the film returned to its place – the pulse fluttered – stopp'd – went on – throb'd – stopp'd again – moved – stopp'd – shall I go on? No.' Dickens's in contrast is a rhetoric of intensification. Its characteristic action is to disarm mental activity and to build up emotional activity until a point of climax is reached, at which the reader experiences an emotional catharsis. The method is the same whether the emotion to be roused is pity or anger:

> She was dead. Dear, gentle, patient, noble, Nell was dead. Her little bird – a poor light thing the pressure of a finger would have crushed – was stirring nimbly in its cage; and the strong heart of its child mistress was mute and motionless for ever.[68]
>
> The light is come upon the dark benighted way. Dead! Dead, your Majesty, Dead, my lords and gentlemen. Dead, Right Reverends and wrong Reverends of every order. Dead, men and women, born with Heavenly compassion in your hearts. And dying thus around us every day.[69]

Critics of eighteenth-century sentimental comedy have struggled with the notion of 'tears and laughter' being intermingled. Frank Ellis brings Voltaire into the debate:

> The alternation of l'attendrissement and laughter in sentimental comedies (Comedies attendrissantes) has been criticised, Voltaire says: 'mais ce passage… n'est pas moins naturel aux hommes…c'est ainsi malheureusement que le

genre humain est fait' (But this change is nonetheless inherent in man…It is unfortunately the way man is made). 'La comédie,' Voltaire adds, 'peut donc attendrir, pourvu qu'ensuite elle fasse rire les honnêtes gens' (Comedy can draw tears as long as it also…makes the audience laugh). Both of Voltaire's ideas found their way to [eighteenth-century] England.[70]

Dickens's power depends first on the separation of the humorous and sentimental registers and then upon the intensification of emotion around value words. Earlier, more complex connotations of words like 'sentiment' or 'rapture' are effortlessly excluded. Words like 'generous' no longer carry a physical connotation as in 'generous with her favours'; 'frank' loses the earlier implication of physical vigour and comes to mean simply 'ingenuous'; 'pure' no longer means specifically 'sexually undefiled', 'chaste', and is dephysicalised to vaguely mean 'good'. When King Claudius describes Hamlet as 'remiss, most generous and free of all contriving' each adjective, especially in the mouth of an enemy, carries its own full, precise, descriptive weight. In Dickens, neither hero nor villain is allowed access to such words. Each has his own identifying register. In *Nicholas Nickleby* there is Ralph Nickleby's snarling parody of the Mantalinis' stylised emotional displays and his sneering account of the goodness/foolishness of his niece and nephew. In Shakespeare, there is a powerful and precise vocabulary of goodness. From the earlier eighteenth-century heroic dramas of Cibber and Steele through to Dickens, however, 'good' adjectives are used cumulatively in often repetitive adjective trains. Someone described as 'pure' is also by implication 'good – honest – innocent – true – open – generous', as Nell is 'Dear, gentle, patient, noble'. The effect is a deliberate blurring of meaning, discouraging mental activity but intensifying emotional response by a process of accumulation.

What is involved in Dickens is the setting up and policing of rival value systems. Sterne's quite different vision emerges for example in his chapter in *Tristram Shandy* on 'whiskers' in which he draws together, as he says, 'the extremes of Delicacy and the beginnings of Concupiscence' in a moral circularity.[71] Increasingly, in the nineteenth century, the displacement of the sexual into the spiritual terms became the norm, leading to Dickens's 'bodiless heroines' and to the rigid separation of the humorous from the sentimental register – for humour, as Sterne shows in the very conception of his work, anarchically moves between the physical and the spiritual, gaining its effects from the confusing of the two. Nineteenth-century sentimentalism, as George Meredith argued, makes the mistake of trying to deny the existence of the physical and to present all human experience in spiritual terms: this, says Meredith, is to ignore the fact that the 'original impulse' of sentimentalism is 'the grossly material, not at all the spiritual'.[72] As a moving force in literature and in society, though, nineteenth-century sentimentalism is at least arguably 'civilising' in that it substitutes harmless tears for violent action. Dickens was surely right to be proud of the social usefulness of his writings – one thinks of the Canadian trappers who wept over the death of Little Nell. The paradox is that the function of sentimentalism is in fact not opposed to but is analogous to that of humour. Smiles (so close, as Darwin observed, to the bared teeth of aggression) turn away wrath; tears (a displaced version of more potent fluids) channel off sexual aggression. The sentimentalist and humorous responses complement each other as an elaborate system of cultural appeasement gestures – and no one comprehends this as satisfyingly as Sterne.

To Thackeray, however, Sterne represented the betrayal and undermining of one mode by the other: 'the foul Satyr's eyes leer out of the leaves of Sterne's work constantly'.[73] Thackeray praised Dickens, in contrast, for triumphing precisely by intensifying the 'serious', the spiritual, the innocent, and separating it from the humorous, the earthly, what was 'merely' physical and therefore impure:

> the very thought of Sterne makes one grateful for the innocent laughter and the sweet and unsullied page which the author of *David Copperfield* gives to my children.[74]

Whether the author of *Oliver Twist* and *Our Mutual Friend* supplied only 'innocent laughter' is perhaps another question. Dickens's relationship to the sentimentalist register is a complex one and culminates, for me, in the supreme sentimentalist achievement of *Dombey and Son*. In this novel he selectively read and simplified Sterne, while learning from him the techniques of producing the crucial sentimental catharsis. Sterne arouses the emotions of his readers and anticipates with scientific rather than moral interest their laughing and their crying. His novels are, after all, Lockean in their effect, whatever his overtly anti-Lockean stance. It is the *process* of 'emoting' which fascinates him. 'Attitudes are nothing, madam – 'tis the transition from one attitude to another – like the preparation and resolution of the discord into harmony – which is all in all.'[75] Reading Sterne is a carnivalesque experience in an unpoliced literary world. It is paradoxical but tempting to say that whatever the reader is capable of imagining, is true. Sentimentalism too, as Sterne reveals, is itself potentially carnivalesque; it can, after all, be a radical mode, both ethically and emotionally unsettling.

# Chapter 3

# SENTIMENTALISM AND ITS DISCONTENTS IN EIGHTEENTH-CENTURY DRAMA: GOLDSMITH AND SHERIDAN

**'Humanity, Sir, is a jewel. I love humanity.'**[1]

The plays of Oliver Goldsmith and of Richard Brinsley Sheridan officially depend for their power on their attacks on eighteenth-century sentimental comedy. Certainly their earliest critics believed this and the playwrights themselves registered their disapproval of the prevailing mode in two classic attacks on sentimentalism. Here is Goldsmith:

> In these plays almost all the Characters are good, and exceedingly generous... If they happen to have Faults or Foibles, the Spectator is taught, not only to pardon, but to applaud them, in consideration of the goodness of their hearts. It is only sufficient to raise the characters a little, to deck out the Hero with a Ribband or give the Heroine a Title; then to put an insipid Dialogue, without Character or Humour, into their mouths, give them mighty good hearts...make a Pathetic scene or two, with a sprinkling of tender melancholy Conversation through the whole, and there is no doubt that all the Ladies will cry, and all the Gentlemen applaud.[2]

Sheridan's sharpest attack is contained in a paean of praise to the rival Muse of Comedy:

> Yet thus adorned with every grateful art
> To charm the fancy and yet reach the heart –
> Must we displace her? And instead advance
> The goddess of the woeful countenance –
> The sentimental muse! Her emblems view,
> *The Pilgrim's Progress*, and a sprig of rue!
> View her – too chaste to look like flesh and blood –
> Primly portrayed on emblematic wood![3]

The triumph of sentimental comedy in the early eighteenth century, in the plays of Richard Steele, Colley Cibber, and others, was by the 1760s so complete that it had become linguistically and dramatically stultifying. Goldsmith and Sheridan, representing a new generation of playwrights and playgoers, self-avowedly aimed to recapture the old spirit of comedy, to 'charm the fancy and yet reach the heart'. As Sheridan's line suggests, however, the plays can only be read fully in terms of the convention against which, but within which, they were written. What becomes evident from such a contextualised reading is the paradox that the comic vigour they express is not inimical to, but is in fact the completion of, the sentimentalist response. Despite their protestations, what emerges and was handed down to Dickens, via his childhood reading, his theatre-going and his adult acting, is the *inextricability* of sentimentalism and 'anti-sentimentalism'. Sentimentalism in Dickens's direct predecessors was thus purveyed by its discontents: it always contained elements of self-critique, a self-reflexivity which is part of its textual and rhetorical complexity. I shall begin this chapter with a summary of the biographical evidence for the presence of Goldsmith and Sheridan in Dickens's works and then go on to look more closely at the key plays themselves.

The direct influence of Goldsmith and Sheridan on Dickens is easily evidenced. Dickens was born a Georgian and the literary world he entered as a child was still very much an eighteenth-century world. We know from Forster that he had read *The Citizen of the World* and *The Vicar of Wakefield* as a schoolboy and that he was given a copy of Goldsmith's periodical, *The Bee*, by his schoolmaster on his departure from Chatham.[4] Dickens refers several times in his letters to Beau Tibbs, Goldsmith's 'shabby aspirant to fashionable society', a figure who has his descendants in *Sketches by Boz*. Tony Lumpkin is quoted ('I can't abear to disappoint myself'); Dickens borrows from *The Vicar* the line 'it is easier to conceive than to describe'; and of course 'Boz' itself was derived from the nickname 'Moses' of Dickens's younger brother, which derived from Moses Primrose, the Vicar's second son.[5] Philip Collins points out that Dickens's fifth son, Henry Fielding Dickens, was nearly christened instead 'Oliver Goldsmith Dickens'.[6] What is most astonishing, though, is the number of references to Goldsmith's first comedy, *The Good-Natured Man* (1768). Dickens's favourite phrase in his letters (according to Graham Storey and Kathleen Tillotson) was from the first scene of that play, 'in concatenation accordingly'. He uses this egregious phrase variously to describe a horse, a bedroom, a stage set, an ale cellar, preparations for theatricals – and baby Alfred Dickens.[7] Its frequent recurrence suggests not only Dickens's love of order and sequence, but more importantly his ear for other writers' phrase making. The voices of his predecessors haunt his work and are heard within his 'inimitable' style, as are the sounds of the words he learnt as an amateur actor. The influence of amateur theatricals in his adult life was, I argue in the following chapter, powerful in his work as well as in his life and, in the light of this, it is worth noting that he rehearsed *The Good-Natured Man*, playing the eponymous hero, for amateur production in 1847. He had already written of his fondness for that play and, in a letter to Bulwer in 1840, linked it explicitly to Bulwer's own play, *Money*:

> Let me thank you for the copy of your comedy [*Money*] received this morning. I told Macready when he read it to me a few weeks ago that I could not call to mind any play since *A Good-Natured Man* so full of real, distinct, genuine character.[8]

References to Sheridan's plays too continually resurface in the *Letters*. *The Rivals* (1775), Sheridan's first play, is a particularly potent presence. Fag's 'I was sly, Sir, devilishly sly!' re-emerges as a verbal tag of Major Bagstock in *Dombey and Son*. Many references are linked to performances of Sheridan's plays. Dickens's first sight of Macready on stage was in *Pizarro*; he saw *The Duenna* and *The Critic* and refers twice to Lord Burleigh from that play. There is a reference in a cancelled paragraph of *The Old Curiosity Shop* to Sir Benjamin Backbite from *The School for Scandal*, and Dickens probably saw that play with Macready in 1841.[9] He certainly discussed in detail the possibility of producing it while he was in Canada. Three critical references to Sheridan's two major plays suggest the extent of Dickens's knowledge – as well as documenting the continued play-acting in which he indulged long after his 'assumptions':

> [*The School for Scandal*] is…usually considered the most impracticable and difficult play in the whole Theatrical Calendar, the parts being without exception 'characters' which require very delicate manipulation.[10]
>
> [Writing to tell Macready of a party the latter had missed] Oh! That you had been in Clarence Terrace on Nina's birthday!… Perhaps you are a Falkland [from *The Rivals*] enough (I swear I suspect you of it) to feel rather sore – just a little bit, you know; the merest trifle in the world – on hearing that Mrs. Macready looked brilliant – blooming, young and handsome; and that she danced a country dance with the writer hereof (Acres to your Falkland) in a through spirit of beaming good humour and enjoyment.[11]
>
> [Considering with an unknown correspondent which play to produce] *The Rivals* is more droll, as a mere piece of drollery, but *The School for Scandal* is a more delightful piece of comedy.[12]

Finally, on one of his stays at Rockingham Castle, 'we got up in the Great Hall some scenes from *The School for Scandal*'. This was with Mary Boyle as Lady Teazle and Dickens as Sir Peter – and that particular piece of role playing continued for years, in Dickens's semi-flirtatious letters to Mary in the guise of Sir Peter.[13]

## Oliver Goldsmith

Like Laurence Sterne, Oliver Goldsmith has suffered a wild oscillation in critical estimation for much of the past two centuries. Mid-twentieth-century critics such as Robert Hopkins and Ricardo Quintana argued that Goldsmith never succumbed to the sentimentalist spirit of the age but remained always a sceptic. Goldsmith's technique, says Hopkins, 'is to appear to join the enemy [sentimentalism] and then bore from within'. Quintana agrees:

> It used to be thought that despite Goldsmith's declared views, it [*The Good-Natured Man*] must be considered a sentimental comedy…today, few who read it against its full Georgian background are likely to miss its satiric intent and its characteristic Goldsmithian irony.[14]

Against this unanimous twentieth-century chorus one must set the (almost unanimous) reactions of the nineteenth century – notably that of Goethe:

> The influence that Goldsmith and Sterne exercised upon me, just at the critical point of my development, cannot be estimated. This *high benevolent irony*, this just and *comprehensive* way of viewing things, this gentleness to all opposition, this equanimity under every change, and whatever else all the kindred virtues may be termed – such things were a most admirable training for me, and surely these are the sentiments, which in the end lead us back from all mistaken paths of life.[15]

Goethe's pairing of Goldsmith with Sterne and his sense of the 'high benevolence' of their authorial stance produce a reading more complex than Dickens's later selective reading of both writers as pure sentimentalists. Goethe's reading is an holistic one: he recognises Goldsmith's irony, but regards it as part of the final sentimental effect. A reading of his own seminal sentimentalist novel, *The Sorrows of Young Werther* (1774), however, suggests in his own writings a complete *lack* of irony, benevolent or otherwise. Instead, there is the intensification of a single, emotional, response to the exclusion of all other possible responses. When the American New Critics came to define sentimentalism, they were quick to recognise, and to condemn, such intensification. It seems likely, from Cleanth Brooks' definition, that *he* would put Goethe and Dickens together as true sentimentalists and place Sterne and Goldsmith together as ironists:

> The sentimentalist takes a short cut to intensity by removing all the elements of the experience which might conceivably militate against the intensity…the

sentimental poet makes us feel that he is sacrificing the totality of his vision in favour of a particular interpretation. Hence the feeling on reading a sentimental poem that the intensity is the result of a trick.[16]

The false note in that definition is surely the weasel word 'trick'. The 'trick' Brooks objects to is the rhetorical technique of intensification, which I am arguing is central to the sentimental register and evident in sentimentalist writing from Goethe to Dickens. Thus the New Critics continued into the twentieth century the binary readings of the nineteenth, simply reversing the binary so that irony was valued at the expense of sentiment.

The notion of Goldsmith as an ironist at odds with his age did not occur to most Victorians. In one of those seminal acts of misreading which, as Frank Kermode and John Bayley have shown, are a driving force in literature,[17] Victorian aesthetic theory elided art and life and allowed contemporary readers and audiences to identify the generous Irish poet with his own fictional 'Good-Natured Man'. This is Thackeray's account:

> [Goldsmith's] sweet and friendly nature bloomed kindly always in the midst of life's storm and rain and bitter weather. The poor fellow was never so friendless but he could befriend someone; never so pinched and wretched but that he could give a crust, and speak his word of compassion. If he had but his flute left, he could give that, and make the children happy in the dreary London court.[18]

Goldsmith had already anticipated such an account and had demolished it in advance, in his 'Elegy on a Mad Dog':

> A kind and gentle heart he had,
> To comfort friend and foes;
> The naked every day he clad
> When he put on his clothes.[19]

There were, of course, cynical Victorians who did see the other side of Goldsmith. Thomas Babington Macaulay, a latter-day Georgian born after his time, reads Goldsmith as an out-and-out humorist:

> A canting, mawkish play, entitled *False Delicacy*, had just had an immense run. Sentimentality was all the mode. During some years more tears were shed at comedies than at tragedies; – a pleasantry which moved the audience to anything more than a grave smile was reprobated as low.

Macaulay mourns the omission of the bailiff scene – 'the best scene in *The Good-Natured Man*' – as a result. *She Stoops to Conquer* he sees as a triumph despite the fact that sentimental comedy still reigned and Goldsmith's comedies were not sentimental. *The Good-Natured Man* had to be funny to succeed. The success of *She Stoops to Conquer* he saw as being simply the triumph of genius; it was, he says, 'an incomparable *farce* in five acts'.[20]

The tendency to simplify Goldsmith and Sheridan as *either* ironists or sentimentalists continues today. A recent critic presents the commonly held current view that 'despite the mockery of false benevolence, it is still benevolence that is the chief virtue in both Goldsmith and Sheridan'.[21] This, I think, is to miss Goldsmith's complex effect – and it is worth examining that effect, that cultural poise, in more detail, in specific scenes from the plays, to see exactly what was lost when the plays were reassessed in the nineteenth century.

## *The Good-Natured Man* (1768)

*Young Will Honeywood, the eponymous 'good-natured man' (the part rehearsed by Charles Dickens in 1847) has all the characteristics of the earlier eighteenth-century sentimental hero, being open-hearted, uncontrollably generous and liable to give his money to unfortunate friends rather than to his creditors. His uncle, Sir William Honeywood, initiates the action of the play by having his nephew arrested for debt, in order to teach him a lesson about the need for self-control. Honeywood is in love with and is loved by Miss Richland, but is too bashful to propose to her and goes so far as to recommend to her the suit of his rival, Lofty, who he believes arranged his release from prison. Eventually, thanks to Miss Richland's clear-sightedness and refusal to act the sentimental heroine, the misunderstandings are resolved, Honeywood realises that it was she who arranged his release and the two are finally united.*

At every point in *The Good-Natured Man*, Goldsmith works to undermine the triumphant (and triumphalist) sentimentalist rhetoric he had inherited from Richard Steele. He begins with a scene surely consciously recalling the opening scene of Steele's *The Conscious Lovers* (1722): in each, an honest servant discusses with his concerned, good-hearted master the disturbing behaviour of the young hero of the play. Sheridan uses the theme again in *The School for Scandal* and it does suggest the awareness of the two later playwrights of a shift in values between the generations – roughly between the early and late eighteenth century. Whereas in Steele, the 'conflict' is the fear of giving pain between a father and son who turn out to share the same values, Goldsmith's master and servant in contrast prove by the end of their exchange that *neither* is a reliable narrator. It is worth examining in detail where the audience's sympathies are directed during the first few lines:

> SIR WILLIAM: Good Jarvis, make no apologies for your honest bluntness. Fidelity like yours is the best excuse for every freedom.
> [Audience: Pro-Jarvis]

| | |
|---|---|
| JARVIS: | I can't help being blunt, and being very angry too, when I hear you talk of disinheriting so good, so worthy a young gentleman as your nephew, my master. All the world loves him.<br>[Audience: Anti–Sir William] |
| SIR WILLIAM: | Say, rather, that he loves all the world; that is his fault.<br>[Audience: Pro-nephew] |
| JARVIS: | I am sure there is no part of it more dear to him than you are, though he has not seen you since he was a child.<br>[Audience: Pro-nephew, Anti–Sir William] |
| SIR WILLIAM: | What signifies his affection to me; or how can I be proud of a place in a heart, where every sharper and coxcomb find an easy entrance?<br>[Audience: ?] |
| JARVIS: | I grant you that he is rather too good-natured; that he is Distanced too much every man's man; that he laughs this minute with one, and cries the next with another; but whose instructions may he thank for that?<br>[Audience: Distanced from nephew] |
| SIR WILLIAM: | Not mine, surely? My letters to him during my employment in Italy, taught him only that philosophy which might prevent, not defend, his errors.<br>[Audience: Distanced from Sir William] |
| JARVIS: | Faith, begging your honour's pardon I'm sorry they taught him any philosophy at all; it has only served to spoil him.<br>[Audience: Distanced from Jarvis – comic contempt?] |

By the time Sir William and Jarvis set out their conflicting values explicitly, the audience is struggling for orientation – quite unlike their nineteenth-century successors, who never needed to when reading a Dickens novel:

| | |
|---|---|
| SIR WILLIAM: | I have been now for some time a concealed spectator of his follies, and find them as boundless as his dissipation. |
| JARVIS: | And yet, faith, he has some fine name or other for them all. He calls his extravagance, generosity; and his trusting everybody, benevolence. It was but last week he went security for a fellow whose face he scarcely knew, and that he called, an act of mu- mu- munificence; ay, that was the name he gave it. (Act I)[22] |

It is now obvious that this is not the oppositional approach of Dickens and the later sentimentalists. Goldsmith demands of the audience a much more delicate judgement – that between balance and excess. He refuses to simplify the issues to make the audience's response easier, nor will he close the scene with a word of consolation, as in Steele's original where the servant ends with a warm, affectionate speech. Goldsmith instead ends with a complex moment of triple-vision, in which all three characters are suddenly seen in perspective:

> JARVIS: Well, go thy ways, Sir William Honeywood. It is not without reason that the world allows thee the best of men. But here comes thy hopeful nephew; the strange, good-natured, foolish, open-hearted – And yet, all his faults are such that one loves him still the better for it. (Act I, 6)

Here the intensifying rhetoric of sentimentalism is critiqued in various ways. 'The world allows thee' suggests the public nature of its values – a feature taken to its satiric extreme by Sheridan with Joseph Surface and by Dickens, of course, with Pecksniff ('his hand in his waistcoat as though he were ready, on the shortest notice, to present his heart for Martin Chuzzlewit's inspection').[23] 'His hopeful nephew' suggests the idealising register used to identify stock situations and characters – which Dickens can use satirically as in describing the loathsome Grandfather Smallweed in *Bleak House* as 'the excellent old gentleman' and his wife as 'the venerable partner of his respected age'.[24] The interrupted adjective train simulates rising emotion through punctuation and the dissolving of morally distinct concepts ('strange, good-natured, foolish, open-hearted') into one large simple concept, 'love'. In the adjective train is 'good-natured', one of several key terms which Goldsmith removes from automatic approbation during the course of the play and holds up for linguistic and ethical scrutiny. Hopkins notes a similar process being applied to 'genteel' in Goldsmith's *Essays*: 'Earlier, "genteel" was an honorific word representing good manners and good taste. By the time Goldsmith finished with the word, it was thoroughly pejorative.'[25] Later in this play, the key term 'good-natured' itself is critiqued by the comic characters. The landlady, recommending a drink, says: 'Just a thimbleful to keep the wind off your stomach. To be sure, the last couple we had here, they said it was a perfect nosegay. Ecod, I sent them away good-natured' (Act V, 68). The audience is being forced to reconsider its vocabulary of value. This is subversive drama for the 1760s; the bond of sentimental solidarity of the mid-1750s is broken. How, in such a fluid linguistic culture, is one to judge between benevolence and extravagance? One is reminded of F. R. Leavis's contrast between Gibbon and Swift: 'Gibbon's irony, then, habituates and reassures, ministering to a kind of judicial certitude or complacency. Swift's is essentially a matter of surprise and negation: its function is to *defeat habit*'.[26]

This 'defeating of habit' continues in the presentation of the heroine. The heroine of the earlier sentimental comedy of Steele and his contemporaries was a charmingly passive object, her language tightly prescribed by conventions derived ultimately from medieval courtly love. Goldsmith's Miss Richland in *The Good-Natured Man* is, as her name suggests, disconcertingly empowered. The lovers meet on stage for the first time as the bailiffs are about to arrest the hero for debt. Despite this inauspicious setting, Goldsmith puts in the mouths of his two protagonists the conventional courtesies about mutual obligation:

> MISS RICHLAND: You'll be surprised, sir, with this visit. But you know I'm yet to thank you for choosing my little library.
>
> HONEYWOOD: Thanks, Madam, are unnecessary, as it was I that was obliged by your commands. (Act III, 30)

Miss Richland increasingly distances herself from the sentimental register by refusing to be passive. While Honeywood is pushed about by his creditors, *she* gives orders:

> Sir, my directions have been given, and I insist upon their being complied with. (Act III, 33)

Goldsmith extracts humour from the excesses of sentimental cliché: when Honeywood nobly pleads on behalf of his friend's suit to the woman he himself loves, Miss Richland, who seems comically ignorant of the rules of the sentimental game, responds as if he had asked her on his own behalf: 'Well, it would be affectation any longer to pretend ignorance; and I will own, Sir, I have long been prejudiced in his favour.' In refusing to play the game of sentiment she exposes the 'affectation' Goldsmith sees in it. Resistance to sentimentalism is set up on another front in Miss Richland's rejection of public 'affectation' (her key term of condemnation) in favour of private expressions of emotion. Honeywood's sentimentalist mask, public altruism hiding private emotional hedonism, is exposed at many points particularly in his (private) asides:

> LEONTINE: I now see through all your low arts; your ever complying with every opinion; your never refusing any request; your friendship as common as a prostitute's favours, and as fallacious; all these, Sir, have long been contemptible to the world, and are now perfectly so to me.
>
> HONEYWOOD: (Aside) Ha! Contemptible to the world! That reaches me. (Act V, 53)

The conclusion of the love-plot shows a woman very much in control – both of the situation and of the male language of rationality. It is the hero who breaks down and utters broken expressions of emotion:

> MISS RICHLAND: After what is past it would be but affectation to pretend indifference. Yes, I will own an attachment, which, I find, was more than friendship.
> And if my entreaties cannot alter his resolution to quit the country, I will even try if my hand has not power to detain him. (Giving her hand)
> HONEYWOOD: Heavens! How can I have deserved all this? How express my happiness, my gratitude? (Act V, 59)

Honeywood does, however, remain the hero, he does 'get the girl' and the play ends with benevolence once again officially triumphant. However, Honeywood's final antiphony of platitudes, though obviously 'true', are not to be thought of as being valorised by any authorial voice:

> Yes sir, I now too plainly perceive my errors; my vanity in attempting to please all by fearing to offend any; my meanness in approving folly lest fools should disapprove. Henceforth, therefore, it shall be my study to reserve my pity for real distress; my friendship for true merit; and my love for her, who first taught me what it is to be happy. (Act V, 60)

The chief characteristic of Goldsmith's rhetoric in this play, then, is resistance, as one register refuses to give way to its opposite. Dickens, reading Goldsmith straightforwardly as a sentimentalist, develops only one side of this complex rhetoric, evolving from it his own typical rhetoric of sentimental intensification.

### *She Stoops to Conquer: or, The Mistakes of a Night* (1773)

*Mr and Mrs Hardcastle inhabit an old-fashioned house in the country with his daughter by his first wife and her son, Tony Lumpkin, by her first husband. Sir Charles Marlow has proposed a marriage between his own son and Miss Hardcastle. Young Marlow, painfully shy with women of his own class but over-free with lower-class women, is duped by Tony Lumpkin into mistaking the Hardcastles' home for an inn. Taking Kate Hardcastle for a servant, he flirts outrageously with her while simultaneously insulting her father by treating him as the landlord of the supposed inn. The arrival of Sir Charles Marlow finally clears up the increasingly complicated misunderstandings and Marlow and Kate Hardcastle are united.*

Goldsmith's most obvious contribution to Dickens's artistic vision was his development, in *She Stoops to Conquer*, of that trope of bourgeois cosiness which looks forward to Dickens's comfortable old couples, from the Fezziwigs in *A Christmas Carol* to the Boffins in *Our Mutual Friend*. This begins in Hardcastle's opening lines:

> HARDCASTLE: I love everything that's old: old friends, old times, old manners, old books, old wines; and I believe, Dorothy (taking her hand), you'll own I have been pretty fond of an old wife.[27]

How one reads this opening, however, will be closely linked to how one reads *The Vicar of Wakefield*. It is as well to remember that Samuel Richardson had recognised the convention well enough to be able to parody it as early as 1747 in *Clarissa*:

> And thus may she live, her old nurse and she; and an old coachman; and a pair of old coach-horses; and two or three old maid-servants; and perhaps a very old footman or two…reading old sermons and old prayer-books; and relieving old men and women; and giving old lessons and old warnings.[28]

Sterne had already produced Uncle Toby and Fielding, Parson Adams – but Goldsmith takes sentimentalism further down the social scale and prepares the way for Dickens's creation of, most notably, the Boffins in *Our Mutual Friend*:

> On the hob, a kettle stands; on the hearth, a cat reposed. Facing the fire between the settles, a sofa, a footstool, and a little table, formed a centrepiece devoted to Mrs Boffin… The room itself was large, though low; and the heavy frames of its old-fashioned windows, and the heavy beams in its crooked ceiling, seemed to indicate that *it had once been a house of some mark, standing alone in the country…*
>
> [Mr Boffin says] '…give us a kiss, old lady,' Mrs Boffin who, perpetually smiling, had approached and drawn her plump arm through her lord's, most willingly complied. Fashion, in the form of her black velvet hat and feathers, tried to prevent it; but got deservedly crushed in the endeavour.[29]

Dickens is here consciously using sentimentalism as a powerful voice against the industrial city, against the horrors of the dust-heaps and the death-carrying river. The narrator carries the reader with him ('deservedly crushed') into complicity with the Boffin ethic. In Goldsmith, however, there is a different, resistant, response to the old husband's affectionate advance:

MRS HARDCASTLE: Lord, Mr Hardcastle, you're for ever at your Dorothy's and your old wives. You may be a Darby, but I'll be no Joan, I promise you. (Act I, 69–70)

The ironising of sentimentalist nostalgia and sentimentalist hypocrisy becomes the main theme of the play. The hero Marlow's bashfulness towards 'women of reputation and virtue' and casual promiscuousness with 'creatures of another stamp' is a comical exposé of earlier sentimental drama, with its ludicrous exaggeration of the courtly love ethic. Kate Hardcastle, the heroine, is obliged, in pursuing Marlow, to maintain the disguise of a kitchen maid in order to overcome his bashfulness with women of his own class. Goldsmith thus wittily rings the changes on the earlier sentimental comedy plot of doting wife disguising herself as a mistress in order to rescue her husband from vice. Marlow, in contrast, has to be rescued from the hypocrisy of publicly proclaimed virtue by learning to be honest about sexual desire. Earlier eighteenth-century 'serious' sentimentalism, isolated from comedy, has produced false language, false behaviour and false relationships: that is the burden of Goldsmith's attack on the mode in *She Stoops to Conquer*. The irony is more focussed than in *The Good-Natured Man* and the whole play pursues a single theme. Marlow's liberation from hypocrisy is enacted linguistically. Disguised as a barmaid, Kate tears off the metaphorical layers of the sentimentalist register ('a fig leaf to cover the naked sense') and liberates Marlow to reveal his sexual desire in the register of comedy:

MARLOW: To guess at this distance, you can't be much above forty (approaching). Yet nearer I don't think that much (approaching). By coming close to some women, they look younger still, but when we come very close indeed ...(attempting to kiss her). (Act III, 102)

Goldsmith here dramatises the removal of the sentimental barrier between the sexes and recalls the sexual frankness of Restoration comedy. Kate, assured of success, goes back to 'her own natural manner'. Marlow, realising his mistake, searches desperately for an appropriate rhetoric:

Madam, fortune was ever my smallest consideration. Your beauty at first caught my eye; for who could see that without emotion. But every moment that I converse with you, steals in some new grace, heightens the picture and gives it stronger expression. What at first seemed rustic pleasures now appears refined simplicity. What seemed forward assurance, now strikes me as the result of courageous innocence and conscious virtue. (Act V, 124)

The antitheses should alert the audience to Goldsmith's pervasive irony. 'Simplicity', 'innocence' and 'virtue' all suggest that, far from attaining true vision at last, Marlow is simply reverting to the old sentimentalist hypocrisy and recasting Kate as the sentimental heroine once again. Goldsmith, however, resists such an easy conclusion and has Kate declare her double identity, uniting the 'modest woman' and the flirtatious serving girl. (The difference from Dickens's rhetoric is evident if one tries to imagine a similar splicing of *Bleak House*'s Esther Summerson and *Barnaby Rudge*'s Dolly Varden.)

> KATE: Yes Sir, that very identical tall squinting lady you were pleased to take me for (curtseying). She that you addressed as the mild, modest, sentimental man of gravity and the bold, forward agreeable rattle of the ladies' club ha ha ha. (Act V, 125)

Goldsmith is able to juxtapose the comic and serious modes of vision without rejecting either. His rhetoric is not built on judgement and exclusion but on parallelism and antithesis, leading to a finely achieved balance, as when Tony Lumpkin's comic rhetoric is set against Marlow's serious one. Lumpkin, unrecognised by Marlow, describes his own family in a way which will vilify his half-sister and flatter himself:

> LUMPKIN: The daughter, a tall, traipsing trolloping, talkative maypole – The son, a pretty, well-bred, agreeable youth that everybody is fond of.
> MARLOW: Our information differs from this. The daughter is said to be well-bred and beautiful; the son, an awkward booby, reared up and spoiled at his mother's apron-strings. (Act I, 76–7)

Goldsmith finally resists commitment. His is a rich and poised rhetoric for a sophisticated audience. The complexities of his irony make his plays, like Sterne's novels, strenuous reading or viewing. The ending of *She Stoops to Conquer*, like that of *The Good-Natured Man*, involves a carefully maintained poise. After Kate's revelation of her double identity, she does not speak again; Marlow has a few humorous words about their love, but the closing lines are given to Kate's father, old Hardcastle, who began the play:

> HARDCASTLE: Tomorrow we shall gather all the poor of the parish about us, and the Mistakes of the Night will be crowned with a merry morning; so, boy, take her, and as you have been mistaken in the mistress, my wish is, that you may never be mistaken in the wife. (Act V, 127)

The balance between the two modes is enacted grammatically here, with the semicolon dividing 25 words in the sentimentalist register from 25 words in the rival register of wit. Goldsmith's poise is perfect – and this has led, as has been shown, to a variety of readings and misreadings, by his contemporaries accustomed to the earlier sentimental drama, by the Victorians reading their way into their own version of sentimentalism, and by critics of our own time.

What Dickens derived from Goldsmith thus depended on how prepared he was to recognise the *balance* of the original. The nearest he comes to a Goldsmithian plot is perhaps in *Our Mutual Friend* when Nicodemus Boffin pretends to be a miser in order to educate Bella Wilfer about the wickedness of wealth; however, the moral in the later novel is much simpler than that in Goldsmith's plays: Bella is taught that wealth leads to wickedness and that it is *better* to believe in the Boffins' sentimental vision. Goldsmith's heroes learn that linguistic honesty, upon which emotional honesty depends, is complex and difficult to achieve – and that too complete an adherence to sentimental language can be impoverishing and deceptive. *She Stoops to Conquer* also suggests, in the relationship of the lovers and in the linguistic struggle at its heart, the rescuing of Eugene Wrayburn by Lizzie Hexam – but again, in *Our Mutual Friend* a simpler linguistic solution is propounded. Marlow begins trapped in the register of sentiment; Eugene begins trapped in the register of wit:

> My father having been a shipper of lime before me, and my grandfather before him – in fact we have been a family immersed to the crowns of our heads in lime during several generations – I beg to observe that if this missing lime could be got hold of without any young female relative of any distinguished gentleman engaged in the lime trade (which I cherish next to my life) being present, I think it might be a more agreeable proceeding to the assisting bystanders, that is to say, lime-burners. (161)

Kate liberates Marlow through comedy into a shared silence. Lizzie liberates Eugene by drawing him into her own serious register. She 'frees' him from wit divorced from sentiment into the sunny uplands of sentiment divorced from wit:

> I will fight it out to the last gasp, with her and for her, here in the open field… (813)

Reading Goldsmith selectively, Dickens achieves, through a simpler rhetoric, a similar unsettling of the social conventions of his own day: an aristocrat declares his love for, and goes on to marry, a member of the underclass. (See further discussion of this extract in Chapter 6.)

In *Bleak House*, a more complex effect is achieved. This novel contains strong echoes of *The Good-Natured Man* and in it Dickens achieves perhaps his most Goldsmithian complexity in the sentimental mode. Dickens rehearsed the play (taking the Honeywood part) in 1847, and its ghostly presence can be felt in the novel he began two years later. Here he explores the limits of the reliable narrator through Esther, whose values are approved (like those of the Honeywoods) but who is set off against an omniscient narrator representing wit and even cynicism; the 'telescopic philanthropy' of Mrs Jellyby pursues the theme of public virtue and private failings; Mr Jarndyce, like Sir William Honeywood, is a benefactor who must be seen as a loveable eccentric rather than a voice of truth; and supremely, in the presentation of Harold Skimpole, Dickens showed himself capable not only of Goldsmith's undermining of hypocrisy, but of a true satirist's ferocity which was quite beyond Goldsmith's scope. The different stresses in the respective bailiff scenes are suggestive: the incompetence of Honeywood becomes the venal irresponsibility of Skimpole, through whom Dickens systematically dismantles the previous generation's construction of the 'Romantic child'. Miss Richland and Esther display a similar incomprehension in the face of the bailiffs – intruders from another class who speak in an alien register (social threats in both cases dramatised linguistically). Goldsmith's bailiff is a witty manipulator and pretender, anticipating *Bleak House*'s Reverend Chadband:

| | |
|---|---|
| HONEYWOOD: | Tenderness is a virtue, Mr Twitch. |
| BAILIFF: | Ay, sir, it's a perfect treasure. I love to see a gentleman with a tender heart I don't know, but I think I have a tender heart myself. If all that I have lost by my heart was put together, it would make a – but no matter for that. |
| HONEYWOOD: | Don't account it lost, Mr Twitch. The ingratitude of the world can never deprive us of the conscious happiness of having acted with humanity ourselves. |
| BAILIFF: | Humanity, sir, is a jewel. It's better than gold. I love humanity. People say, that we in our way, have no humanity; but I'll show you my humanity this moment. There's my follower her, little Flanigan, with a wife and four children, a guinea or two would be more to him than twice as much to another. Now as I can't shew him any humanity myself, I must beg leave you'll do it for me. (Honeywood gives money to the follower) (29) |

Dickens's bailiff, Coavinses, is heavy, taciturn, a victim of society yet vaguely sinister – as the lowering presence of the working classes contrives to be throughout *Bleak House*. Goldsmith's ultimately integrated language suggests an essentially stable society. Dickens's divided linguistic world suggests a society divided, potentially revolutionary, heavy with menace:

> 'Did you know this morning, now, that you were coming out on this errand?' said Mr Skimpole.
> 'Know'd it yes'day aft'noon at tea-time,' said Coavinses.
> 'It didn't affect your appetite? Didn't it make you at all uneasy?'
> 'Not a bit,' said Coavinses. 'I know'd if you wos missed today, you wouldn't be missed tomorrow. A day makes no such odds.'
> 'But when you came down here,' proceeded Mr Skimpole, 'it was a fine day. The sun was shining, the wind was blowing, the lights and shadows were passing across the fields, the birds were singing.'
> 'Nobody said they warn't, to *my* hearing,' returned Coavinses.
> 'No,' observed Mr Skimpole, 'But what did you think upon the road?'
> 'Wot do you mean?' growled Coavinses, with an appearance of strong resentment. 'Think! I've got enough to do, and little enough to get for it, without thinking. Thinking!' (with profound contempt).
> 'Then you didn't think, at all events,' proceeded Mr Skimpole, 'to this effect: "Harold Skimpole loves to see the sun shine; loves to hear the wind blow; loves to watch the changing lights and shadows; loves to hear the birds, those choristers in Nature's great cathedral. And does it seem to me that I am about to deprive Harold Skimpole of his share in such possessions, which are his only birthright!" You thought nothing to that effect?'
> 'I – certainly – did – NOT,' said Coavinses. (127)

The two scenes make an instructive counterpoint. Honeywood, the true sentimentalist, is a victim, baffled by the witty bailiff who presents a comic version of his own ideals. Skimpole, the false sentimentalist, *defeats* the menacing bailiff by baffling him with a parody of sentimentalism. Dickens in Skimpole seems to critique the uncomplicated sunny benevolence of Mr Pickwick by transforming it into dishonesty and immaturity. There is added complexity in the refraction of the scene through Esther's 'sentimental heroine' narration. The prose is energised by the clash of registers – a rhetoric of repression and idealisation centred on Esther, in the middle paragraph of the following extract, and a rhetoric of frankness and particularity, in the framing paragraphs, centred on Dickens's ruthless exposure of Skimpole:

> 'Now, my dear Miss Summerson, and my dear Mr Richard,' said Mr Skimpole gaily, innocently and confidingly, 'here you see me as utterly incapable of helping myself, and entirely in your hands! I only ask to be free. The butterflies are

free. Mankind will surely not deny to Harold Skimpole what it concedes to the butterflies!'

I possessed fifteen pounds, odd shillings, which I had saved from my quarterly allowance during several years. I told Richard of my having this little store and I asked him delicately to inform Mr Skimpole, while I should be gone to fetch it, that we would have the pleasure of paying his debt.

When I came back, Mr Skimpole kissed my hand, and seemed quite touched. Not on his own account (I was again aware of that perplexing and extraordinary contradiction) but on ours; as if personal considerations were impossible with him, and the contemplation of our happiness alone affected him. (126)

Dickens seems here to have learnt from Goldsmith how to merge sentimentalism and the comedy of humours in a complex vision in which humour is seen, not as contradicting but as *completing* the sentimentalist response. In both scenes, hypocrisy is certainly attacked but sentimental values, through Esther's and Honeywood's charity, are finally reinforced. When, in the Mr Pecksniff chapters of *Martin Chuzzlewit* and in *Bleak House*, he allows himself to recognise Goldsmith's complex vision, Dickens's own sentimentalist rhetoric becomes complex enough to comment strongly on the hypocrisies of his own society. When he reads 'dear old Goldsmith' simply and narrowly, he produces a different, simpler, rhetoric of intensification, the language of Samuel Pickwick, Mr Brownlow in *Oliver Twist* and the Cheeryble Brothers in *Nicholas Nickleby*.

## Richard Brinsley Sheridan

Where Dickens, I believe, selectively read or even *mis*read Sterne (see previous chapter) and often simplified Goldsmith, I feel sure that at some deep level he *understood* Sheridan. Thomas Sheridan's telling comment on his brother's success suggests a key similarity of temperament between Sheridan and Dickens:

> Talk about the merit of Dick's comedy, there's nothing to it. He had but to dip into his own heart and find there the characters both of Joseph and Charles.[30]

A similar psychological complexity might well be observed in Dickens's own double identification with Charles Darnay and Sydney Carton in *A Tale of Two Cities*, with Wrayburn and Headstone in *Our Mutual Friend*, or even with Edwin Drood and Jasper in his final novel, as Chapter 6 will suggest.

Linguistic excess is another shared feature of the two writers. Mrs Nickleby and Flora Finching's fertile imaginations owe a great deal to *The Rivals'*

Mrs Malaprop, whose comments on Captain Absolute take the 'ghosting' process further back as Sheridan himself ventriloquises Shakespeare:

> Then he's so well-bred – *so* full of alacrity and adulation! – and has *so* much to say for himself – in such good language too! His physiognomy so grammatical! – Then his presence is so noble! – I protest, when I saw him, I thought of what Hamlet says in the Play: 'Hesperian curls! – the front of Job himself! – an eye, like March, to threaten at command! – a station, like Harry Mercury, new–' Something about kissing on a hill. However, the similitude struck me directly.[31]

> 'I think it was in the year eighteen hundred and seventeen; let me see, four and five are nine, and – yes, eighteen hundred and seventeen, that I thought I never should get rid of; actually and seriously thought I never should get rid of. I was only cured at last by a remedy that I don't know whether you ever happened to hear of, Mr Pluck. You have a gallon of water as hot as you can possibly bear it, with a pound of salt and sixpen'orth of the finest bran, and you sit with your head in it for twenty minutes every night just before going to bed; at least, I don't mean your head – your feet. It's a most extraordinary cure – a most extraordinary cure. I used it for the first time, I recollect, the day after Christmas Day, and by the middle of April following the cold was gone. It seems quite a miracle when you come to think of it, for I had it ever since the beginning of September.' (*Nicholas Nickleby*, chapter 27)

> '…oh do tell me something about the Chinese ladies whether their eyes are really so long and narrow always putting me in mind of mother-of-pearl fish at cards and do they really wear tails down their back and plaited too or is that only the men, and when they pull their hair so very tight off their foreheads don't they hurt themselves, and why do they stick little bells all over their bridges and temples and hats and things or don't they really do it!' (*Little Dorrit*, chapter 13)

There are direct quotations from Sheridan too. Jack Absolute's caricatured evocation of Lydia to his father ('She squints, doesn't she? A little red-haired girl?') conjures up visions of Fanny Squeers in *Nicholas Nickleby*, while his modest request to Sir Anthony was borrowed directly by Dickens to introduce Mr Squeers himself as having 'but one eye, and the popular prejudice runs in favour of two' (30):

> JACK: Now, without being very nice, I own that I should rather choose a wife of mine to have the usual number of limbs and a limited quantity of back: and though one eye may be very agreeable, yet, as the prejudice has always run in favour of two , I would not wish to affect singularity in that article. (39)

## *The Rivals* (1775)

*Captain Jack Absolute, son of the wealthy Sir Anthony Absolute, wishes to woo the lovely Lydia Languish, niece of the linguistically challenged Mrs Malaprop. Knowing that Lydia has romantic notions about being pursued by an impoverished suitor, he poses as a lowly sailor, Ensign Beverley. Meanwhile his friend Faulkland, the embodiment of the jealous temperament, makes his lover, Julia, suffer because of his own lack of trust in her. Jack's rival is Bob Acres, a fiery country squire. The misunderstandings are eventually resolved and the two heroes gain their respective brides.*

*The Rivals* is, like Goldsmith's *She Stoops to Conquer*, a play about appropriate language – *in*appropriate language being ridiculed in Lydia's romantic bookishness, in Faulkland's demands upon Julia to play the sentimental heroine ('She might [should] have been temperately healthy, and somehow plaintively gay'),[32] in Bob Acres's country metaphors, in Jack's playing of the dutiful son and of course in Mrs Malaprop's egregious linguistic impropriety, which sets in comic perspective the linguistic travails of the other characters.

Just as Dickens is at many points in dialogue with Sheridan, so Sheridan himself reacted against his predecessor Richard Steele, whose *The Conscious Lovers* was still near the top of the dramatic repertoire in the 1780s. *The Conscious Lovers* contains a paradigm of filial behaviour – self-conscious moralising allied to dullness – which Sheridan neatly parodies in *The Rivals*. Both plays begin with a father wishing a son to marry someone unknown, while the son's affections, unbeknownst to the father, are already engaged elsewhere.

Here is young Jack Absolute about to greet his father:

ABSOLUTE: Now for a parental lecture – I hope he has heard nothing of the business that has brought me here. – I wish the gout had held him fast in Devonshire, with all my soul. (Enter Sir Anthony)
ABSOLUTE: Sir, I am delighted to see you here; and looking so well! – your sudden arrival at Bath made me apprehensive for your health.
SIR ANTHONY: Very apprehensive, I dare say, Jack… Well, Jack, I am glad to see you, though I did not expect it, for I was going to write to you on a little matter of business. Jack, I have been considering that I grow old and infirm, and shall probably not trouble you long.
ANTHONY: Pardon me, Sir, I never saw you look more strong and hearty; and I pray frequently that you may continue so.
SIR ANTHONY: I hope your prayers may be heard with all my heart. Well then, Jack, I have been considering that I am so strong and hearty, I may continue to plague you a long time. (31)

The two characters begin by taking up the early eighteenth-century roles from the sentimental drama, of dutiful son and fond and pathetic old father. Absolute traditionally ripostes to his father's claim of weakness by replacing 'old and infirm' by 'strong and hearty'. Sir Anthony accepts the antithesis and it looks as though young Jack has won the sentimental exchange – until Sir Anthony breaks the rules and routs sentimentalism by taking its stylised language seriously, much as Miss Richland does in Goldsmith's *The Good-Natured Man*.

Two quite different registers are in operation. A close examination of successive lines of the Sheridan dialogue neatly reveals how the sentimentalist register differs from the anti-sentimental one. 'Strong and hearty' as used by Sir Anthony undermines the meanings of the same words used by Jack. The blurring assonance of Jack's conventional formulation contrasts strongly with the deliberate dissonance of Sir Anthony's riposte. The typical sentimental sentence, used in just the same way by Dickens, consists of one simple proposition subject to intensification:

> Pardon me, Sir, I never saw you look so strong and hearty; and I pray
> [Rising action to climax on stress on 'pray']
>
> continuously that you may continue to do so.
> [Falling action]

The sentence moves to disarm analysis. It builds up to an intensified emotional climax, and then falls away. The anti-sentimental sentence mimics the structure of the first, but includes an evaluative 'so', which creates a pause so that the subsequent adjectives are given their full weight rather than glossed over; and hidden in the falling action of the sentence is the shift of register from 'pray' to 'plague' – the assonance helping the disguise: 'Well then Jack, I have been considering that I am *so* strong and hearty, I may continue to plague you for a long time.'

This taking of sentimental language literally in order to expose it as false is a major source of comic satisfaction in both eighteenth- and nineteenth-century comedy. Jane Austen uses it in exchanges between Henry Tilney and Catherine Morland in *Northanger Abbey*; much later, George Meredith uses it between Clara and Willoughby in *The Egoist*; and Dickens builds a whole novel out of it in *Nicholas Nickleby* – in Squeers's assaults on the notion of the Romantic child and especially in the confrontations between Ralph Nickleby and his niece and nephew. Like Goldsmith, Sheridan moves dialogically between the sentimental and anti-sentimental registers and holds them in poise. Lydia and Julia, like Mr Hardcastle in *She Stoops to Conquer*, provide parallel serious and comic endings to the play:

> ABSOLUTE: Well, Faulkland, we have both tasted the Bitters, as well as the Sweets, of Love – with this difference only, that you always prepared the bitter cup for yourself, while *I–*

| | |
|---|---|
| LYDIA: | Was always obliged to *me* for it, hey? Mr. Modesty? – But come, no more of that – our happiness is now as unalloyed as general. |
| JULIA: | Then let us study to preserve it so: and while Hope pictures to us a flattering scene of future Bliss, let us deny its pencil those colours which are too bright to be lasting. – when Hearts deserving Happiness would unite their fortunes, Virtue would crown them with an unfading garland of modest, hurtless flowers; but ill-judging Passion will force the gaudier Rose into the wreath, whose thorn offends them, when its leaves are dropt! (V.iii.252–64) |

Sheridan exuberantly relishes *all* the literary modes he employs. Julia's speech coexists with Lydia's without being undermined by it.

## *The School For Scandal* (1777)

*The rich Sir Oliver Surface, returning unexpectedly from India, decides to test his two nephews, Joseph and Charles. He has heard from his old friend Sir Peter Teazle that Joseph is regarded highly as a moralistic young man, while Charles is dismissed as an extravagant spendthrift. Encountering the two brothers in disguise, Sir Oliver discovers Joseph to be a heartless hypocrite while Charles's extravagance hides a genuine warm-heartedness. Charles is in love with Sir Peter's ward, Maria, who returns his love. Sir Peter has his own problems, having recently married a much younger wife, who seems to be having an affair with the sanctimonious Joseph. All misunderstandings are eventually resolved, Charles is united with Maria, Sir Peter with Lady Teazle and the venal Joseph is exposed for his true colours.*

*The School for Scandal* enacts a linguistic debate very close to Dickens's later concerns. In this play, the older eighteenth-century meaning of 'sentiment' – sententious, judgemental – embodied in Joseph Surface, is brought into confrontation with the meaning of the word as it was to develop into the nineteenth century, personified by Charles. Here are the antecedents of the soft hearts and hard heads of such nineteenth-century dramatists as Bulwer Lytton and of Dickens's Nickleby brothers. Charles Surface, the warm-hearted brother, is not presented, however, as an example to follow – he is wild, embarrassingly irresponsible, irreverent about his ancestors and a comic figure in almost all his appearances. His gaiety and humour contrast with Joseph's dourness, but the audience by the end is dazzled by Sheridan into laughter rather than moral judgement and there is no 'sympathetic' welling of tears for Charles as there is for the Nicklebys.

Sheridan's blatant refusal to judge his characters seems to have been particularly uncongenial to nineteenth-century critics and audiences. It was impossible to sentimentalise the man himself, a man of wit and irreverence in his private life, as they had been able to do with Goldsmith, but Charles

Lamb's comments in his famous essay 'On the Artificial Comedy of the Last Century', anticipate what the Victorians went on to do to Sheridan:

> A player with Jack [Palmer]'s talents, if we had one now, would not dare to do the part in the same manner...he must take his cue from his spectators, who would expect a bad man and a good man...rigidly opposed...Joseph Surface, to go down now, must be a downright revolting villain.[33]

As in the case of Goldsmith, modern critics are hard put to feel confident that they have fully fathomed Sheridan's irony. Mark Auburn hesitates long before coming to a firm conclusion:

> Despite his insight in his last two major comic works into what most would call reality – a demonstration that vice is as much a part of human nature as virtue – his evident faith in well-intentioned men and benevolent providence to expel the vicious from society seems unrealistic. He was a sentimentalist.[34]

Auburn had taken an early step towards this conclusion in plumping for a straightforward interpretation of Sir Oliver's behaviour in testing the two brothers in *The School for Scandal*. 'Sir Oliver', he says, 'whether or not we approve his behaviour – and we are certainly not invited to find fault with it – demands gratitude in return for his money.' In a footnote he makes the point more strongly: 'Sheridan surely...joined his audience in applauding Charles's sentimentality and damning Joseph's ingratitude' (129).

The 'surely' suggest a lingering doubt; and this dubious conclusion springs, I think, from a surprisingly ahistorical approach. Benefactors like Sir Oliver, in the dramas from which Sheridan derived his own theatrical experience, were by no means exempt from criticism. *The School for Scandal* gains a moral interest and complexity if the audience is subtle enough to see through Sir Oliver, with his benevolent egotism, and to realise too that the Teazle reconciliation is not a simple happy ending. At his best Sheridan, like Goldsmith, maintains a poise between wit and sentiment; like Goldsmith, he will not allow his audience to relax into complete reliance on either mode. His dialogue, with its subtle use of dashes to indicate pregnant pauses, keeps the registers of sentiment and humour carefully balanced, even in his conclusion:

> SIR OLIVER: (to Charles and Maria) ...may your love for each other never know – abatement.
> SIR PETER: And may you live as happily together as Lady Teazle and I – intend to do.[35]

As in the case of Goldsmith, twentieth-century critics were reluctant to acknowledge Sheridan's radiant enjoyment of *both* sentiment and irony, usually insisting that he *must* owe allegiance to either one or the other. W. A. Darlington in *Writers and their Work* comments:

> Sentimentality was indeed one of Sheridan's chief weaknesses in private life and his plays succeed because of their essential decency…[he displayed] a natural lack of offence combined with an uninhibited gaiety.[36]

The argument for Goldsmith and Sheridan's playful approach still being called 'sentimental' is that, if emotional excess is purged by humour, then paradoxically the serious values are strengthened. They become dramatically effective, so to speak, only in debate with their opposites. Identifying with the lighter people, the audience can simultaneously admire the moral worth of the serious characters. Here, perhaps, is the key divide between eighteenth- and nineteenth-century versions of the sentimentalist mode. In Goldsmith and Sheridan, who reach back to the Restoration in their use of wit, humour comes near enough to sentiment to purge it of excess. In the nineteenth century, humour tends to move away, to the extremes of farce. It no longer *comments* on sentimentalist values, but uses them casually for ends of its own. No one, in other words, dare poke fun at Kate Nickleby. The broad humour of Fanny Squeers and the Crummles troupe is quite separate and has no creative commerce with the serious parts of the novel at all. Thus the dramatic dialogue between wit and sentiment achieved by Goldsmith and Sheridan tends to be lost in Dickens (although, as has been shown, the treatments of Pecksniff and of Skimpole, revealing the darker side of sentimentalism, are notable exceptions). Generally, it is Dickens's selective reading or even *mis*reading of his eighteenth-century masters which forces him into finding quite a different source of dramatic power in his own work. Where Goldsmith and Sheridan derive their characteristic dramatic voice from the dialogue they set up between the sentimental and the ironic and from the freedom they give their audiences, Dickens's characteristic energy comes precisely from the effort involved in keeping the two registers apart and from the sentimental rhetoric of intensification which results. In Dickens's and his generation's characteristically simplifying or selective readings, then, the rhetorical and ethical poise of Goldsmith and Sheridan is transformed into something very different.

# Chapter 4

# DICKENS AND NINETEENTH-CENTURY DRAMA

**'We would indict our very dreams.'**[1]

We have been spoilt [for enjoying Restoration comedy] with – not sentimental comedy – but a tyrant far more pernicious to our pleasures which has succeeded it, the exclusive and all-devouring drama of common life, where the moral point is everything... We dare not contemplate an Atlantis, a scheme, out of which our coxcombical moral sense is for a little transitory ease excluded. We have not the courage to imagine a state of things for which there is neither reward or punishment. We cling to the painful necessities of shame and blame. We would indict our very dreams.[2]

## Charles Lamb

Charles Lamb is an important liminal figure in the transition between eighteenth- and nineteenth-century literary sentimentalism. His essay, 'On the Artificial Comedy of the Last Century' (1822), cited above, helped to transmit and to fix attitudes to the earlier playwrights, and it is highly significant that what he perceives to be the key difference between the two periods is the rise of judgementalism. On the cusp of two centuries and of two aesthetic theories, already recognising the beginnings of what was to become the moralistic Victorian elision of art and life, Lamb struggles to separate 'real' from acted villainy as he recalls an eighteenth-century performance of *The School for Scandal*:

> When I remember [of Joseph Surface] the gay boldness, the graceful solemn plausibility, the measured step, the insinuating voice – to express it in a word – the downright acted villainy of the part, so different from the pressure of conscious actual wickedness – the hypocritical assumption of hypocrisy – which made Jack so deservedly a favourite in that character, I must needs conclude the present generation of playgoers more virtuous than myself or more dense. (161)

This splendid comment reminds one forcibly that eighteenth-century sentimentalism evolved as a dramatic mode in which gesture *was* character. Twentieth-century 'performative' accounts of personality, from Berthold Brecht to Judith Butler, have made twenty-first century audiences much more receptive to Lamb's theories than were his own contemporaries.[3]

As a child, reading 'as if for life',[4] Dickens devoured *Essays of Elia*, the first volume of which had appeared in 1823 when he was eleven. Lamb's own work in the sentimental mode influenced Dickens profoundly and haunts some of his most successful sentimentalist creations, notably Tom Pinch in *Martin Chuzzlewit*. Before moving on to the main subject of this chapter, the dramas in which Dickens acted, I shall therefore turn briefly to this influential figure, another 'sentimentalist' who was also one of its discontents. In his lifetime, Lamb had found himself the unwilling victim of considerable sentimentalising by his friends. Coleridge's dewy-eyed word-picture in 'This Lime Tree Bower My Prison',[5] in which he three times refers to the 'gentle-hearted Lamb', elicited a sharp and distinctly *un*-sentimental response from its subject, in which the shifts in meaning of the vocabulary of sentiment are vividly evident:

> For God's sake (I never was more serious), don't make me ridiculous any more by terming me gentle-hearted in print, or do it in better verses. It did well enough five years ago when I came to see you, and was moral coxcomb enough at the time you wrote the lines, to feed upon such epithets; but, besides that, the meaning of gentle is equivocal at best, and almost always means poor-spirited, the very quality of gentleness is abhorrent to such vile trumpetings. My *sentiment* is long since vanished. I hope my *virtues* have done *sucking*. I can scarce think but you meant it in joke. I hope you did, for I should be ashamed to think that you could think to gratify me by such praise, fit only to be cordial to some green-sick sonneteer.[6]

Sentimentalism seems here to have become a threat to masculinity: it is already associated with femaleness ('green-sick'-ness being the Elizabethan term for what was seen as the female monthly malady) and with childhood (by 'done sucking' Lamb presumably means being newly weaned); true men, by implication, are not 'poor-spirited' but proud and *not* given to 'sentiment'. In Coleridge's usage, then, the shift from rational sentiment to emotionalism seems already to have been made. There is no reason, however, to think that Dickens ever saw this letter: the first collected edition of Lamb's *Letters* was not published until 1874. To Dickens, as references in his own letters reveal, Lamb remained very much 'the frolic and the gentle' of Wordsworth's loving poetic obituary.[7] In Dickens's time Lamb was held up as a supreme example of self-denial. In keeping his mentally disturbed sister Mary at home and cherishing her even after she had, in a fit of madness, murdered their mother, he had become an icon of the 'good heart'. The Notable Names Database (NNDB) talks of his 'calm self-mastery and loving self-renunciation' which 'will ever give him an imperishable claim to the reverence and affection of all who are capable of appreciating the heroisms of common life'.[8]

Dickens's image of Lamb came from these popular myths and also from the anecdotes of his own friends, Thomas Talfourd and John Forster, both of whom had known Lamb personally in the final years before his death in 1834. What Dickens shares with Lamb is an unexpected combination of quiet literary nostalgia with an energetic love of modern London. The essay 'Dream Children'[9] in particular is a ghostly presence behind the final reverie of Master Humphrey in the last number of *Master Humphrey's Clock* (1841),[10] in which the lonely old man imagines himself surrounded by a loving family and grandchildren. Dickens even includes 'a crippled boy – a gentle, patient child', with whom Master Humphrey particularly identifies, just as in Lamb, the 'limp' of the narrator and then of his beloved brother form a central trope, perhaps suggesting imperfection and vulnerability in a brutal outside world.[11] London is present in the Master Humphrey tale, as it was so vividly in Lamb's imagination too: in his final meditation, the old man turns his thoughts from his own solitude to the bustling city beyond his fireside:

> Amid the struggles of this struggling town what cheerful sacrifices are made; what toil endured with readiness; what patience shown and fortitude displayed; for the mere sake of home and the affections! Let me thank Heaven that I can people my fireside with shadows such as these; with shadows of bright objects that exist in the crowds about me; and let me say, 'I am alone no more.'[12]

For the Christmas Number of *Household Words* in 1852, Dickens contributed 'The Poor Relation's Story', in which he developed another idea he believed in as passionately as Lamb had done – that of the power of imagination to compensate for an empty real life. 'The Child's Story', his other 1852 offering, is also very much in Lamb's wistful, whimsical mode and develops the sentimental notion (there too in Dickens's favourite among Wordsworth's poems, 'We Are Seven') that our beloved dead are not lost to us but remain vividly alive, in a way which collapses the distinction between memory and reality. Dickens commented to Forster about the death of a shared friend, 'But this is all a Dream, maybe, and death will wake us.'[13]

'Sentimentalism' here, in Lamb and Dickens, involves that 'ghostliness' which has fascinated twenty-first century critics. Sentimentalist nostalgia depends upon a semantic confusion between what is real and what is uncanny. In the words of Bennett and Royle: 'the uncanny can be described as the thoughts and feelings that may arise...when the homely becomes unhomely, when the familiar becomes uncomfortably strange or the unfamiliar becomes strangely familiar'.[14] Dickens's ghost stories, as well as the endings of some of his major novels, exploit precisely this deconstruction of the boundary between dream and reality – exactly the rhetorical technique he found in 'Dream Children'. The uncanny is a powerful feature in Lamb's essay. The narrator, Elia, talks to his children, Alice and John, about their family history and particularly about his own grandmother. It seems to be a simple genre piece. However, in the final paragraphs Lamb movingly reverses presence and absence, the 'real' children fade and re-emerge as figments of Elia's imagination:

> We are not of Alice, nor of thee, nor are we children at all. The children of Alice call Bartrum father. We are nothing; less than nothing, and dreams. We are only what might have been, and must wait upon the tedious shores of Lethe millions of ages before we have existence, and a name.[15]

There is an extra twist, when Lamb's own 'real life' is read in conjunction with his writing: the 'story' of Great-Grandmother Field, told to the children Alice and John, deconstructs: what was told as 'fancy' is Lamb's own family history: Great-Grandmother Field actually lived, beyond the pages of *Essays of Elia*. A *true* story has been narrated to doubly fictional listeners (listeners who are not even real in their own story) – so that the acts of telling and listening become problematised. The 'implied listeners', the children, John and Alice, shift uncannily into the realm of imagination, for they have never been born. How real then to Charles Lamb are we, the 'real' listeners – ourselves born so long after the writing of the tale?

'Dream Children' directly influenced *Master Humphrey's Clock* and the essay 'A Child's Dream of a Star', but its spirit and the themes of the unlived and of the healing power of fancy are there in much of Dickens's most effectively sentimental work, as in his incantatory vision of Louisa Gradgrind's future, at the end of *Hard Times*:

> Herself again a wife – a mother – lovingly watchful of her children, ever careful that they should have a childhood of the mind no less than a childhood of the body... Did Louisa see this? Such a thing was never to be.[16]

Lamb is, on this evidence, a seminal influence: both he and Dickens developed the sentimentalist tradition they had inherited from the eighteenth century into an oppositional force in an industrial age. Both developed that powerful sentimental quality, nostalgia, as a stylistic weapon in the preservation of individual histories against the anonymity of industrial society; anticipating postmodernism, both could – and in Lamb's case, often did – use the sentimental tradition to undermine the certainties of the realist mode.

Lamb ghosts Dickens's work in many places. The 1860s' collection of essays *The Uncommercial Traveller* clearly borrows from his essay style and several features of what might be called the myth of Charles Lamb are important in Dickens's novels: there are characters such as Mr Wemmick in *Great Expectations* who prove their sentimental worth by caring for unworthy or demanding family members; the toil of long hours of office work is memorably captured in the figure of Bob Cratchit in *A Christmas Carol*; and the noble, uncomplaining brother-figure is apotheosised in *Martin Chuzzlewit*'s Tom Pinch in a way which seems to draw its emotional energy from Dickens's own mythologising of Charles Lamb. Dickens's sentimentalist expostulations to and about Tom suggest the character's huge emblematic importance to his creator. Words like 'gentle', 'nostalgic', 'innocent' and 'domestic', embodied in Tom Pinch, carry a heavy freight of responsibility in Dickens's crusade to prove that imagination *can* ultimately overcome the harshness of the real world and may even be able to redeem it. Finally, Lamb's own refusal to indulge in direct moralising anticipated Dickens's fury with George Cruikshank for his 'Frauds on the Fairies'.[17] Lamb belonged emotionally to the earlier aesthetic of Goldsmith and Sheridan: literature and especially drama was to him open, complex, nuanced. Literature was not to be equated simplistically with life.

## Dickens on the Nineteenth-Century Stage

> [I]t is something to have seen *The School for Scandal* in its glory…
> 
> …We must love or hate – acquit or condemn – censure or pity – exert our detestable coxcombry of moral judgment upon everything. Joseph Surface, to go down now, must be a down-right revolting villain.[18]

A history of sentimentalism might, as Charles Lamb's observation suggests, be written in a history of productions of *A School for Scandal*. It is worth noting that Dickens's favourite actor/comedian, Charles Mathews, at an early stage in his career played Joseph Surface under the direction of Sheridan himself. It would surely be possible to establish a lineage of moralising 'sentimental' hypocrites from Surface to Pecksniff. Mathew's direct impact on the novels has already been charted (for example by Paul Schlicke)[19] but the triangular relationship, via Sheridan, is as far as I know unexplored. Mark Auburn suggests (without following Lamb) that one could imagine a 'heavily sentimental' *School for Scandal*,[20] with Charles sitting in a nostalgic haze amid his ancestors' portraits and with a strong stress on the Teazles' reconciliation – but that, equally, one could imagine a strictly comic, more Restoration, production. The unique poise of this play must certainly have been lost on an early nineteenth-century audience which, if Lamb is to be believed, had already begun to desire above all not to *enjoy* but to *judge* correctly, to allocate praise and blame appropriately, to apply to art the 'coxcombical moral sense' it applied to life. Julia Swindells describes the emergence in the early nineteenth-century theatre of the 'new, moral actor' and suggests that a mixed audience, including working people, responded to and reinforced 'English bourgeois sentimental drama'.[21] In addition, the resurgence in the early nineteenth century of the tenets of neo-classical criticism meant that Johnsonian accusations could be levelled against contemporary writers. '[H]e makes no just distribution of good and evil, nor is always careful to show in the virtuous a disapprobation of the wicked.' This is actually Samuel Johnson himself,[22] but it is the substance of Thackeray's attack on *Oliver Twist* in 1840: '[I]n the name of commonsense, let us not expend our sympathies on cut-throats and other such prodigies of evil!'[23] This is precisely the 'coxcombical moral sense' Lamb had feared and derided in the essay quoted at the beginning of the chapter.

The early eighteenth-century sentimental comedy of Colley Cibber, Richard Steele and their contemporaries had allowed no dramatic debate between rival visions, but was an extended apologia for the prevailing mode. Even 'humour' characters had to be tested morally. The later eighteenth century, the generation which produced Goldsmith and Sheridan, involved, as we have seen, a complex poise between wit and sentiment and a complex relationship with a complex audience. Thereafter, from the 1790s onwards, as art and life become elided in aesthetic theory and Thackeray's 'common-sense' demands that an audience waste no sympathy on reprobates, an increasingly apologetic tone can be detected – epitomised in the titles of three plays closely associated with Dickens: Ben Jonson's bold *Every Man in His Humour* (Dickens played Bobadil in 1845, while writing *The Cricket on the Hearth*); Elizabeth Inchbald's diffidently apologetic *Every One Has His Fault* (1793); and Bulwer Lytton's even more limply good-hearted *Not So Bad As We Seem* (1851), in the premier of which, for the Guild of Literature and Art, Dickens starred as the good-hearted rake, Lord Wilmot.

Elizabeth Inchbald was an undoubted influence:[24] Dickens read her collection of *Farces* as a child, saw her plays when he was a young man and produced and acted in the best of the farces, *Animal Magnetism*, in January 1857, when it was performed after *The Frozen Deep*. In the play, Dickens played a doctor who is duped into believing that he can 'magnetise' everyone around him. The significance, in relation to Dickens's use of mesmerism, cannot be overestimated and the role may have led him to question his own powers – though it never led him, like Prospero, to 'burn my books' and his commitment to mesmerism seems to have continued. Two months after the success of *Not So Bad As We Seem*, Dickens produced Charles Mathews's farce, *Used Up*, in which he played another figure who questions his own powers: an aristocrat, rather anticipating Eugene Wrayburn in *Our Mutual Friend*, who is bored and weary of the world but is restored to life by experiencing the realities of rural living.

My argument in this chapter will be, firstly, that the safe confines of the sentimentalist tradition gave Dickens access to potentially deviant modes of vision. Creating on stage the heroes of *Not So Bad As We Seem* and *The Frozen Deep*, he acted out, in publicly acceptable form, subversive impulses which threatened to engulf him both as man and as writer. Secondly, I want to suggest that Dickens's acting 'ghosted' his novels; that the words he uttered on stage and the ideas and emotions he *embodied* there, uncannily haunt the major works, in a way that has not yet been thoroughly explored. The Preface to *A Tale of Two Cities* (1859) suggests the physical nature of the process:

> When I was acting, with my children and friends, in Mr Wilkie Collins's drama of *The Frozen Deep*, I first conceived the major idea of this story. A strong desire was upon me then, to *embody it* in my own person.[25]

Dickens, as his letters attest, became totally absorbed in all his 'assumptions'; references to and quotations from the most apparently insignificant productions can be found in his correspondence years after they occurred. Critics generally accept that his theatrical experience fed the novels both directly (as in the creation of, for example, the Crummles troupe in *Nicholas Nickleby* or Mr Wopsle in *Great Expectations*) and indirectly (as the theme of *The Frozen Deep* re-emerges in *A Tale of Two Cities*). The extent of Dickens's debt to the contemporary theatre is also explored by Adrian Poole in the close links he uncovers between the plots of three plays by James Sheridan Knowles, *The Hunchback*, *The Daughter* and *The Secretary*, and the plot of *Our Mutual Friend*.[26] Juliet John, Paul Schlicke and Sally Ledger have all recently explored Dickens's involvement in the popular drama of his day.[27] The specific focus of this chapter, however, is on Dickens's experience of assimilating sentimental popular culture by acting in it.

## *Every Man in His Humour*

Dickens was producer, director and stage manager in an amateur production of Ben Jonson's *Every Man in His Humour* in the autumn of 1845.[28] His enjoyment of the role of Bobadil was palpable:[29] he used Bobadil's oaths in his letters – 'By the foot of Pharoah!' and 'By the body of Caesar!' and signed himself 'Bobadil'.[30] His letters contain detailed discussions of his costume:

> *Be very careful that the colours are bright; and that they will shew well by Lamplight...* I wish the tops of the boots, the gauntlets, and the hat-brim to be very large... I wish particularly to see the red of which you propose to make Bobadil's breeches and hat. I want it to be a very gay, fierce, bright colour.[31]

This is not dissimilar to his method of construction of his written characters, via their costumes. Mr Pecksniff, for example, in the second chapter of *Martin Chuzzlewit*, has a very detailed 'costume': 'white cravat...fastened behind...two jutting heights of collar... hair, just grizzled with iron-grey...all brushed off his forehead, and...bolt upright... plain black suit...dangling double eye-glass'.[32] This externalising approach, having been roundly condemned by modernist critics prizing interiority, is now much more likely to make sense to twenty-first century readers used to the notion of 'identity as performance' which has been developed in recent critical theory, and particularly in gender studies.[33]

Jonson's play, which dramatises the 'purging' of the humours of the main characters, centres on a misunderstanding between a wild (but basically good-hearted) young man and his father, who pursues his son through his 'low' surroundings. A Sam Weller–ish servant takes the side of the boy and contrives to dupe the father. After a series of complications, the young hero and his mistress are united, with the father's approval.

Bobadil is usually written off as merely another example of the *miles gloriosus*, the braggart soldier, inherited from classical comedy. There is, however, more to him than this and one can see readily what drew Dickens to him. Two performances are going on simultaneously: alongside the bravado and the verbal wit, Bobadil yearns for social acceptance. Deeply embarrassed to be found in poor lodgings by his hanger-on, Matthews, he maintains his dignity by explaining that he chose the place on purpose because 'I love a cleanly and quiet privacy, above all the tumult and roar of fortune.'[34] He struggles between the need to preserve a veneer of gentlemanly reticence and the desire to boast of his great military exploits. The latter impulse usually triumphs:

> ...at the beleaguering of Strigonum...in less than two hours, seven hundred resolute gentlemen, as any were in Europe, lost their lives upon the breach... By St George, I was the first man that entered the breach; and had I not effected it with resolution, I had been slain, if I had a million of lives... (III.i.41)

Bobadil has the turn of invention of Falstaff, without Falstaff's incorrigibility and self-confidence: 'We will have a bunch of radish, and salt, to taste our wine; and a pipe of tobacco to close the orifice of the stomach' (I.iv.34). Jonson's imagination leaps towards absurdity, revealing him as an antecedent of *Hard Times*'s Josiah Bounderby (with his 'turtle soup and venison' fantasy of the factory workers' demands), though Jonson uses the traditional military metaphors of his own time. Bobadil fantasises about training a select corps of nineteen men to work with him to defend the entire country:

> I would choose them by an instinct, a character that I have; and I would teach these nineteen the special rules, as your *punto*, your *reverso*, your *stoccato*, your *imbroccata*, your *passada*, your *montanto*... This done, say the enemy were forty thousand strong, we twenty would come into the field, the tenth of March, or thereabouts; and we would challenge twenty of the enemy; they could not, in their honour, refuse us; well we would kill them; challenge twenty more, kill them... (IV.v.60)

Bobadil's complete absorption in his own fantasy, as absolute as Dickens's in his, does not protect him from eventual exposure: in the end, revealed as a fraud and a coward, he is splendidly dignified in defeat, a figure of genuine pathos. His fate is, after a sound beating, to be exiled from the rest of the company: '[W]hile we are at supper, you...shall penitently fast in my court without, and if you will, you may pray there, that we may be so merry within, as to forgive, or forget you, when we come out' (V.i.141).

The role of the outsider who uses inventiveness and braggadocio to gain social acceptance might be said to have been made for Dickens; it might even have provided a useful compensatory activity, during the winter of 1845 to 1846, to the composing of the sentimental *The Cricket on the Hearth*. Dickens himself seems to have realised his need for such activity: he observed in a letter to George Cattermole that 'I have been bottled up so long that I bless this play for serving as a corkscrew'.[35]

### *Not So Bad As We Seem* or *Many Sides to a Character* (1851)

> I think it most admirable. Full of character, strong in interest, rich in capital situations and certain to go nobly... I know from experience that I could find nobody to hold the play together in Wilmot if I didn't do it. I think I could touch the gallant, generous, careless pretence, with the real man at the bottom of it, so as to take the audience with him from the first scene... Therefore I throw up my cap for Wilmot, and do hereby devote myself to him, heart and head![36]

Thus wrote Charles Dickens in a letter to Sir Edward Bulwer Lytton on 5 January 1851. Lytton's play, which was given its title in a postscript to that letter, was *Not So Bad As We Seem*,[37] an indifferent costume drama set in the reign of George I and written to inaugurate the short-lived Guild of Literature and Art over which the two literary lions had collaborated. The cast included Augustus Egg, John Forster, Mark Lemon, Frank Stone, John Tenniel and Wilkie Collins. According to Forster, the play was performed 'for the first time at Devonshire House on 16 May 1851, before the Queen and Prince and as large an audience as places could be found for. The success abundantly realised expectations; and, after many representations at the Hanover Square Rooms in London, strolling began in the country, and was continued at intervals for considerable portions of this and the following year.'[38]

In *Not So Bad as We Seem* there are several foreshadowings of Dickens's later novels: the heroine, Lucy, in her almost maternal devotion to her father, anticipates another Lucie in *A Tale of Two Cities*: the exiled, supposedly guilty mother, the mysterious veiled 'Lady of Deadman's Lane' for most of the play, perhaps contributed to Lady Dedlock in *Bleak House* (begun in November of that year); but it is in the presentation of the dandy, Lord Wilmot, that Dickens I think learned, rather than simply borrowed, from Bulwer Lytton. Wilmot is shadowed by an adoring friend and imitator, Softhead, as Eugene Wrayburn in *Our Mutual Friend* is by the similarly lightweight Lightwood; his foil is the self-made man, Hardman. Their confrontation over the girl they both love looks forward to that between Wrayburn and Bradley Headstone:

> HARDMAN: Ay, smile. You have wealth, rank, fashion and wit; I have none of these, and I need them not. But I say to you – that ere the hand on this dial moves to that near point in time, your love will be hopeless and your suit will be withdrawn.
>
> WILMOT: The man's mad. Unless, sir, you wish me to believe that my life hangs on your sword, I cannot quite comprehend why my love should go by your watch.
>
> HARDMAN: I command you, Lord Wilmot, to change this tone of levity.[39]

Wilmot, though presented as a dandy and a cynic, is obviously a 'safe' rebel, a Georgian buck tailored, in every sense, to suit Victorian tastes. He is a straightforward, monochrome version of Goldsmith's Honeywood and of Sheridan's Charles Surface, as the opening exchange makes clear:

> LADY: I have heard much of Lord Wilmot's eccentricities – but also of his generosity and honour.
>
> SMART: Yes, Madam, nobody like him for speaking ill of himself and doing good to another. (I.i.413)

Where Goldsmith's opening dialogue in *The Good-Natured Man* is designed to *dis*orientate the audience, to throw each member back on to individual judgement, Lytton's dialogue panders to the demands of the audience's shared 'moral sense', in Lamb's terms. Smart, the valet, reliably guides everyone to safe approval of the hero. Wilmot's 'witty' entrance, which follows, is not true wit, independent and subversive, but a literary quotation (from Pope) which aligns him with the establishment through the established tradition of English literature:

> And sleepless lovers, just at twelve, awake? Any duels today, Smart? No – I see something more dangerous – a woman. (I.i.413)

These coded references to the unmentionable rake hero of Restoration drama are necessary to give meaning to the 'pretence' which is the play's chief source of emotional interest. The pretence is no more, dramatically, than a development of the heroic bashfulness of Goldsmith's Marlow in *She Stoops to Conquer*. Wilmot's identifying 'humour' is that he cannot bear his good heart to be seen. (*Bleak House*'s John Jarndyce, with his 'wind in the east' is an obvious descendant.) The moral – and dramatic – centre of the play is Wilmot's sentimental 'melting' of Hardman:

> *[Hardman holds Wilmot's father's life in his hands and can thus blackmail Wilmot into withdrawing all claim to the girl he loves.]*
> WILMOT: Sir, I cannot argue with, I cannot rival, the man who has my father's life at his will, whether to offer it as a barter, or to yield it as a boon. Either way, rivalry between us is henceforth impossible. Fear me no more!… I depart.
> HARDMAN: (Aside) His manliness moves me… (To Wilmot) You will do it, my lord.
> WILMOT: Ay, indeed – and when my father is safe, I will try to think I wronged you. (Aside. And not one parting word to – to – S'death – I am unmanned. Show such emotion to him – No! No! – And if I cannot watch over that gentle life, why, the angels will!) I – I go sir, fulfil the compact; I have paid the price (Exit). (V.ii.480)

What is going on here seems to be the revelation of a yielding female nature suppressed within the male and identified by tears. Eve Kosofsky Sedgwick and other critics have explored the complex mid-Victorian constructions of masculinity and identified the homoerotic charge in the contemporary rhetoric of maleness – what Dickens meant (talking about his next major role, in *The Frozen Deep*) as touching 'the real man at the bottom of it'.[40] The assumption is that the male wants not only to dominate but to be dominated and nineteenth-century sentimentalist rhetoric operates by simulating that desire in forcing tears from the hero through the cruelty of the 'hard' character – who then repents and is himself 'melted'. Linguistically, the move is shown by the rejection of the register of wit in favour of the sentimental register. Anticipating Eugene Wrayburn, Wilmot reveals his true worth to the Victorian audience by frequently abandoning the abbreviated half-sentences of his 'cynical' register for the Latinate periods which are one of the many linguistic resources of sentimentalism:

> WILMOT [cynical]: Hush! Must not shock Mr. Hardman, the most friendly, obliging man, and so clever – will be a minister one day. But not one of our set. (I.i.416)
>
> WILMOT [sentimental]: My dear Duke, forgive me if I dismiss with a jest a subject so fatal, if gravely entertained. (I.i.420)

The sentimentalised dandy figure becomes for Dickens a type of hedonism, of freedom of emotional expression, to set against the emotional restraint, the self-repression, of Hardman and of Bradley Headstone. The conflict, in Lytton's and in Dickens's own personalities and in the habitus of mid-Victorian society, between restraint and frankness, repression and expression, asceticism and hedonism, was neatly dramatised in the casting of the 1851 production. Dickens's foil as Wilmot was the Hardman of the dour, 'self-made' John Forster; introduced into the company and into Dickens's acquaintance as Smart the valet was the young Bohemian, Wilkie Collins. During the provincial tour of the play which Forster refused to join 'because', observed Dickens unsympathetically, 'he thinks he is not appreciated as Hardman', Collins began to usurp Forster's place as Dickens's foil in private life. Forster's only written reference to a development which must have deeply hurt him is the last sentence of his chapter 'In Aid of Literature and Art', in his two-volume *Life* of his friend, in which he quotes from one of Dickens's letters to him, 'you have no idea how good Tenniel, Topham and Collins have been in what they had to do' and comments: 'These names, distinguished in art and letters, represent additions to the company who had joined the enterprise; and the last of them, Mr Wilkie Collins, became, for the rest of the life of Dickens, one of his dearest and most valued friends.'[41] Distancing himself from Forster, Dickens perhaps saw for the first time in perspective the ideals of hard work, restraint and respectability upon which both men had built their careers; drawing closer to Collins, he could for the first time openly acknowledge the attractions of idleness, carelessness and hedonism. In the role of the debonair, generous Wilmot, nightly confronting the narrow and unlikeable Hardman/Forster, he must surely have been increasingly tempted to try a new role for himself. The crucial developments in Dickens's life – the separation from his wife Catherine and the liaison with Ellen Ternan – could never have happened without such a re-casting. In laying claim to the part in the first place, he probably saw himself still as the delicate, almost effeminate young man of the Cruikshank and Maclise sketches, though according to R. H. Horne, a fellow actor, he looked on stage more like 'the captain of an East Indiaman' – vigorous, weather-beaten and authoritative.[42] The almost adolescent enthusiasm with which at the age of 39 he opted for Wilmot surely suggests a man approaching middle-age, who 'hath ever but slenderly known himself' and who seeks through play-acting to explore a possible new identity.

For two years, within the safe confines of Victorian approval, Dickens acted out the part of the dandy, a character who stood opposed to all that Hardman, Podsnap and John Forster (so intimately linked with both) stood for. His subsequent novels show an increasingly tragic reworking of the Wilmot/Hardman confrontation: in *Little Dorrit*, Henry Gowan gains Pet from Arthur Clennam; in *Great Expectations*, Pip's pride is dismantled in an awful parody of Hardman's fate; and finally, in *Our Mutual Friend*, Dickens can in Headstone castigate fiercely and cruelly qualities that had formally sustained him, while acknowledging, in Wrayburn, the attractiveness of formally despised aristocratic dilettantism.

## *The Frozen Deep*

Wilkie Collins had his own well-developed scepticism about Victorian values, as evidenced in his novels, particularly *No Name* (1862); however, in *The Frozen Deep* (1857) he produced, with Dickens, a dramatic *tour de force* confirming and reinforcing nineteenth-century sentimentalist tradition. The title itself is a metaphorical version of the sentimentalist mask, the 'surface' which so fascinated Dickens hiding the good heart of the sentimental hero. It anticipates Dickens's construction of Headstone, linking sentimentalism with hidden passions in a way which particularly excited him: 'No man knows till the time comes what depths there are within him.'[43] Like the Lytton play, *The Frozen Deep* is about the nature of the hero's heart, and involves Renunciation (implicitly capitalised), which developed from the eighteenth century into an even more popular theme during the mid-Victorian period, as the values of the 'good heart' became increasingly linked to Christianity. Wardour (his 'ardour' carefully hidden under watch and 'ward') begins as a sullen potential villain, soured by his rejection by Clara Burnham. He has vowed vengeance upon Clara's favoured lover, Frank Aldersley, and his opportunity comes when Chance throws them together on an ill-fated expedition to the Arctic. Against all expectations, Wardour's 'good heart' triumphs and the final scene contains Dickens's greatest *coup de théâtre*, when Wardour staggers on stage, carrying the injured Frank to safety, and dies at Clara's feet. The play seems to have been inspired, as R. L. Brannan explains,[44] by the 'manly fortitude' of Sir John Franklin on his fatal expedition to the Arctic in 1845. Dickens's angry defence of Franklin's memory (against charges of cannibalism) is a significant example of his use of the sentimentalist register for polemical purposes:

> Utilitarianism will protest 'they are dead; why care about this?' Our reply shall be, 'Because they are dead, therefore we care about this. Because they served their country well, and deserved well of her, and can ask, no more on this earth, for her justice or her loving-kindness; give them both, full measure, pressed down and running over. Because no Franklin came back, to write the honest story of their woes and resignation, read it tenderly and truly in the book he has left us. Because they lie scattered in those wastes of snow…therefore cherish them gently, even in the breasts of children. Therefore, teach no-one to shudder without reason, at the history of their end. Therefore, confide with their own firmness, in their fortitude, their lofty sense of duty, their courage, and their religion.'[45]

The passage is written in the style of Mr Chadband in *Bleak House*, built on anaphora ('Because… Because… Because… Therefore… Therefore') which substitute emotional intensification for rationality: '*Because* they are dead, therefore we care about this' (my emphasis). Dickens obviously feels that this is a place to set up his ideological battle line between sentimentalism and utilitarianism. The point, implied in the final two sentences, is that Franklin and his team were not the sort of men to stoop to cannibalism. However, the drift of the passage is a generalised, non-intellectual, emotional warmth which is deliberately dissociated from and indeed actively suppresses rational activity. This is, as Juliet John has argued, a conscious privileging of the non-intellectual, the instinctive, over the rational.[46] Dickens undermines the logic of 'because' and 'therefore' with sentimental vocabulary: 'cherish', 'gently', 'breasts' and especially 'children': '*Because* they lie scattered in those wastes of snow…therefore cherish them gently in the breasts of children' (my emphasis). It would be difficult to extract a paraphrasible meaning from that sentence. Instead of denotation it produces, through well-established *connotation*, a powerful if generalised emotion. Ironically, though he can't hear it in his own prose, Dickens is perfectly able to detect this method being used by other preachers, and parodies it wonderfully in *Bleak House*'s Mr Chadband:

> You are a human boy, my young friend. A human boy. O glorious to be a human boy. And why glorious, my young friend? Because you are capable of receiving the lessons of wisdom, because you are capable of profiting by the discourse which I now deliver for your good, because you are not a stick, or a staff, or a stock, or a stone, or a post, or a pillar. Oh be joyful![47]

A serious value system is in operation in the Franklin passage: spontaneous emotion is glorified even in an apparently casual alliterative phrase such as 'tenderly and truly', the words being linked not only by assonance but by Dickens's central belief that *truth* is to be found in the heart rather than in the head. It is a verbal combination he uses frequently, for example at Mrs Dombey's death, where it occurs in a metaphor anticipating the Collins play: 'depths of tenderness and truth'. Despite the Romantic setting of the Arctic wilderness, *The Frozen Deep* is still a monument to sentimentalism. The hero stands romantically against the world but his heroic qualities spring not from the Romantic will, but from the sentimentalist 'good heart'.[48]

Various elements in the play are particularly important in revealing the use Dickens made of conventional material. There is the blending of sentimentalism with Romanticism, which involves the move from a domestic to an heroic setting; there is the idealisation of male friendship which was to become a major feature of nineteenth-century sentimentalism; there is the linking of sexual desire with death, evident in *Clarissa* and powerfully linked with Keats's Romanticism and with Goethe's *The Sorrows of Young Werther* (see Chapter 1); most interestingly of all, and linked with this, is the continuation of sentimentalist displacement: the hero purifies his physical desires by offering his surrogate, Aldersley, to the heroine. In death, he at last earns his moment of emotional coition with her:

> Nearer, Clara – I want to look my last at you. My sister, Clara! Kiss me, sister, kiss me before I die! (Act the Third)[49]

Dickens is moulding Collins's text to meet his own emotional needs, within the safe public disguise of sentimentalist conventions.

Unlike the very real Arctic wilderness in which Sir John Franklin and his unfortunate crew had met their ends, the Arctic wastes in *The Frozen Deep* are as irrelevant to Dickens's central concerns as were the Alps to *Little Dorrit*.[50] The external world is merely a projection of the internal world of the 'good heart' within which the actual drama takes place. The symbolic significance of these arctic conditions for Dickens was not only their metonymic representation of the frozen heart. A letter to Forster, quoted by Brannan, suggests another connection:

> Again I am beset by my former notions of a book whereof the whole story shall be on the top of the Great St Bernard. As I accept and reject ideas for *Little Dorrit*, it perpetually comes back to me. Two or three years hence, perhaps, you'll find me living with the Monks and the Dogs a whole winter – among the blinding snows that fall about that monastery. I have a serious idea that I shall do it, if I live.[51]

Dickens is here surely thinking of an article by Henry Morley which he had published in *Household Words* 14 February 1857, entitled, 'The Lost English Sailors' (145–7):

> Shut up in Arctic monasteries – with no monkish souls, men have learnt energetically to respect and help each other, to trust in each other, and have faith in God. The entire series of books written by Arctic Sailors, except only one or two, bears most emphatic witness to the fine spirit of manhood nourished among those who bear in company the rigours of the frozen sea.

As well as foreshadowing the Christmas book, *No Thoroughfare*, which Dickens and Collins wrote together in 1867, both the letter and the article suggest the mid-Victorian sentimental construction of male friendship, linked both with arctic conditions and its spiritual equivalent, the purity of monastic life. Critics, notably Eve Kosofsky Sedgwick, have identified here another, autoerotic, strand of sentimentalism.[52] Dickens confessed to a 'sort of sacred joy' when he read about the comradeship between Franklin and his men. What is involved is the sentimentalist displacement from the sexual to the 'innocent'; the latter then becomes charged with an emotional intensity which parallels the original sexual response.

What Barbara Hardy identifies as the 'topos of inexpressibility'[53] became a major feature of nineteenth-century sentimentalist rhetoric, in which the rational basis of eighteenth-century male friendship was gradually lost in an exploration of the 'female' tenderness which could subsist between two men. That it stirred Dickens's imagination is particularly evident in the Nicholas/Smike relationship in *Nicholas Nickleby* and in the highly charged emotion between Eugene and Mortimer in *Our Mutual Friend*. The tenderness between the last two has an explicitly female quality about it and may even owe something to the highly popular contemporary account of the death of

Admiral Lord Nelson, with his final (misreported?) words to his companion, 'Kiss me, Hardy!':

> Eugene (as he lies apparently dying): Touch my face with yours, in case I should not hold on till you come back. I love you, Mortimer. Don't be uneasy for me while you are gone.[54]

Sedgwick suggests that the central emotional transaction in much nineteenth-century literature, whatever the overt plot, is 'between men'. Here both the suppressed eroticism and the suppressed Christian discourse of sentimentalism are in play: female, but also Christian, virtues of tenderness and passivity displace male ones of vigour and aggression. Sentimentalism successfully reinscribes dangerous sexuality as harmless friendship, while retaining the emotional charge of the original. Dickens in *The Frozen Deep* anticipates *Our Mutual Friend* by making the estrangement of the good-hearted Crayford and Wardour, and their eventual reconciliation a strong subsidiary plot-line, rivalling the heterosexual love-interest in Wardour's dying speech:

> Stay, someone was here and spoke to me just now. Ah! Crayford! I recollect now. (Embracing him.) Dear Crayford! Come nearer! My mind clears, but my eyes grow dim. You will remember me kindly for Frank's sake?

In *The Frozen Deep* Dickens and Collins attempt to combine male and female virtues in a way peculiar to their own time: eighteenth-century sentimentalism, with its delicate feminine connotations, is subsumed into an heroic setting and embodied in a man full of the 'heroic and tremendous' virtues of fortitude and courage. The actual feminine interest, in the heroine, is deliberately muted and Collins emphasises the difference between the two sets of virtues by separating them in the construction of the play. Act I is a domestic drama involving the womenfolk mourning at home for their lost men; Act II is an heroic drama of friendship and betrayal among the men-folk in the Arctic; and the two come together in Act III, which reveals the final sentimentalist tableau, as Richard Wardour, having carried Frank on stage, dies in Clara's arms. The sentimental tableau is a particular feature of *The Frozen Deep* and its domestic significance was recognised by at least one reviewer: Act I, he said, was 'one of those sweet picturesque views so thoroughly English, with a village church and spire in the distance, standing out in relief against the strong red lights of a fine sunset'.[55] Another review itself employs sentimentalist rhetoric to describe the sentimentalist rhetoric of the play. It is a rhetoric based on stasis, not movement, the stress being on nouns, not verbs, and on the use of anaphora to disarm intellect to produce a generalised emotion. The proclaimed 'naturalism' of the play is inadvertently revealed to rely on a similar extreme stylisation:

> Of the effect of this scene…it would be difficult to convey an adequate idea. The weary, lonely grief of the four companions, the spirit of quiet, gentle sorrow that moves over the whole performance; the sweet, sad melody sung by the two young ladies…the awful forebodings of the Scotch nurse; the deep yet melancholy sympathy of the evening light and the solemn stealing in of the white moonrise; the wretchedness and the terror of the ladies, and the shuddering awe of Esther's vision (not raved out, according to transmitted fashion, but all quiet and intense) – these are elements contributed to the general effect which is new to our stage, because based on Nature instead of on tradition.[56]

That this play exemplifies sentimentalism after it had absorbed the effects of the Romantic movement is evident from the link established between Wardour's desire for Clara and his death. Eighteenth-century comedy generally retained the New Comedy structure of lovers' reunion and happy ending. Wardour's indifference to life and commitment to death, in contrast, reveal the influence of the intervening Romantic Byronic hero. Unlike the heroes of sentimental comedy, whose purpose is to be reintegrated into society, he stands irretrievably outside, a dangerously subversive force. However, in the mid-Victorian version, the Byronic hero's destructive sexuality must be moderated into religious worship, part of Victorian medievalism and of the medieval courtly love ethic, before it can become socially acceptable. Women here are adored objects rather than characters in their own right:

> WARDOUR: The only hopelessness and wretchedness in this world, is the wretchedness that women cause.
> CRAYFORD: Ay, and the only unalloyed happiness, the happiness they bring.
> WARDOUR: That may be your experience of them. Mine is different. All the devotion, the patience, the humility, the worship, that there is in Man, I laid at the feet of a Woman. (Act the Second, 133)

Dickens's use of capital letters in the prompt copy (followed here) indicates both the emphasis he wanted on the spoken word, and the emblematic quality of the male and female roles. His aim is to show Wardour transcending the passions of jealousy and desire and achieving a formal act of renunciation, and he pursues this theme in typical sentimentalist style, by carefully minimising extraneous matters. Brannan skilfully shows how Dickens altered Collins's original script to reduce interest in the other characters and focus on Wardour's struggle. The heroine, Clara, is presented by Collins as also engaged in a struggle (with guilt over her hasty dismissal of Wardour). Dickens cut several of Collins's speeches for Clara so as to reduce her from being a parallel dramatic centre of interest to a simple tableau angel. In Act I she is sketchily presented, acting merely as a device to set up the tension between the two men. In Act III, she returns as the Angel in the House, a cherished object. Her friends and old nurse talk of her in iconic terms, before she eventually appears, borne in like an icon:

> Enter Clara… with Lieutenant Crayford and Lucy, on either side, leading her. (Act the Third, 150)

Clara is then given a set speech in which love of God, love of Nature, love of the past, love of England and sexual love come together in an expression of undifferentiated emotion. Clara clearly *embodies* all the things she describes:

> I see so much of the Mercy and Goodness of the Great Creator all around me – such brightness and beauty to delight us in the Earth and Heaven – such a blessed ending to all the past anxiety and sorrow of Lucy, and Caroline, and Rose, that I cannot lose hope. The very waves looked joyful as we walked along the shore just now. The poor stunted bushes on the cliff rustled as happily in the sweet air as the tall Elm Trees in our English home. When I heard them, I thought of the Trees that Frank and I used to walk under. Shall I see those Trees again, when we get back to England – and not see Frank! Shall I never, never shew him the withered leaves of his Nosegay, which I have kept here so long, for his sake! O! I must hope, and you must help me by hoping too. (Act the Third, 151)

By being invested with such a weight of emotional significance, Clara acquires the stature she needs for the final scene where her only actions are to 'fall on Frank's bosom' and eventually to kiss Wardour as he dies, accompanied by the tears of the audience.[57]

There is always a political dimension to the public (including theatrical) expression of emotion. It is no coincidence that sentimental tears were rife in literature and on stage at the time of the French Revolution. The influence of Goethe and especially of *The Sorrows of Young Werther*,[58] on the development of the Romantic movement suggests the liberating power, both politically and personally, of emotional expressiveness. The conflicted discourses of emotion during the Victorian period indicate a continuing fear of revolution, lasting into the 1850s.

In *The Frozen Deep* Dickens is well aware of the power his ability to draw tears from an audience gives him. In a letter to Mrs Richard Watson he explains:

> All last summer I had a transitory satisfaction in rending the very heart out of my body by doing that Richard Wardour part. It was a good thing to have a couple of thousand people all *rigid and frozen* together, in the palm of one's hand – as at Manchester – and to see the hardened Carpenters at the sides crying and trembling at it night after night.[59]

There is certainly, however, in Dickens's case, an even more important erotic/psychological liberation taking place. Wardour's ability to draw tears from Clara at the climax of *The Frozen Deep* is crucial to the dramatic catharsis. It is the final act of emotional, and very public, coition which Dickens had been preparing in his intensification of the role of Wardour. His description of the Manchester performance, in which professional actresses, the Ternans, replaced his daughters and friends, suggests almost grotesquely the place of public tears in Victorian society:

Maria Ternan (playing Clara) said to Dickens before the performance:

> 'Oh Mr Dickens...I can't bear it...I cried so much when I saw it that I have a dread of it...' She had to take my head up as I lay dying, and put it on her lap, and give me her face to hold between my two hands. All of which I showed her elaborately (as Mary had done it before) that morning. When we came to that point at night, her tears fell down my face, down my beard (excuse my mentioning that hateful appendage), down my ragged dress – poured all over me like Rain, whereupon Lemon [playing Aldersley], the softest-hearted of men, began to cry too, and then they all went at it together. I think I never saw such a pretty little genuine emotion in my life.[60]

This is a revealing moment in the development of nineteenth-century sentimental rhetoric but also in the emotional development of Dickens himself. Eroticism 'safely' displaced into tears becomes publically acceptable and can be explored without, it seems, any danger to the social order. It was in the context of the catharsis provided by the Wardour role that Dickens fell in love with Maria's sister, Ellen, who, acting in a minor role, was looking on. Dickens recognised it as a turning point in his life in a letter to Collins, 21 March 1858:

> The domestic unhappiness remains so strong upon me that I can't write and (waking) rest one minute. I have never known a moment's peace or content since the last night of *The Frozen Deep*.[61]

Brannan, puzzled by Dickens's fevered search for mass publicity for this play, eventually puts it down, unconvincingly, to Dickens's social conscience:

> His reasons for seeking publicity are not clear...he may have hoped that large numbers of people would share his faith in the nature of man, his faith in the power of noble sentiments, which the action of *The Frozen Deep* affirms. He may have hoped that the play would stimulate interest in the new expedition to search for Franklin... One can be certain only that Dickens had a highly unusual desire to publicise an amateur theatrical. (62)

That 'desire', I would argue, sprang not so much from social conscience as from the urgent intimacy of Dickens's relationship with his audience. The enacting of such a public 'little death' enabled him to explore in front of them what Stedman calls the 'repression and release'[62] economy of his society and of his own temperament. Whether it be in dramatic roles or in the public readings of his novels, there is the same compulsion to reveal himself emotionally. The relationship of Dickens with his audience was thus on a level of intimacy and single-minded intensity quite unknown to any of his eighteenth-century predecessors. The original casting (with the young Wilkie Collins as Aldersley being carried by Dickens and given as a partner to his daughter Mary) suggests, as in dreams, an exploration of incest taboos. I have already suggested the significance to Dickens of Collins's frank hedonism in contrast to his own middle-aged self-repression. The play satisfied his psychological needs in a variety of ways: it allowed him to vent the frustrations within his own marriage in railing against 'women' in general; it allowed him masochistically to offer up his own spoilt emotional life for the sake of the youthful Collins and Mary – while paradoxically stealing from them the most thrilling response from the audience; and, most of all, it allowed him, as sentimentalism always did and does allow its practitioners, to exhibit and explore his own deviant and illicit impulses within the safe confines of public approval – to escape from the contemporary pressure to 'indict our very dreams'.

As with all his 'assumptions', Dickens went on acting the part long after the performances were over. Life in this case abetted him by imitating the plot of the play during Dickens's and Collins's subsequent holiday in Cumberland. Collins lamed himself on a mountain descent, and Dickens wrote to Georgina Hogarth: 'How I enacted Wardour over again in carrying him down, and what a business it was to get him down:...but he was got down somehow, and we got off the mountain, somehow; and now I carry him to bed, and into and out of carriages, exactly like Wardour in private life.'[63] Later, he wrote, how 'I long to be back in Richard Wardour's clothes...' In a letter to Collins written shortly after Catherine's enforced departure from the marital home, he added a PS: 'I miss Richard Wardour's dress and always want to put it on. I would rather, by a great deal, act [than give public readings]'.[64] As in the play, so in the subsequent novel, *A Tale of Two Cities*, which it haunts, there is an obviously respectable 'shadow-self' in the shape of Charles Darnay. He is the Frank Aldersley figure, who is on hand to retain public approval, leaving Dickens free, in Wardour and Sydney Carton, to explore the dangers of deviance.

It does not take excessive commitment to Freudian analysis to be persuaded that any increase in psychological subtlety and in deviance in the novels written after *The Frozen Deep* could well be evidence of the creative use to which Dickens put the erotic strand of Victorian sentimentalism. In Dickens's stage life, Lord Wilmot, in *Not So Bad As We Seem* (1851) had been a contradictory figure: a rake in a world which had been emptied of sex. Sexuality could only emerge on stage and into mid-Victorian public discourse, as it does in *The Frozen Deep* (1858), through the encoding of sentimentalist 'melting'. George Meredith recognised its erotic potential when, in 1885, he memorably and shockingly defined sentimentalism as the 'fire flower, or pinnacle flame-spire, of sensualism'.[65] What was always, particularly in the eighteenth century, the socially subversive potential of sentimentalism, re-emerges in *The Frozen Deep* in its Victorian form: it is now only through this popular and 'safe' rhetoric that not only Dickens but the emotionally policed mid-Victorian theatrical public can explore otherwise taboo areas of sexual expression.

# Chapter 5

# THE EARLY NOVELS AND *THE VICAR OF WAKEFIELD*

'Everything in our lives, whether of good or evil, affects us most by contrast.'[1]

The plots of Dickens's early novels are all structured around the preservation of sentimental values – the good heart, innocence, benevolence – in a changing and potentially dangerous world. This seems initially to involve a very severe segregation of good from evil. Sentimental characters and scenes are cordoned off from the darker forces in each novel in a way critics have assumed to be simplistic and unchallenging. This chapter will seek to show, however, that even in these early novels Dickens is prepared to take risks, both ethical and stylistic, to critique the sentimental values he is at pains to propagate. I shall refer briefly to *The Pickwick Papers* and *Oliver Twist* before turning to the three novels which are most germane to my examination of the sentimentalist tradition, *Nicholas Nickleby*, *The Old Curiosity Shop* and *Martin Chuzzlewit*. I begin however, with some brief comments on Dickens's own favourite novel, *The Vicar of Wakefield*.[2]

## *The Vicar of Wakefield*

Oliver Goldsmith's masterpiece was a great influence on the sentimentalism of Dickens's early novels and a particularly powerful presence behind *The Battle of Life* – indeed, Dickens suggested that his characters in that most untypical Christmas book should be depicted in the illustrations 'in the coats and gowns of dear old Goldsmith's day'.[3] Goldsmith's masterpiece, said Dickens, is a book 'of which I think it is not too much to say that it has perhaps done more good in the world, and instructed more kinds of people in virtue, than any other fiction ever written'. Dickens's praise of *The Vicar* is contained (characteristically) in a letter appealing for help for Goldsmith's great-nephew and he reads the novel very obviously as a moral tract.[4] Goethe,

Thackeray, Fanny Burney and many others read *The Vicar of Wakefield* exactly as Dickens did, completely missing what modern readers assume to be Goldsmith's irony. Clive T. Probyn sums up neatly the central question still unresolved about this novel: 'Is *The Vicar of Wakefield* consistently or only intermittently an ironic novel? Is it a sentimental romance, or a parody of romance, or both?'[5] As in the case of Goldsmith's plays, the problem seems to hinge on the text's addressivity, on the relationship established between the sentimental narrative voice and the readership.

*Dr Primrose and Deborah, his wife, live with their six children in blissful rural seclusion until, on the eve of their son George's marriage to Arabella Wilmot, they lose all their money through the bankruptcy of a merchant with whom they have invested. The marriage cannot take place, George is sent off to town to work and the family move in much reduced circumstances to live on the land of Squire Thornhill. They are helped by a mysterious eccentric, Mr Burchell. A series of further calamities befall the family as their daughter Olivia is seduced by Squire Thornhill, their house is destroyed by fire, Dr Primrose is thrown into debtors' prison by the unrepentant Thornhill, and hears there of Olivia's death and his other daughter Sophia's abduction. Then comes a dramatic turning point as George appears badly injured and recognises Burchell as the good Sir William Thornhill. 'Burchell' and Sophia, Arabella and George are married in a double wedding, it turns out that Olivia was legally wed to Thornhill after all, and happiness and fortune are restored to the worthy Vicar.*

Goldsmith's story of a domestic rural idyll destroyed by a series of melodramatic occurrences and in the end restored by a parallel series of implausible coincidences contains obvious anticipations of *Nicholas Nickleby*, with the very salient difference that the anti-sentimental principle, the enemy of the 'good' characters, is embodied in the *Vicar* by an eighteenth-century hypocrite in the mould of Joseph Surface, whereas Dickens in *Nickleby* has to resort to an outright melodramatic villain, Ralph Nickleby. The problem of evil seems much less of an issue to Goldsmith and the eighteenth-century novelists: *everyone* is implicated in sentimentalist rhetoric and may be redeemed, whereas in Dickens a different emotional economy is at work, the intensity of evil seeming to act as a necessary balance to the intensity of goodness.

This 'sentimental economy' is very evident in Goldsmith's treatment of tears. Here is the Vicar telling Arabella Wilmot of the awful events that have befallen his family:

> 'My little family are now dispersing fast, and poverty has brought not only want, but infamy upon us.' The good-natured girl let fall a tear at this account; but as I saw her possessed of too much sensibility, I forebore a more minute detail of our sufferings.[6]

Miss Wilmot, as the sentimental heroine, must be spared too many tears. Even the hypocritical villain, Thornhill, is spared, in the final exposure scene, and in fact never quite gives up his sentimentalist rhetoric:

> Mr Thornhill's assurance had entirely forsaken him: he now saw the gulph of infamy and want before him and trembled to take the plunge. He therefore fell on his knees before his uncle, and in a voice of piercing misery implored compassion. Sir William was going to spurn him away, but at my request he raised him... [Thornhill] was going to express his gratitude for such kindness in a set speech; but the Baronet prevented him by bidding him not aggravate his meanness, which was already all too apparent. (165)

This is a world away from the terrible suicide of Ralph Nickleby. The problem of evil is one, apparently, which nineteenth-century sentimentalism has to solve for itself: it is without precedent in the eighteenth-century forebears. From *The Vicar*, however, Dickens did learn, not only the need for the establishment of a 'community of good' within a naughty world but also the importance of contingency. Goldsmith's protagonist disarms disbelief at the series of coincidences which lead to the book's conclusion by observing:

> Nor can I go on, without a reflection on those accidental meetings which, though they happen every day, seldom excite our surprise but upon some extraordinary occasion. To what a fortuitous concurrence do we not owe every pleasure and convenience of our lives. (159)

Dickens was to set up the same narrative parameters in *Little Dorrit*, though there is a signal difference. Dickens misses Goldsmith's 'double-voiced discourse': the Vicar's balanced periods are not those of the implied author. The Vicar's voice is constantly ironised. The contrast between the 'pleasure and convenience' lauded by the character and the extreme events he has reported – the ruining of his daughter, the destitution of his family – defamiliarise the text, undermine its complacency and mingle sentimentalism with irony in the reader's response. Dickens's randomness, in contrast, has a fairytale quality about it – 'chance' leading to dramatic shape and to closure. Both writers overtly restore equilibrium in their conclusions. The sentimental tableau at the end of *The Vicar of Wakefield* superficially anticipates many such in Dickens:

> As soon as dinner was over, according to my old custom, I requested that the table be taken away, to have the pleasure of seeing all my family assembled once more by a cheerful fire-side. My two little ones sat upon my knee, the rest of the company by their partners. I had nothing now on this side of the grave

to wish for, all my cares were over, my pleasure was unspeakable. It now only remained that my gratitude in good fortune should exceed my former submission to adversity. (169–70)

Once again, however, Goldsmith demands a complex response from the reader: the balanced Latinate periods are 'sentimental' in the earlier sense of rational and moralistic – a sense which the whole action of the novel has already ironised. Dickens chooses to read the resolution as a simple restoration to a prelapsarian state and it is this that he attempts, quite *un*ironically, to recreate, particularly in the early novels where the influence of Goldsmith is most apparent. *Nicholas Nickleby*, for example, ends with Smike's wept-over grave and *Martin Chuzzlewit* with the apotheosis of Tom Pinch. Irony is ruthlessly excluded from both endings.

In this chapter I shall be arguing that this dramatised opposition of sentimentalism and irony is precisely what gives Dickens's early novels their power. They are novels of affect as well as of satire, but they operate precisely by keeping the two modes ruthlessly apart. This construction of rigidly separate rival discourses derives from Dickens's enthusiastic but highly selective reading of his predecessors. Paradoxically, though, it is these early novels which are most obviously haunted by the voices of the earlier writers, in their characterisation, their plots and their language.

One way of approaching the difference between Dickens and his predecessors is to address Clive Probyn's question (is *The Vicar of Wakefield* a romance or a parody of romance, or both?) through theorists such as Roland Barthes who in his essay 'The Death of the Author' shifts the balance away from authorial intent and towards the power of the text itself.[7] Narrative theory and particularly Wolfgang Iser's concepts of the 'implied reader' and the 'implied author' help too.[8] In the case of late eighteenth-century sentimental writers, there seem to be at least two implied authors – the ironist and the sentimentalist – and at least two implied readers, the sentimentalist (implicitly constructed as female) and the man-of-the-world ironist. This is most revealingly suggested by Laurence Sterne in his letter to 'Hannah' (already quoted in Chapter 2), in which he mischievously observes that the writing of *A Sentimental Journey* 'will make you cry as much as ever it made me laugh – or I'll give up the business of Sentimental writing and write to the Body'.[9] Sentimental writing, according to my argument, very often writes 'to the Body' – even, as Chapter 4 has suggested, the sentimental writing of Dickens. Q. D. Leavis, in her pioneering study of the eighteenth-century reading public, frequently distinguishes between simple and complex styles and responses.[10] These might well be linked in Iser's terms, with the number of implied readers involved in the reception of the text. Instead of the plural and complex implied readership of Sterne and Goldsmith, Dickens's relationship with his 'Readers' (always capitalised in the prefaces to the novels) is notoriously intimate, exclusive, simple and intense. The concept of the 'implied reader' thus acquires a particular potency when applied to his novels. Probyn suggests that, in contrast, Goldsmith 'provides space for his readers' – space, presumably, for a *variety* of responses.

In what follows I shall not be seeking to establish a linear narrative from simple to complex sentimental effects in Dickens's novels, nor suggesting that 'complex' is aesthetically, morally or intellectually better than 'simple'. Each of the novels needs to be read carefully for the range of sentimental effects created: there is no straightforward 'development'. In *Martin Chuzzlewit*, for example, Pecksniff is constructed complexly; in *Edwin Drood*, the Rosa Bud/John Jasper scene employs a simple, intensified rhetoric. These are stylistic choices from a wealth of possibilities offered by the tradition Dickens inherited. In all cases, though, it is important to set the novels in their cultural and literary contexts: the sort of acontextual close reading to which they are still being subjected leads to reductiveness and makes it impossible to recognise Dickens's important reworkings of literary tradition.

## *The Pickwick Papers*

The picaresque structure of this novel suggests that it is 'sentimental' in an eighteenth- rather than a nineteenth-century sense, concerned with public benevolence rather than with the evoking of an intense emotional response. R. Robison explores Mr Pickwick's debt to Sterne's Uncle Toby, David Parker likens him to Don Quixote,[11] and many other studies of the novel seem compelled to address the literary provenance of the central figure in an attempt to identify the novel's real concerns. Dickens himself thought the creative process worthy of mention and at this early stage in his career seemed to feel no need to link imagination to real life: 'I thought of Mr Pickwick, and wrote the first number'.[12] Pickwick is more than an embodiment of sunny benevolence. He begins, rather, as a *critique* of benevolence-in-the-form-of-philanthropy – again, a very eighteenth-century figure, much in the manner of Goldsmith's 'Good-Natured Man'. The novel's effects are complex, as in *The Vicar of Wakefield*. Pickwick aspires, he says, to 'benefit the human race' but, as David Parker points out, at the beginning of the novel 'humanity in the abstract is the object of his benevolence' and only later does he learn the value of individual sympathy.[13]

For modern readers, the most moving episode in *Pickwick Papers* is Mr Pickwick's incarceration in the Fleet Prison – reminiscent of Dr Primrose's fate and a bold testing of the benevolent sentimentalism of the earlier chapters. There is certainly stylistic uncertainty at this point in the novel – the threat of subversion from a different genre altogether, the Newgate Novel, and Pickwick's eighteenth-century (or to be more accurate, Georgian) benevolence is tested in the new nineteenth-century moral world of individual (Romantic) sympathy. The novel's final paragraph delivers the moral sentiments of the previous century:

> Nearly the whole of my previous life having been devoted to business and the pursuit of wealth, numerous scenes of which I had no previous conception have dawned upon me – I hope to the enlargement of my mind, and the improvement of my understanding. If I have done but little good, I trust I have done less harm, and that none of my adventures will be other than a source of amusing and pleasant recollections to me in the decline of life. God bless you all! (872)

This is a rational account – indeed, very literally a rationale – of the narrative itself. Pickwick talks in the style of Dr Johnson and of Jane Austen of 'the enlargement of my mind and the improvement of my understanding'. There is no mention here of sympathy or the good heart. Yet the Fleet Prison scenes have announced a new approach to emotion. The old man, 'his limbs...shaking with disease, and the palsy...fastened on his mind' (657) or the 'young woman with a child in her arms, who seemed scarcely able to crawl, from emaciation and misery...[who] burst into such a passion of grief, that she was compelled to lean against the wall for support' (636) announce a new and dreadful mode of experience for readers and for reformers alike. Can abstract eighteenth-century benevolence survive this Romantic demand for individual sympathy, which disrupts the novel (and the eighteenth-century novel form) irretrievably? Pickwick himself, as Parker points out, turns away from eighteenth-century benevolence and towards nineteenth-century sentimentalism for the answer, as is evident when he meets the starving Job Trotter and Alfred Jingle:

> Yes; in tattered garments, and without a coat: his common calico shirt, yellow and in rags; his hair hanging over his face: his features changed with suffering, and pinched with famine, – there sat Mr Alfred Jingle; his head resting on his hand, his eyes fixed upon the fire, and his whole appearance denoting misery and dejection! (657)
>
> 'Good fellow... Ungrateful dog – boyish to cry – can't help it – bad fever – weak – hungry. Deserved it all; but suffered much – very.' [He] sat down on the stairs, and, covering his face with his hands, sobbed like a child...
>
> 'Come here, sir,' said Mr Pickwick, trying to look stern, with four large tears running down his waistcoat.
>
> 'Take that, sir.'
>
> ...Must we tell the truth? It was something from Mr Pickwick's waistcoat pocket, which chinked as it was given into Job's hand, and the giving of which,

somehow or other, imparted a sparkle to the eye, and a swelling to the heart, of our excellent old friend, as he hurried away. (659)

The sentimental narrator has now lost his ironising tone and himself is moved by Pickwick's evolving benevolence. Even though the ending of the novel reads like a return to the eighteenth century, the key moment in a sentimental reading of the novel is again the 'topos of inexpressibility'[14] – the point at which the eighteenth-century novel form admits its inadequacy to deal with nineteenth-century sympathetic identification:

I have seen enough... My head aches with these scenes, and my heart too. Henceforth I will be a prisoner in my own room. (707)

## *Oliver Twist*

Dickens's account of the relationship of good and evil in the preface to the third edition of *Oliver Twist* is instructive in relation to his later development of sentimentalism. 'I confess,' he says, 'I have yet to learn that a lesson of the purest good may not be drawn from the vilest evil... [It was] in this spirit, when I wished to show, in little Oliver, the principle of Good surviving through every adverse circumstance,' that 'I bethought myself of those who figure in these volumes' (62) – in other words, the criminals, prostitutes and abused children for whose presence in the novel he had been criticised. The balancing of good and evil upon which the novel is built is extreme and radically unstable. Steven Connor sees the partitioning as being impossible to sustain since 'what characterises the haunts of wickedness and vice in the novel is not only their darkness and oppressiveness, but also their instability' and yet what impels the novel, he argues, is 'the desire for moral segregation of the pure from the impure'.[15] His implication is that the linguistic energy of the novel comes precisely from the rhetorical effort expended in trying to maintain what turns out to be an impossible state of affairs.

The climax of this rhetorical effort in *Oliver Twist* is Oliver's physical collapse in the middle of the novel and his rebirth into the new Brownlow world. Brian Cheadle points out that the savagery and casual cruelty of the first half of the novel *needs* to be balanced by what have been called the 'sentimental' sections.[16] However he seems to conclude from this that these sections cannot therefore be called 'sentimental' at all. I would argue rather that Dickens's central thesis is *about* sentimental values: in worshipping money, he says, industrialised society is 'putting entirely out of sight any considerations of heart, or generous impulse or feeling' (73). The clash of registers is at its most brutal at the moment of Oliver's collapse – when Fang the barbaric magistrate refuses to give Oliver any support 'let him [fall down] if he likes' and the cruelly comic narrative voice points out the brutality:

> Oliver availed himself of the kind permission, and fell heavily to the floor in a fainting fit. The men in the office looked at each other, but no one dared to stir. (64–5)

From this point, with that denial of all human sympathy and insistence upon the separateness of individuals, the novel turns about, brings in Mr Brownlow and the bookseller, and transfers Oliver to a new, safe, domestic, rural space, the sentimental space. This space has a natural affinity with death, as have all such spaces in Dickens. Here, Oliver falls into a sleep which is specifically likened to death:

> [He] fell into that deep tranquil sleep which ease from recent suffering alone imparts; that calm and peaceful rest which it is pain to wake from. Who, if this were death, would be roused again to all the struggles and turmoils of life; to all its cares for the present; its anxieties for the future; more than all, its weary recollection of the past. (69–70)

In this sentimental space, weeping is part of the emotional economy: as Oliver recovers, his old nurse 'forthwith began to cry most violently'.

> 'Never mind me, my dear,' said the old lady. 'I'm only having a regular good cry. There; it's all over now; and I'm quite comfortable.' (70)

In this brutal novel, which deals with prostitution, child abuse, violent death and capital punishment, Dickens struggles to maintain the plausibility of the belief that the world can be sustained by the 'good heart'. Sentimental values here are *not* linked with excess, but are carefully calibrated to provide a necessary balance to the horrors that Dickens, through them, has had the courage to describe.

## *Nicholas Nickleby*

Just as Fagin manifests himself in the most sentimental space of all, Oliver's bedroom at Mr Brownlow's, so the sentimental Nickleby family are flung into the world of Ralph Nickleby and usury and have their vocabulary of sentiment shredded in the encounter. *The Vicar of Wakefield* haunts this novel, in the innocent, unworldly family as well as in subsequent details of the plot. The opening scene involves, as so often in Dickens, analysis of a single word.

Kirstie Blair's work on the place of the heart in Victorian culture suggests what is at stake, both culturally and ethically.[17] The scene needs to be quoted at length for the battle of registers to emerge:

> A lady in deep mourning rose as Mr Ralph Nickleby entered, but appeared incapable of advancing to meet him, and leant upon the arm of a slight but very beautiful girl of about seventeen, who had been sitting by her. A youth, who appeared a year or two older, stepped forward and saluted Ralph as his uncle…
>
> 'You didn't mention in your letter what my brother's complaint was, ma'am.'
>
> 'The doctors could attribute it to no particular disease,' said Mrs Nickleby, shedding tears. 'We have too much reason to fear that he died of a broken heart.'
>
> 'Pooh!' said Ralph, 'there's no such thing. I can understand a man's dying of a broken neck, or suffering from a broken arm, or a broken leg, or a broken nose; but a broken heart! It's nonsense, it's the cant of the day. If a man can't pay his debts, he dies of a broken heart, and his widow's a martyr.'
>
> 'Some people, I believe, have no hearts to break,' observed Nicholas, quietly.

There are two further references to the heart during the scene:

> '[W]hat do you mean to do for your bread, sir?'
>
> 'Not to live upon my mother,' replied Nicholas, his heart swelling as he spoke.
>
> …[The contrast between himself and his nephew] galled Ralph to the heart's core, and he hated Nicholas from that hour. (24)

Blair's work reveals the process by which the physical and the metaphysical heart were confused during the period. She argues that 'the rapid rise of physiological and medical explanations of bodily processes meant that the embodied heart assumed a vital role in culture and literature'.[18] She reveals the cultural value placed, in a newly industrialised world, upon this central feature of sentimentalist rhetoric:

> The uneasy power of the heart in many Victorian texts is…so emphatic because the heart seemed to be losing much of its traditional resonance being replaced by new theories and beliefs.[19]

Charles Bell's medical account of the heart, discussed in the Introduction,[20] is in a way yet another exploration of sentimental values: it might finally answer the question posed by Ralph Nickleby: *can* a physical heart be 'broken'?

The sentimental reading (the metaphorical heart) is presented in the *Nickleby* scene as superior to the 'worldly' reading (the physiological heart). Interestingly, however, Mrs Nickleby is drawn away from the sentimental party because *she* finds a resonance in Ralph's words: recalling the one thousand pounds her husband had lost, 'these dismal thoughts made her tears flow faster, and in the excess of these griefs she (being a well-meaning woman enough, but weak withal) fell...to deploring her hard fate' (25). The possession of the 'good heart' rather than the 'hard heart' is obviously central to the scene – but the heart here is also revealed to have the potential for darker emotions such as envy and jealousy. Ralph's heart is presented as darkened rather than hard: he *can* respond to his niece Kate's innocence and beauty. Dickens experiments with the word and with its social and cultural implications in his linking of Ralph with capitalism and with a decadent aristocracy, both very specifically described as 'heartless'.

One other issue held up for analysis here is the notion of sentimentalism as ultimately self-indulgent. Why exactly does Nicholas's 'heart swell' when he asserts that he will not live off his mother? Is it pity for that widowed figure? (Identifying with others is after all one of the sentimental commandments, as in Charles Bray's contemporary account of the education of the feelings.)[21] Is it rather the notion of *himself* striking an heroic pose that moves him so much? This would link back to Sterne's notion of the sentimental response as being ultimately about the 'feeler' rather than the object of pity: as Marcus Wood points out, writing of slavery, empathy and pornography, observing oneself is the most moving experience of all![22] Dickens here, without irony but with sharp perceptiveness, records acutely what makes the sentimental heart 'swell'. Ralph and Nicholas are set up as balanced antagonists on either side of a debate about the nature of the human heart.

In examining different aspects of sentimental rhetoric, Dickens shows himself to be keenly aware of the effects he creates. The shedding of tears is first ruthlessly ironised – through Mrs Nickleby's weeping at the thought of the lost thousand pounds – but later in the scene shown as *genuine* evidence of the family's sentimental credentials:

> The simple family, born and bred in retirement and wholly unacquainted with what is called the world – a conventional phrase which, being interpreted, often signifieth all the rascals in it – mingled their tears together at the thought of their first separation; and, this first gush of feeling over, were proceeding to dilate with all the buoyancy of untried hope on the bright prospects before them. (28)

This is very obviously echoing Goldsmith's Primrose family – but, whereas Mrs Deborah Primrose attempts 'to ease her heart by reproaches',[23] the childlike Nicklebys' effulgence of tears is recognisably Victorian.

Dickens's desire to keep absolute goodness separate from the threats posed by the outside world distances him from the more complex positions of his predecessors, Goldsmith, Sheridan and Sterne, and emerges as peculiarly of his own time, part of the anxiety expressed by scientists such as Charles Bell: the heart is important both metaphorically and literally, in the newly industrialised world, and needs to be carefully preserved. Dickens is at pains to support this research in his fiction: the 'good heart' is alive and well, he declares triumphantly, in the actual existence of the Cheeryble Brothers:

> Those who take an interest in this tale will be glad to learn that the BROTHERS CHEERYBLE live; that their liberal charity, their singleness of heart, their noble nature, and their unbounded benevolence, are no creations of the Author's brain; but are prompting every day (and oftenest by stealth) some munificent and generous deed in that town of which they are the pride and honour. (xlii)

The brothers were apparently based on William and David Grant, Manchester businessmen and philanthropists, whom Dickens may have met on a visit to the city in 1838. In order to prop up these constructed figures, his embodiments of benevolence, the central pillars of his sentimental rhetoric, Dickens does in the 1830s exactly what the prescient Charles Lamb so abhorred in the 1820s: he collapses the distinction between fact and fiction, insisting on justifying fiction by the standards of real life. A similar 'protesting too much' can be sensed in all three early novels in the assertion of the truth of sentimental values. *Nicholas Nickleby* borrows more from the conventions of melodrama than from those of sentimental drama. Yet the whole novel is underpinned by the desperate assertion of the truth of benevolence. The rawness of the genre battle, between 'realism' on the one hand and sentimentalism on the other, is a sign of the raw world into which the novel emerged.

In that raw world, a new and emblematic character emerges. The figure of Smike has no precedent in eighteenth-century sentimental tradition yet he is the source of the greatest emotional response in the novel. Here Dickens rings the greatest changes on the tradition he has inherited and prefigures the creation of Jo in *Bleak House*. Comments on Jo cast light back on the earlier figure:

> Homely filth begrimes him, homely parasites devour him, homely sores are in him, homely rags are on him: native ignorance, the growth of English soil and climate, sinks his immortal nature lower than the beasts that perish.[24]

In *Nicholas Nickleby* Dickens had not yet found such a powerful rhetoric to implicate the whole of English society in his attack. Smike is an almost allegorical figure of victimhood who literally has no place in the world: 'In the churchyard we are all alike, but here there are none like me.'[25]

Places in *Nicholas Nickleby* are deeply implicated in the presentation of sentimental values. The apparently random journeyings between Devonshire, London, Yorkshire and Portsmouth suggest an increasingly desperate search for that 'stable space', that static condition, in which such values can be safe. The final place, of course, is Smike's grave, just outside the haven where the new Nickleby idyll is re-established. At the end of the novel, the central energy of evil is extinguished and the equilibrium of family life is restored – producing a stasis which is presented as a victory for goodness. The tone is elegiac, and the return of Nicholas to his father's home as well as the focus on the grave suggests a sentimentalism which is both static and conservative – despite earlier moments of radicalism, for example in the treatment of Sir Mulberry Hawk or of Kate Nickleby at the milliner's. The metaphorical, unworldly heart remains the central organ of value. Kate and Nicholas's dead father had 'the kindest and gentlest heart that ever ached on earth [and it has] passed to the peace of heaven'.[26] The 'aching heart' suggests the nostalgia – literally the 'pain of the past' – which is fundamental to this type of conservative sentimentalism. Dickens's solution in this early novel to the problem posed in the first sentence of the present chapter – how to preserve the values of the 'good heart' in a dark and dangerous world – is a return to the past, the re-inhabiting of earlier spaces, the imposing of stasis upon change. Nicholas literally returns to his father's house and finds 'all the peace and cheerfulness of home restored'. Nothing must be changed: 'none of the old rooms were ever pulled down, no old tree was ever rooted up, nothing with which there was any association of bygone times was ever removed or changed'.[27] This can only be a temporary solution. The novels which immediately followed – *The Old Curiosity Shop* and *Martin Chuzzlewit* – show a much more complex attitude to the past and to the preservation of sentimental values.

## *The Old Curiosity Shop*

*The Old Curiosity Shop* is perhaps the novel most often cited in condemnations of Dickens's 'sentimentality'. However, it can be and has been read as a powerful indictment of the industrial world, using almost Bunyanesque allegory to make its point. The circumstances of this novel's emergence say a great deal about the needs and nature of mid-Victorian sentimentalism. Dickens began the novel in eighteenth-century mode, deliberately likening it to Oliver Goldsmith's periodical, *The Bee*. However, the discursive approach of discussing ideas was inimical to the mid-Victorian taste for the sentimental release of tears. In the fourth number, the child and grandfather were introduced, encountered by

Master Humphrey in the London streets; after another three numbers, Master Humphrey bowed out 'for the convenience of the narrative' and the novel was eventually published as *The Old Curiosity Shop*.[28] The title itself identifies clearly various features of nineteenth-century sentimentalist rhetoric: 'Old' implies nostalgia, while the 'Curiosity Shop' suggests an accumulation of emotion-laden objects to produce an intensified response. The same technique is used in presenting the premises of the Little Midshipman in *Dombey and Son*: in both cases, the 'shop' is devoid of customers, the proprietor thereby proving his morally praiseworthy inadequacy to succeed in a capitalist world. These shops are spaces in which the 'Community of the Good' can be established and the good characters in each of the novels duly gravitate there, setting up an oppositional sentimental community within but against the industrialised world.

The move from a disparate 'desultory' collection of friends telling individual tales to the focus on a single character, the 'little-child story', as Dickens put it, is crucial to the sentimental effect: the intense focus on a single figure is what Dickens went on to achieve with the Richard Wardour figure in *The Frozen Deep* (see discussion in Chapter 4) – paring away other characters' speeches to build up a focused response on the sentimental hero/heroine. This could be seen as analogous to the way tears well up, accumulate and eventually *overflow* the eyes. The 'overflow' effect (explored by Darwin in *On the Expression of Emotion in Man and Animals*)[29] is crucial to a successful, completed, sentimental response.

*The Old Curiosity Shop*, as Norman Page and others have observed, is built on polarities, on binary oppositions – and this is a deliberate principle of construction: 'Everything in our lives' in the narrator's words, 'whether of good or evil, affects us most by contrast.'[30] This principle of contrast, as has been seen, is particularly important to sentimental writing and is closely linked to the educational and psychological theories of the time which themselves derive, unexpectedly, from Locke's theory of association. Charles Bray and other contemporary educationalists stressed the importance of educating the emotions by means of contrasting experiences.[31] Over half of the 73 chapters of the novel are set in London and the remainder are beyond the city – though not where one might expect, in a countryside embodying better, purer values, but rather 'on the road', with all the sense of homelessness and insecurity that implies. Though Nell does eventually find a peaceful end in a country church, she had earlier wandered through an England ravaged by industrialisation. The confrontation with the factory furnace and the industrial workman is a key moment (chapter 45). By applying some of the terms and expectations of narrative theory, one can begin to see how unexpectedly transgressive the use of polarities actually is. Dickens's binary here is more complicated than 'country versus city', just as the novel itself is more complex than it is usually credited as being. Identifying the underlying binaries upon which the allegorical effects are built suggests the complexity of Dickens's poetic effects. 'Home' versus 'abroad' is obviously present beneath 'city' versus 'country'. However, 'home' is a place of sadness, a transgressive spot within the city, while 'country' is a place of wandering. 'Community' versus 'isolation' is also complicated by the fact that the communities Nell and her grandfather encounter are very often flawed. Dickens's clusters of value words suggest (as in the case of *Dombey and Son* – see Chapter 6) a deconstructive reading. Even in the opening paragraphs, night is linked with the countryside and day with the city. Nell moves, then, from day into night, as from life into death. In structural terms, the oppositions of movement and stillness, and of change and stasis, suggest most clearly the shape of the narrative. The traditional narrative pattern of disequilibrium to equilibrium *is* finally imposed but with significant differences:[32] Nell dies away from home, and home (in the shape of Kit Nubbles and the long-lost uncle) follows her and attempts (unsuccessfully?) to re-establish itself elsewhere in the final chapters. Images of stillness are set against images of energy, and, though it is the latter in Quilp and Dick Swiveller, which have attracted most critical attention and praise, it has not generally been acknowledged how greatly the two are interdependent. The extreme physical energy and activity of the first two (Dick's surname itself suggesting the flexibility and movement, both physical and verbal, which give him his significance) are essential to set off Nell's preternatural stillness. Quilp's extravagant energy ('I really don't believe he's human' concludes Mrs Nubbles)[33] is given as much excessive attention as is Nell's passivity, for the very good reason that one critiques the other: rhetorically as well as in the structure of the plot, they could not exist alone. Quilp's death is an exact counterpart of Nell's in its being the summation of his frenetic activity, just as hers is the summation of her heroic passivity: it takes three separate processes finally to kill off this prodigy of energy:

> ...he staggered and fell; and next moment was fighting with the cold, dark water... Another mortal struggle and he was up again, beating the water with his hands... The resistless water...driving him under it, carried away a corpse. (528)
>
> Tired of the ugly plaything, it flung it on a swamp – a dismal place where pirates had swung in chains...and left it there to bleach... There was something of the glare upon its face. The hair, stirred by the damp breeze, played in a kind of mockery of death...about its head, and its dress fluttered idly in the wind. (528–9)
>
> The general supposition being that he had committed suicide...the verdict was to that effect. He was left to be buried with a stake through his heart in the centre of four lonely roads. (569)

Quilp ends the novel, like Nell herself, as an icon, though of exactly the opposite sort: buried with a stake through his heart at the centre of a lonely crossroad, he is transformed linguistically into a vampire, just as Nell is transformed linguistically ('So we shall know the angels in their majesty')[34] into a saint. Those readers such as Edward FitzGerald who read only the 'Nelly-ad' parts of the novel, and those like Thackeray who read only the comic parts (as I observed in the Introduction) , missed the dialectic upon which it is constructed and the rhythms which underlie its prose.

I have been arguing that in the earlier novels, Dickens cannot allow the rhetorics of sentiment and humour to comment upon each other as they do so fruitfully in Goldsmith and Sheridan, whom he selectively reads as thorough-going sentimentalists. In this novel he adds to the repertoire of sentimentalism the figure of the 'Romantic child' which he has inherited from Wordsworth – though that figure is used in a Victorian, rather than in a Romantic, way. Nell is insulated from all criticism, from humour and from any suspicion of irony. There are, however, several 'Nell surrogates' who are enriched by their places in the humorous sections of the story, and through whom the innocent child figure *is* analysed and demystified. Chief among these is the Marchioness, who satisfies several of the criteria for the role of sentimental child victim, being little, young and bullied. Gabriel Pearson argues that 'The Marchioness, as soon as she appears, disables Nell's childhood by showing what real hardship and terror can do.'[35] I would argue rather that she allows Dickens to critique and complicate his own sentimental rhetoric by addressing the same figure of the suffering child in a different register. The suspicion that the Marchioness is herself the child of Quilp shows Dickens's implicit recognition (never openly declared) of the ultimate interdependence of the two rhetorics of sentiment and humour. Algernon Swinburne unwittingly recognises the interlocking of the two modes in his own conversion of Nell into a Quilpian grotesque: Nell, he says, is unreal, 'a monster as inhuman as a baby with two heads'.[36] He is of course right: she is (and has to be) as extreme in her sentimental world as Quilp is in his grotesque one. Pearson intuits something similar when he comments that Quilp's 'resurrection scene almost parodies Nell's apotheosis' and that 'Monster begets monster and Nell, in her turn, [is] a monster of goodness.'[37] That is precisely the point: the two are like the two figures in a weather-house: they gain significance only in terms of each other's movement.

Quilp's wife, another Nell surrogate, is described as pretty, weak and innocent, but is presented without any attempt at pathos, through the insulating rhetoric of humour – which, in twenty-first century narratological terms, makes the 'sentimental narrator' as callous a voice as that of as Quilp himself. The small boy in the village who becomes Nell's friend and is the first to mourn her death is yet another change rung by Dickens on the 'sentimental heroine' figure: he shows that what is being explored now, in the mid-nineteenth century, is the immolation of *innocence* rather than of femaleness. Dickens later in his career was perfectly capable of capturing a child's world through a child's eyes – through Little Paul Dombey or Pip in *Great Expectations*. It is notable that Nell's vision, in contrast, is not particularly 'childlike': Dickens's focus, in this very Victorian novel, is not on the moral superiority of the 'Romantic child', but on the suffering of innocence in the industrial world. The presence of a Quilp figure is unimaginable within Wordsworth's vision of the Romantic child; however, it is crucial to Dickens's vision of a radical, anti-industrial, anti-capitalist sentimentalism.

The last Nell-surrogate, unexpectedly, is Dick Swiveller himself, who quells any tendency in the reader to disbelieve in Nell's plight, by parodying it himself – Dickens, as it were, 'getting his retaliation in first'. Dick's own (drunken) account of himself is pure sentiment:

> Left an infant by my parents at an early age…cast upon the world in my tenderest period, and thrown upon the mercies of a deluding dwarf, who can wonder at my weakness! Here's a miserable orphan for you. (179)

These surrogates of Nell suggest Dickens's efforts to develop in a variety of ways, rather than merely to reinscribe the sentimental response. Increasingly in the later scenes, however, he focuses as he would do in *The Frozen Deep* on the lonely figure of the central sentimental character who is to elicit sentimental tears. A long series of paragraphs leading up to the revelation of the dead body are not otiose but are crucial stages in accumulating the reader's emotions until they reach that 'overflowing' effect which is the function of nineteenth-century sentimental prose to elicit. They are paralleled, as has already been suggested, by the series of comic paragraphs describing the stages of Quilp's protracted death, which produce their own blackly comic catharsis in a burst of horrified laughter, as he is buried like a vampire, with a stake through his heart.

Although the story is obviously allegorical in tone and intent, the circumstances of its construction result, in Gill Ballinger's words, in an 'improvisatory and episodic' effect.[38] I would argue that this, paradoxically, adds to the power of the tale: the stillness and certainty of allegory are undermined by the contingency of the picaresque – assertions of meaning, therefore, are constantly threatened by narrative disorder, by the possibility of randomness. This is a very prophetic, almost twenty-first century, deconstruction of allegory, presenting it as a precarious assertion of meaning in a world that postmodernist readings make meaningless. The very *precariousness* of the narrative's authority, in other words, adds to its effect. Ballinger identifies one particularly postmodernist moment (though she does not read it as such): the return of Master Humphrey as the 'single gentleman' at the end of the story, 'notwithstanding his declaration when he introduced Nell in the original machinery that his night-walking adventure "was fictitious"'.[39]

The ultimate coherence of Dickens's poetic vision emerges, however, in the way the opening paragraphs do still 'cast their shadows before' the later ones, despite their different and improvisatory provenance: there is at the beginning of the novel a churchyard – a city churchyard, with death in its city form: 'a noisy churchyard' where the buried soul 'had no hope of rest for centuries to come' (9). The image later to be used in the death of Paul Dombey makes an early appearance: a river which passers-by imagine will 'grow wider and wider until at last it joins the broad vast sea' (exactly the image Matthew Arnold was to use a few years later in 'The Future').[40] There is the captive bird at sunrise, 'whose cage has hung outside a garret window all night long, [singing] half mad with joy!' which foreshadows Nell's little bird whose frail life eventually proves stronger than her own (11).

The figure of Nell herself has respectable sentimental predecessors in the mid-eighteenth-century plays of Richard Steele, for example, and the even earlier plays of Thomas Otway. She is, like Oliver Twist, less a character than a space for the projection, by author and reader, of the absolute values of goodness and purity. The whole novel is given its meaning through the juxtaposition of Quilp's frenetically active death and the still tableau of Nell's deathbed:

> She was dead. No sleep so beautiful, so calm, so free from trace of pain, so fair to look upon...
> She was dead. Dear gentle, patient, noble Nell, was dead...
> She was dead, and past all help, or need of it... (557)

The reifying, indeed, deifying, of Nell's body, to which so many later readers have objected, has to be set against the ruthless deconstruction of the notion of identity elsewhere in the novel. The powerful sentimentalist rhetoric of anaphora surrounding Nell asserts permanence; the rest of the novel insists on flux. One moment which is to resonate again at the very end of the book is Nell's first visit to the graveyard which is to be her final resting place. There she meets an old woman tending her long-dead husband's grave:

> [S]he spoke of the dead man as if he had been her son or grandson, with a kind of pity for his youth, growing out of her own old age, and an exalting of his strength and manly beauty as compared with her own weakness and decay; and yet she spoke about him as her husband too, and thinking of herself in connexion with him, as she used to be and not as she was now, talked...as if he

were but dead yesterday, and she, separated from her former self, were thinking of the happiness of that comely girl who seemed to have died with him. (138)

It is that knowledge of the precariousness of human identity against which the insistent rhetoric of sentimentalism militates: Dickens's dialectic demands belief in the permanence of Nell's goodness even while simultaneously insisting that nothing lasts. When Arnold said that 'we have to turn to poetry...to console us', he was identifying a key function of sentimentalism – but he was by no means rejecting the continuing reality of tragedy.[41]

The cruelty of the nineteenth-century world is revealed through comedy as well as through the tragedy of Nell. The characters in the Jolly Sandboys discuss the fate of other outsiders and marginal figures – and there is pain behind the laughter: as one of the showmen comments, 'Once get a giant shaky on his legs, and the public care no more about him than they do for a dead cabbage stalk' (152). The cruel treatment meted out to physical weakness is a recurrent and shocking revelation in the story of Nell and her grandfather: comedy here reinforces the horror. The sentimental rhetoric of sympathy in this novel is also socially radical.[42] George Gissing argued that its first readers recognised that there was radical potential in *The Old Curiosity Shop*. He implies in doing so that there is a radical potential in sentimentalism itself (see Introduction). To him, harsh realist that he is and denizen of the 'mean streets', Nell's death is 'fresh and original'. Writing at the turn of the century, he reminds his readers that 'Dickens spoke with a new voice on behalf of children; at a time when children were horribly neglected, and often horribly ill-used, he found a way of calling attention to their unregarded lives.'[43]

One of the ghostly voices from the sentimental tradition haunting this novel, as I have suggested, is Oliver Goldsmith. An even stronger presence is Charles Lamb, whose essay 'Dream Children', as argued in Chapter 4, haunts several of Dickens's works. The ontological instability of 'Dream Children' is evident particularly in the closing pages of *The Old Curiosity Shop*:

> Did Kit live a single man all his days, or did he marry? Of course he married, and who should be his wife but Barbara... When Kit had children six and seven years old, there was a Barbara among them, and a pretty Barbara she was. Nor was there wanting an exact facsimile and copy of little Jacob... Of course there was an Abel...and there was a Dick... The little group would often gather round him of a night and beg them to tell again the story of good Miss Nell who died... (573–4)
>
> Such are the changes which a few years bring about, and so do things pass away, like a tale that is told! (575)

This is ultimately a novel not about certainty but about the uncertainties of fiction, which critiques the very possibility upon which its emotional power rests: *can* there be such a creature as Nell, an embodiment of permanent values, or will she prove to have been a fiction, crafted by human wishes, created, as the text half suggests, by the desire of Master Humphrey? The book begins and ends on the fragility of human imagination: it is self-reflexive and deconstructive in a way which, as I have suggested, anticipates postmodernism. Sentimentalism here works strangely to enact its own destruction: '[D]ay', says Master Humphrey, 'too often destroys an air-built castle at the moment of its completion, without the smallest ceremony or remorse' (6). Dickens's self-reflexivity is both bold and risky at this point: he reminds his readers that his own art too is just such an 'air-built castle' – not, as his critics suggest, an unproblematic window on a world he insists is real, but a chimera, its optimistic sentimental values asserted only temporarily against all the contradictory metafictional evidence. The narrative voice itself turns out to be the equivalent of that 'day' of human reason, ruthlessly destroying what the 'night' of imagination has built. At the end of the novel, the text powerfully recalls Master Humphrey's own opening words, as he destroys his own dream-world 'without the smallest ceremony or remorse': the sentimental narrator engineers his own destruction, as he insists that the reader *accept* that Nell will be forgotten – that she was, despite all the emotion we have been encouraged to invest in her, simply a chimera – a cluster of words on a page:

> [Kit] sometimes took them to the street where she had lived; but new improvements had altered it so much, it was not like the same. The old house had been long ago pulled down, and a fine broad road was in its place. At first he would draw with his stick a square upon the ground to show them where it used to stand. But he soon became uncertain of the spot, and could only say it was thereabouts, he thought, and that these alterations were confusing. (574–5)

The 'Old Curiosity Shop' itself is here figured as having been 'drawn with a stick', 'a square upon the ground'. Its sentimental values, its nostalgia, its giving a home to the absolute goodness of Nell, are destroyed in favour of 'a fine broad road': the road of social improvement, of the future. Stasis in the end succumbs to change. The novel is thus both a celebration and a critique of Victorian sentimentalism. No one is more aware of sentimentalism's power than Dickens and in the death of Little Nell he draws supremely on that power, using it to challenge society. In the end, however, goodness and evil both prove chimeras, vanishing once the act of reading is over, and leaving not a wrack behind:

> Such are the changes which a few years bring about, and so do things pass away, like a tale that is told!

## A Note on *A Christmas Carol*

In *A Christmas Carol* change certainly does take place but it is not as real as it at first appears. Read as an exploration on the trope of consumption, this novella emerges as much more conservative than the sentimental narrative voice tries to suggest. It contains many of the emotive features of the mode: contrast between the good heart and the hard heart; nostalgia for a lost childhood; the grave as the centre of the novel; Tiny Tim's vulnerability and fictional death in Scrooge's vision. Dickens seems to be testing out each sentimental feature – ringing the changes on it, testing its potential to be transferred from the ghostly to the real life of the novel. What *is* eventually transferred is not as radical as it seems: whilst the Cratchit family feast upon the economical goose in Scrooge's third-stave dream, their actual Christmas dinner is somewhat of a disappointment. Consumption of the 'dream' goose is verbally and sentimentally scrumptious, while the fate of the 'real' goose does not make it into words at all: there is no representation of this meal in the text. Even Scrooge's generosity at the end can be read negatively as merely reinforcing the master/servant relationship between him and Bob Cratchit.[44] I deal with this novella more extensively elsewhere.[45]

## *Martin Chuzzlewit*

*Martin Chuzzlewit* is particularly indebted, in plot and character, to eighteenth-century drama. *The School for Scandal* is there in the focus on appearance, on 'Surface' and on the exploration of the paths of two young men in opposite directions. Joseph and Charles have a benefactor, Sir Oliver, who governs the action of the play, just as Old Martin ultimately adjudges the fortunes of Young Martin and of his cousin, Jonas. The test he sets for his younger relatives is derived from the test that Sir Oliver, in the Sheridan play, sets for his two young nephews, and disguise is central to both. Through disguise, the cant values of the age are, in both play and novel, extensively explored and critiqued and, by the end of each work, they have been painfully revised. Mr Pecksniff owes a great deal to eighteenth-century notions of 'sentiment' in his determination to deliver a moral precept on every occasion. *The School for Scandal*, like *Martin Chuzzlewit*, pivots on that word, 'sentimental'. Here is the first mention of Joseph Surface:

> LADY SNEERWELL: ...I have found him out a long time since. I know him to be artful, selfish and malicious – in short, a sentimental knave.
>
> SNAKE: Yes, yet Sir Peter vows he has not his equal in England; and above all, he praises him as a Man of Sentiment.[46]

F. W. Bateson's gloss on this extract, in his 1979 edition of *The School for Scandal*, touches on the history of sentimentalism in several instructive ways which lead directly back to *Martin Chuzzlewit*. He says, of 'a sentimental knave':

> ...the paradox depends upon the two conflicting contemporary senses of the word *sentimental* (a term not recorded until the later 1740s): i) as the English adjective of Fr. s*entiment* (=aphoristic moral generalization of some special moral issue); ii) as the primarily English shorthand for the enjoyment of private emotion for its own sake (primitive form of romanticism), as in parts of Sterne's *Sentimental Journey* (1776). Sheridan was responsible for modern figurative sense ('the true sentimental and nothing ridiculous in it', *The Critic*).[47]

The entangled roots of the adjective 'sentimental' result in the strange anomaly at the heart of *Martin Chuzzlewit*: that the term may be used to describe both Pecksniff *and* Tom Pinch. This touches on the *doppelganger* relationship between the two which has always caused such confusion in responses to this novel. Pecksniff is (borrowing Bateson's term for Surface) a 'sententious aphorist';[48] Tom Pinch is a figure who both responds emotionally to events himself and is a cause of emotion in readers – a further complication in the use of the term. As in the case of Quilp and Little Nell, it is, rhetorically, only the excess of the 'good' sentimental figure that makes possible the excess of the comic monster. This process begins, as has been shown, very simply in *Nicholas Nickleby* in melodramatic mode, with Ralph Nickleby's frankness in his pursuit of evil being balanced by Nicholas's frankness in pursuit of good. In the subsequent novels the process becomes more complicated and the balancing figures evolve more specific forms of interdependence, so that Quilp's demonic energy is set off by Nell's passivity and here, Pecksniff's superhuman, glorious selfishness is enabled by Tom's monumental unselfishness. In *Dombey and Son*, the process reaches perhaps its most effective expression in the 'hardness versus softness' of the two principals (see Chapter 6). This might explain the strange rhetorical effect of the final apotheosis of Tom Pinch being expressed in the register of Pecksniffian hyperbole. Here is Pecksniff:

> 'Forgiveness,' said Mr Pecksniff, 'entire and pure forgiveness is not incompatible with a wounded heart; perchance when the heart *is* wounded, it becomes a greater virtue. With my breast still wrung and grieved to its inmost core by the ingratitude of that person, I am proud and glad to say, that I forgive him. Nay! I beg,' cried Mr Pecksniff, raising his voice, as Pinch appeared about to speak, 'I beg that individual not to offer a remark: he will truly oblige me by not uttering one word: just now; I am not sure that I am equal to the trial. In a very short space of time, I shall have sufficient fortitude, I trust, to converse with him as if these events had never

happened. But not,' said Mr Pecksniff, turning round again towards the fire, and waving his hand in the direction of the door, 'not now.' (20)

And here is the Pecksniffian sentimental narrator extolling Tom Pinch:

> Ah Tom, dear friend, old friend!
> Thy head is prematurely grey, though Time has passed between thee and our old association, Tom. But, in those sounds with which it is thy wont to bear the twilight company, the music of thy heart speaks out: the story of thy life relates itself.
> Thy life is tranquil, calm and happy, Tom. In the soft strain which ever and again comes stealing back upon the ear, the memory of thine old love may find a voice, perhaps; but it is a pleasant, softened, whispering memory, like that in which we sometimes hold the dead, and does not pain or grieve thee, God be thanked! (831–2).

Rhetoric reveals more about the interconnectedness of Pecksniff and Pinch than mere exposition of plot or character. Even their names suggest that they are part of a shared cluster of values: a 'peck' and a 'pinch' would have been synonymous in mid-Victorian English. Mr Pecksniff proclaims his disinterested kindness to Old Martin and

> [throws] himself back in the easy-chair: so radiant with ingenuous honesty, that Mrs Lupin almost wondered not to see a stained-glass Glory, such as the Saint wore in the church, shining about his head. (37)

This prefigures the final apotheosis of Tom Pinch:

> From the Present, and the Past…thy strain soars onward to the Future. As it resounds within thee and without, the noble music, rolling round ye both, shuts out the grosser prospect of an earthly parting, and uplifts ye both to Heaven! [49]

In his apostrophising of the female sex, after the brutalising of Mercy by Jonas, the sentimental narrator's voice alarmingly merges into Pecksniff's:

> Oh women, God-beloved in old Jerusalem! The best among us need deal lightly with thy faults, if only for the punishment thy nature will endure, in bearing heavy evidence against us, on the Day of Judgment! (457)

The book (in the writing of which, as Dickens observed in his preface to the first edition, he had kept 'a steadier eye upon the general purpose and design' than in the earlier novels) is overtly about 'selfishness'.[50] It is *unselfishness* rather than later nineteenth-century *tenderness* which becomes the focus of the sentimental response: the emotion elicited for the sentimental characters is proportionate to their embodying unselfishness and benevolence, and so has a public, rational base. Therefore, unexpectedly, and despite the tears elicited by the Pinches, this is much more an eighteenth- than a nineteenth-century version of sentimentalism. This earlier, public sentimentalism continued into the nineteenth century in the work of educationalists such as Charles Bray, who argued that the education of children should focus upon the eradication of selfishness and the substitution of 'benevolence'. Bray's 1838 description might very well provide a blueprint (an appropriately architectural term?) for Dickens's construction of Tom Pinch. Bray writes of 'benevolence':

> Uses: desire of the happiness of others; universal charity, mildness of disposition, and a lively sympathy with enjoyment of all animated beings... (3)
>
> We esteem and honour that man most who subdues the passions which directly refer to himself, and cultivates those which have their source in benevolence – who resists his own gratification, and enters warmly by sympathy into what others feel. (199)

In the education of children he observes that, '[i]f properly treated, they will in time learn to prefer the happiness and comfort of others to their own; but for this we must wait patiently.[51]

Dickens in Pecksniff and Pinch is presenting a 'Disquisition upon the Moral Feelings' in the manner of Bray. He too is fascinated by the notion of the education of such feelings and though he presents his two principals as inexplicably and immutably themselves, he explores in a much more empirical way the forces which made Jonas Chuzzlewit. Here he seems to combine Lockean associationism with a pre-Darwinian version of the notion of adaptation to environment. His clearest expression of the process is contained in the preface to the Cheap Edition (1849):

> I conceive that the sordid coarseness and brutality of Jonas Chuzzlewit would have been unnatural, if there had been nothing in his early education, and in the precept and example always before him, to engender and develop the vices that make him odious. But, so born and bred: admired for that which made him hateful, and justified from his cradle in cunning, treachery, and avarice; I claim him as the legitimate issue of [his] father...nothing is more common in real life than a want of profitable reflection on the causes of the many vices and crimes that awaken general horror... Let the reader go into the children's side of any prison in England, or I grieve to say, of many workhouses, and judge whether

those are monsters who disgrace our streets people our hulks and penitentiaries, and overcrowd our penal colonies, or are creatures whom we have deliberately suffered to be bred for misery and ruin. (xiii)

Here one can perhaps catch a glimpse of the inception of Magwitch, emerging fully formed a decade or so later in *Great Expectations*. Yet Dickens's philosophical problem is that the characters into whom he puts the most rhetorical energy and complexity are conceived as absolutes, inexplicable in terms of environment, standing uncompromisingly outside debates about nature and nurture. This suggests that they exist primarily as rhetorical tropes, as balancing figures of speech, so that the impact on the reader of Pecksniff's breathtaking misuse of key words like 'forgiveness', 'virtue' and 'fortitude', in the example above, is increased by the contrasting use of the same words in the plain language of Tom and Ruth Pinch. Yet this opposition deconstructs, much as it does in *Dombey and Son*, because that 'plain language' is overwhelmed by the sentimental narrator's blandishments. The narrative voice, as has been shown, abandons plain language for the overblown rhetoric of Pecksniff himself. Steven Marcus perceptively remarked that this novel is Joycean, 'for language itself is one of its subjects'.[52] I would suggest rather that in this novel various linguistic registers are set loose in a textual free-for-all whose outcome is open ended, ambiguous and undecidable.

Another sentimental exploration Dickens conducts in *Martin Chuzzlewit* is into the nature of tears. The 'hydraulic' theory of emotion is explained well by Dylan Evans (2001): the hydraulic model, he says, 'envisions emotions as forces that seek discharge by any means necessary'[53] and Michael Slater notes the 'sentimental effusions which well up whenever little Ruth Pinch gets anywhere near to the Temple Fountain'.[54] This suggests that there is something extreme and grand in Dickens's outrageous sentimentalism in this novel – which rises to the heights of his achievement with Pecksniff. It is almost as if he set himself the linguistic task of seeing just how far sentimentalist rhetoric would stretch by producing the most caressing and intrusive narrative voice and the smallest, meekest sentimental heroine possible. Even the commandeering of the Temple Fountain (an actual place in London) as a grand metonym for the 'crystal fountain' of the eyes, boldly giving an outward and visible sign of the 'sluicing' process he was producing in his readers, suggests that physicalisation of emotion which he adapted from Sterne.

Oh! foolish, panting, frightened little heart, why did she run away?
 Merrily the little fountain played, and merrily the dimples sparkled on its sunny face. John Westlock hurried after her. Softly the whispering water broke and fell; roguishly the dimples twinkled, as he stole upon her footsteps.

> Oh, foolish, panting, timid little heart, why did she feign to be unconscious of his coming! Why wish herself so far away, yet be so flutteringly happy there! (685)

Much later Ruth discovers Tom's own need for tears, in his unrequited love for Mary, and provides them for him:

> More closely yet, she nestled down about him; and wept as if her heart would break.
> 'Don't. Don't,' said Tom. 'Why do you hide your face, my dear?'
> Then, in a burst of tears, it all broke out at last.
> 'Oh Tom, dear Tom, I know your secret heart. I have found it out! You couldn't hide the truth from me. Why didn't you tell me? I am sure I could have made you happier if I had, if you had! You love her, Tom, so dearly!'
> Tom made a motion with his hand as if he would have put his sister hurriedly away; but it clasped upon hers, and all his little history was written in the action. All its pathetic eloquence was in the silent touch. (762)

*Martin Chuzzlewit* is the novel in which, more than any other, Dickens was overtly experimenting with language; in writing it, he wrote to Forster, 'I feel my power now, more than I ever did'.[55] Yet everything in the novel, as in the scene above, seems to privilege *gesture* over language. Emotions in this novel are noticeably physicalised. 'Pathetic eloquence' – that is, eloquence which both enacts emotion to and elicits emotion from the reader, is everywhere visible, as it is on the eighteenth-century stage, through gesture and posture. Sometimes, as in the sentimental tableaux of family life struck by the Pecksniff family, the sentiments acted out are manifestly and comically false:

> The young lady...resumed her stool, reposed one arm upon her father's knee, and laid her blooming cheek upon it. Miss Charity drew her chair nearer the fire...and looked towards her father. (15)

On many other occasions, though, similar 'stage business' is used without irony to convey character. Young Martin's moods, for example, are read by Mark Tapley through very precise theatrical descriptions: before the voyage to America, Mark finds Martin

> seated moodily before the dusty grate, with his two feet on the fender, his two elbows on his knees, and his chin supported, in a not very ornamental manner, on the palms of his hands. (245)

Similarly, when Mark realises the extent of his new master's selfishness and what a challenge this will be to keeping up his own optimism, his response is embodied in his features rather than in soliloquy. When Martin looks at him,

> he turned away, as being suddenly intent upon certain preparations for the journey, and, without giving vent to any articulate sound, smiled with surpassing ghastliness, and seemed by a twist of his features and a motion of his lips, to release himself of this word:
> 'Jolly!' (245)

Readers are here very clearly spectators. Examples might be multiplied: throughout this immensely theatrical novel, actions speak louder than words. Words, in fact, are heavily compromised by being handed over at the beginning of the novel to, of all people, Pecksniff, whose account of them prefigures Lewis Carroll's Humpty Dumpty, but is also surely an implicit critique of the deliberately vague and generalising techniques of sentimentalist rhetoric:

> Mr Pecksniff was in the frequent habit of using any word that occurred to him as having a good sound, and rounding a sentence well, without much care for its meaning. And he did this so boldly, and in such an imposing manner, that he would sometimes stagger the wisest people with his eloquence, and make them gasp again. (14)

A deconstructive reading might see this as a textual undermining of text – a self-critical comment by Dickens on the factitiousness of the 'power' he acknowledged to Forster and which he exercises, with unconsciously Pecksniffian afflatus, in the apostrophising of Tom Pinch.

Sentimentalism is therefore very thoroughly analysed and critiqued in *Martin Chuzzlewit*. The central sentimental figure *acts out* innocence as though he were the author's favourite actor, Charles Mathews, performing in one of the farces Dickens so enjoyed as a boy:

> The perfect and entire satisfaction of Tom; his surpassing appreciation of the husky sandwiches, which crumbled in his mouth like sawdust; the unspeakable relish with which he swallowed the thin wine by drops, and smacked his lips, as though it were so rich and generous that to lose an atom of its fruity flavour were a sin; the look with which he paused sometimes with his glass in his hand, proposing silent toasts to himself; and the anxious shade that came across his contented face when, after wandering round the room, exulting in its uninvaded snugness, his glance encountered the dull brow of his companion; no cynic in

the world, though in his hatred of men a very griffin, could have withstood these
things in Thomas Pinch. (93–4)

*Martin Chuzzlewit* attacks, through Pecksniff, the false language and false
appearances which betray the sentimental vision while validating exactly that
language and those appearances in other parts of the novel. The free and open
expression of emotion which is part of both the eighteenth- and nineteenth-
century habitus of the sentimentalist mode is attacked in Mercy Pecksniff's
effusiveness while being validated in Ruth Pinch's tears. Mary Graham, the
sentimental heroine, in contrast, is praised by the narrative voice, as is Tom
Pinch, for the ability to *contain* emotion. She is:

> …timid and shrinking in her manner, and yet with a greater share of self-
> possession and control over her emotions than usually belongs to a far more
> advanced period of female life. (28)

'Surface' is explored more extensively and subtly in this novel than in any
other of Dickens's works, as befits its textual haunting by *The School for Scandal*.
Clothes *are* personality:

> …the very fetch and ghost of Mrs Gamp, bonnet and all, might be seen hanging
> up, any hour of the day, in at least a dozen of the second-hand clothes shops
> about Holborn. (315)

Mrs Gamp and Pecksniff in particular build up their identities with each
item of their theatrical costumes. Pecksniff is introduced in a passage in
which the items of costume are donned and tried out for effect, one after
the other:

> His very throat was moral. You saw a good deal of it. You looked over a very
> low fence of white cravat (whereof no man had ever beheld the tie, for he
> fastened it behind), and there it lay, a valley between two jutting heights of
> collar, serene and whiskerless before you. It seemed to say, on the part of Mr.
> Pecksniff, 'There is no deception, ladies and gentlemen, all is peace: a holy
> calm pervades me.' So did his hair, just grizzled with an iron-grey, which was all
> brushed off his forehead, and stood bolt upright, or slightly drooped in kindred
> action with his heavy eyelids. So did his person, which was sleek, though free
> from corpulence. So did his manner, which was soft and oily. In a word, even
> his plain black suit, and state of widower, and dangling double eye-glass, all
> tended to the same purpose, and cried aloud, 'Behold the moral Pecksniff!'
> (11–12)

Dickens too dons the character and puts on his costume as he does with equal energy the role of Tom Pinch. One is reminded of his directorial tendency to commandeer all the parts in the plays in which he acted and of his antics in front of the mirror while he was writing, witnessed by another Mary, his daughter, Mamie:

> I was lying on the sofa endeavouring to keep perfectly quiet, while my father wrote busily and rapidly at his desk, when he suddenly jumped from his chair and rushed to the mirror which hung near, and in which I could see the reflection of some extraordinary facial contortions he was making. He returned rapidly to his desk, wrote furiously for a few moments, and then went back to the mirror. The facial pantomime was resumed, and then turning toward, but evidently not seeing, me, he began talking rapidly in a low voice... Ceasing this soon, however, he returned once more to his desk, where he remained silently writing until lunchtime.[56]

Sentimentalism in these early novels is thus performed more than it is preached. Only in *Martin Chuzzlewit* is it the actual subject of the novel, which enacts the linguistic struggle between eighteenth-century public aphorisms and the nineteenth-century private tender heart. Evil in Pecksniff is the very eighteenth-century evil of sentimental hypocrisy – but in Jonas Chuzzlewit it escapes from that model and, as in the examples of Bill Sikes and Ralph Nickleby, extends into the nineteenth-century mode of murder and melodrama. This necessitates the escape too of the sentimental figure into an equally extreme position of rhetorically buttressed sainthood. Smike, Little Nell and Tom Pinch have to reach the rhetorical heights they achieve in order to balance, linguistically and emotionally, the grandeur of their adversaries. Goldie Morgentaler expresses an earlier, more limited view that 'sentimentality too often threatens to smother the reader, especially in the sections dealing with Tom and Ruth Pinch',[57] an account which does not do justice to these novels as complex linguistic constructions. There is much of Smollett and of Fielding in the long and playful chapter titles of these early works. Linguistic rather than moral exuberance is their overriding characteristic and the rhetoric of sentimentalism rises to the challenge of adapting to that exuberance, becoming a tool for both radical and conservative positions in responding to nineteenth-century social change. In *Martin Chuzzlewit*, the young hero does not achieve sentimental status until chapter 33, when he eventually acquires the identifying adjectives 'frank and generous'. By then, the enemies of 'the good heart' have been variously examined and society's need for the sentimental 'good heart' has been conclusively proved.

The intensity of the rhetoric used of Tom Pinch may well have had an extra-literary prompting in the figure of Charles Lamb (see Chapter 4). Dickens's concluding passages in *Martin Chuzzlewit* are a virtuoso exercise in Lamb's own sentimentalist style, of a piece with the bravura performances in the rest of the novel in a variety of linguistic modes:

> Thou glidest now, into a graver air; an air devoted to old friends and byegone times; and in thy lingering touch upon the keys, and the rich swelling of the mellow harmony, they rise before thee. The spirit of that old man dead, who delighted to anticipate thy wants, and never ceased to honour thee, is there, among the rest: repeating, with a face composed and calm, the words he said to thee upon his bed, and blessing thee! (832)

The ghosts of both Lamb and Goldsmith haunt this passage.[58] A comparison with key passages from the earlier writers suggests the nature of the haunting. Here is Goldsmith:

> …we loved each other tenderly, and our fondness increased as we grew old. There was in fact nothing that could make us angry with the world or with each other. We had an elegant house, situated in a fine country, and a good neighbourhood. The year was spent in moral or rural amusements; in visiting our rich neighbours, and relieving such as were poor. We had no revolutions to fear, nor fatigues to undergo; all our adventures were by the fireside…[59]

Here is Lamb:

> Then I told them how for seven long years, in hope sometimes, sometimes in despair, yet persisting ever, I courted the fair Alice W—n, and, as much as children could understand, I explained to them what coyness, and difficulty, and denial meant in maidens – when suddenly, turning to Alice, the soul of the first Alice looked out from her eyes with such a reality of representation, that I became in doubt which of them stood before me, or whose that bright hair was, and while I stood gazing, both the children gradually grew fainter to my view, receding, and still receding till nothing at last but two mournful features were seen in the uttermost distance.[60]

Dickens's expostulation to his beloved readers is different from Goldsmith's wry, ironised first-person narrative; different from both is Lamb's intimate, quiet request that his readers reverse their understanding of what they have just read. All three narrative voices are euphoric, but readers of Goldsmith and Lamb need to be alert, uneasy, ready to reread, reinterpret. Dickens's readers, in contrast, are in a tight authorial embrace, forced to read in only one way. Lamb and Goldsmith suggest plurality – in response, in rereading, in audience; Dickens insists on singleness. It is this intensity of reader response which is to characterise the further changes rung on the sentimentalist tradition in Dickens's later novels.

# Chapter 6

# THE LATER NOVELS

### 'What the Waves were always saying'[1]

The sentimental bond between Dickens and his implied (and actual) readership provides the real emotional heart of each of the great novels. It involves, as I shall argue in this chapter, several key aspects of the nineteenth-century sentimentalist tradition, including its evolution from eighteenth-century moralising to individual emotional sympathy, and its confusion between the theatrical and public on the one hand and the Romantic and private on the other. The unique closeness of Dickens and his readers is so generally accepted (even by critics who object to it) that I feel obliged to include Virginia Woolf's perverse comment to prove my point through the blatant inappropriateness of hers:

> Of all the great writers Dickens is both the least personally charming and the least personally present in his books. No-one has ever loved Dickens as he loves Shakespeare or Scott.[2]

Robert Garis provides one example of a much more common response:

> I have phrased my answer to Dickens's dilemma in direct discourse because one tends to feel a warm personal attachment to the manager of the Dickens theatre.[3]

Benjamin Jowett, who delivered the sermon at Dickens's funeral service, expressed the same sense of attachment on behalf of the first generation of Dickens's readers:

> [N]o-one was ever so much beloved or so much mourned. Men seem to have lost, not a great writer only, but one whom they had personally known.[4]

At the end of the twentieth century Peter Ackroyd, liberated by the deregulations of postmodernism, was able to invite his subject *into* his biography and to interview a ghostly Charles Dickens to powerful effect in his monumental *Dickens* (1990).[5]

The gradual modulation of Dickens's sentimental narrator's voice from that of editor (in *The Pickwick Papers*, very much in the eighteenth-century tradition of Addison and Steele) to the nineteenth-century's 'sympathetic friend' is charted by Bradley Deane in *The Making of the Victorian Novelist*.[6] The impulse behind the evolution of the nineteenth-century novel narrator might be linked back to neo-classical didacticism, with its aim to *teach* by delighting, to *guide* the reader, in Dr Johnson's phrase, towards a 'just distribution of good [and] evil'.[7] However, just as the word 'sentimental' shifted in meaning from suggesting moral judgement to signifying emotional responsiveness, so Dickens's narrative persona, far from remaining as a moralising guide, rapidly acquired the attributes of a warmly affectionate friend. This is obvious from the outset in *Pickwick*, in the eponymous hero's comical attempts at sententiousness. Shades of the earlier function haunt *Master Humphrey's Clock*, until the intradiegetic narrator is ousted by the sentimental extradiegetic narrator of *The Old Curiosity Shop*.[8] The novels' prefaces are testament to the close bond between this 'sympathetic friend' and his readers, as well as to the need such a bond satisfied in the actual (as well as the implied) author:

> If any [of my readers] have felt a sorrow in one of the principle incidents on which this fiction turns [that is, Little Paul's death] I hope it may be a sorrow of the sort which endears the sharers in it, one to another. This is not unselfish in me. I may claim to have felt it, at least as much as anybody else; and I would fain be remembered kindly for my part in the experience. (Preface to the First Edition, 1848)

The relationship, though so blatantly public, was revealingly envisaged by Dickens as a private one:

> The many friends [*The Old Curiosity Shop*] has won me, and the many hearts it turned to me when they have been full of private sorrow, invest it with an interest, in my mind, which is not a public one, and the rightful place of which appears to be 'a more removed ground'. (Preface to the First Cheap Edition, 1848)

The strong desire of the sentimentalist author to be *physically* involved in the eliciting of emotion is evident in the preface to *A Tale of Two Cities*, quoted in Chapter 4:

> When I was acting, with my children and friends, in Mr. Wilkie Collins's drama of *The Frozen Deep*, I first conceived the major idea of this story. A strong desire was upon me then, to *embody it in my own person* [my emphasis].

One recalls once again Mamie's revelation of her father's mode of composition – leaping up from his desk to grimace into a mirror, as he embodied his characters.

## Dombey and Son

*Dombey and Son* is, for me, Dickens's greatest triumph in the sentimentalist tradition. It enacts with the reader the sentimental 'melting' process which is its central theme and it was from *Dombey* that Dickens first conceived the idea of direct interaction with his audience through the public readings. He thus returned the sentimentalist tradition back to the stage, thereby recognising the very public presentation of private emotion.

One reason for the peculiar intensity of the novel may be the author's own strong identification with all three central figures. Here, more painfully than anywhere else, Dickens confronts, and through sentimentalist conventions is able to begin to reconcile, the divisions in his own nature. There is from the beginning a protectiveness in his attitude to Mr Dombey, the character whose personality and value system the plot itself ruthlessly exposes and destroys. Forster notes his 'dread of caricature in the face of his merchant hero'.[9] The projected 'humour' figure becomes a potentially tragic one. This cold, hard, prosperous man is one of several characters (Bounderby in *Hard Times* and Headstone in *Our Mutual Friend* being others) upon whom, in the later novels, Dickens rings fantastic changes on his own life story and whom he makes to bear the guilt for his own ever-increasing success. At the same time, Mr Dombey allows him to explore his simultaneous awareness of emotional failure and isolation. Dickens's own passionate 'marriage' to his audience is transformed in *Dombey* into the nightmare opposite he dreaded: the coldness of rejection by his public. There is a poignant anticipation in Dombey's response to Edith's rebellion of events in Dickens's private life eleven years later:

> Do you know who I am, Madam? Do you know what I represent?... People to say that Mr Dombey – Mr Dombey! – was separated from his wife!... You're absurd! (629)

Early in the novel Dombey is shown projecting his own vulnerability onto his baby son:

> He wiped blinding tears from his eyes as he [paced up and down the room]…and often said… 'Poor little fellow!' (20)

As in the case of Nicholas Nickleby's tears, these are the displaced tears of sentiment, apparently for another person but actually for oneself, which

Dickens was so sharp in identifying: 'he pitied himself through the child' (20), adds the narrator, astutely. It is exploring this psychological identification of adult with child, in creating the inner life of Little Paul and in setting himself the strangely modernist task of presenting the child's death exclusively through the child's eyes, that Dickens seems to have been enabled to make the connection between his own adult and child selves. While composing the Mrs Pipchin chapters, he wrote earnestly to Forster, seeming to conceive the idea of autobiography in the act of writing:

> I hope you will like Mrs Pipchin's establishment. It is from the life, and I was there – I don't suppose I was eight years old… Shall I leave you my life in MS when I die? There are some things in it that would move you very much.[10]

Thus he approaches circuitously the most painful part of his childhood: he had, as he must have been aware, moved into lodgings at the house of Mrs Roylance, Mrs Pipchin's original, not at eight years old but at twelve, when, in 1824, his father had been sent to the Marshalsea Prison and he himself had begun work at Warren's Blacking Factory. It was only after regaining access to his own childhood through the writing of *Dombey and Son* that Dickens could begin the novel more generally recognised as triumphantly autobiographical, *David Copperfield*.

Paul is close to his creator not only in being, as young Charles had been, a sickly child kept indoors, but also in his love for his elder sister. Florence owes a great deal to Dickens's sister Fanny, who protected Charles as Florence does Paul. However, in life it was Charles, not Fanny, who was neglected. It was Fanny who seemed destined for a glittering career (as a singer) while Charles was cast away by his parents into the blacking factory. When Fanny was presented with the Royal Academy Silver Medal, Dickens wrote in the autobiographical fragment he showed to Forster:

> …the tears ran down my face. I felt as if my heart were rent. I prayed, when I went to bed that night, to be lifted out of the humiliation and neglect in which I was. I never suffered so much before.[11]

Dickens penned these words while tracing the neglect of the fictional Florence and while watching Fanny herself die of consumption: in fiction, he reverses the fates of the sickly boy and the beautiful older sister (while giving his dying sister's name to Paul's dying mother). Florence's immolation thus achieves a particular intensity, while her characterisation remains necessarily vague. Her experience, as well as Paul's and Mr Dombey's, is filled with the surreal intensity of her creator's remembered life: it is this triple identification which is new and rare and which gives the book its particular power.

The almost physical presence of the author projected via his narrator is never more evident than in the crucial scene in *Dombey and Son* in which Dombey and Florence find themselves alone together:

> Florence entered, and sat down at a distant little table with her work: finding herself, for the first time in her life – for the very first time within her memory from her infancy to that hour – alone with her father, as his companion. (482)

Read within a twenty-first century horizon of expectations, the interpolated expansion of the 'for the first time in her life' sounds like the simple hyperbole we distrust as sentimental. Only by setting the scene back into the literary context of early eighteenth-century domestic sentimentalism which Dickens knew so well can we, as belated readers, pick up the heroic force of the interpolation. Lady Easy, in Colley Cibber's *The Careless Husband* (1704),[12] also slighted by one who should have loved her, enters a similar domestic scene – her husband and the maid (who is his mistress) asleep on two chairs – and responds 'Protect me, Virtue, Patience, Reason/Teach me to bear this killing sight!' Much later in the century, Fanny Burney's Evelina meets her long-lost father in a drawing room and they kneel to each other, weeping and uttering passionate expressions of love:

> Oh Sir…that you could but read my heart! – that you could see the filial tenderness and concern with which it overflows![13]

Sentimentalist rhetoric often asserts emotions by naming them, and Dickens follows the tradition here by unequivocally proclaiming and expanding on the major significance of this moment. On the stage, the choreography speaks for itself; in the novel, the narrator must step forward in his narratorial persona to deliver the anticipated speech which is, as in the tradition of sentimental drama to which it belongs, an expansion, by repetition and anaphora, of the identity and significance of the heroine:

> She, his natural companion, his only child, who in her lonely life and grief had known the suffering of a broken heart…who…who…who had, all through, repaid the agony of slight and coldness, and dislike, with patient unexacting love, excusing him, and pleading for him, like his better angel!
> She trembled and her eyes grew dim. (482)

The intimate closeness of Florence and the narrator here is evident in the very slight shift of viewpoint, so slight that at first the syntax suggests that the speech has been 'delivered' by Florence herself. However, while in sentimental comedy the heroine did (perforce) assert her own powers, in the epistolary novel a doubling technique had developed whereby the heroine proclaimed her emotion, while her reputation and loveliness (which could not be 'seen' in the novel) were proclaimed by her admirers. A double or triple layer of emotion was thus built up. It is Dickens's narrator here who takes on the role of Florence's admirer, 'embodying in his own person' the emotions inherent in the situation. The relationship between this dramatic narrator and Florence is ardent and intense; in successive paragraphs his rhetoric intertwines with Florence's own, as if he caressed her:

> [Dombey's] figure seemed to grow in bulk before her... She yearned towards him, and yet shrunk from his approach. Unnatural emotion in a child... Unnatural the hand that had directed the sharp plough, which furrowed up her gentle nature...![14]

Mr Dombey – as contained and private as the other two, Florence and the sentimental narrator, are articulate and public – attempts to escape, so to speak, from the glare of the footlights and the threat of public exposure:

> ...withdrawing into a shadowy corner at some distance, where there was an easy chair, [he] covered his head with a handkerchief, and composed himself to sleep.

The handkerchief, the traditional prop of sentimental comedy, is used by Dickens with supreme originality. Cibber's Lady Easy had triumphed as virtue over vice by covering her wayward husband's sleeping head with a handkerchief – in a simple act hiding his guilt from the world and thereby poignantly proclaiming her own virtue. Sterne's characters perform extreme acts of sentimental intercourse by weeping together and exchanging handkerchiefs. Here, Dombey takes this symbol of emotional engagement (the gauntlet, as it were, in the sentimental lists) and uses it to protect himself from Florence's terrifying encroaching tenderness. And yet the symbol is still pregnant with its earlier life in the eighteenth-century sentimental tradition. Even when misused in the interests of hardness and detachment, the handkerchief magically softens the bearer. As in a fairytale, Dombey, covered by the handkerchief, is able to see clearly for the first time. He perceives Florence's tenderness and, like almost all the characters in the novel, falls under its spell:

> Once attracted, [he] seemed to have no power to turn his eyes away.

The narrator, invisible, goes over to him, as on a stage, and tries to probe beneath the anti-sentimental mask:

> And what were his thoughts meanwhile…[w]as there reproach to him… Had he begun to feel…?

The vision is a complex one. The identification between narrator and Dombey is suggested but is incomplete. This is not indirect free speech but a more theatrical address to the reader:

> Meaner and lower thoughts, as that his dead boy was now superseded by new ties, and he could forgive the having been supplanted in his affection, *may have* occasioned them [my emphasis].

Unlike the narrative voices in Thackeray or George Eliot, Dickens's narrator, an actor among actors, accepts the limitations of his vision and turns them to dramatic advantage. The readers are forced, like Florence, to search for access to Dombey's inner self: forced, in fact, to enact the novel's central movement. But then the long-anticipated melting begins, visible even to the narrator:

> As he looked, he softened to her, more and more.

Dombey's emotions and, correspondingly, the reader's, are at first blurred ('As he looked, she became blended with the child he had loved') and then elevated to the spiritual plane: 'As he looked, he saw her for an instant by a clearer and brighter light…as the spirit of his home' (484).

Anaphora builds up the emotion in the character and correspondingly in the reader – but then comes, at the moment of highest tension, the dramatic interruption: the entrance of Edith. The whole scene is a remarkable *tour de force*, built on the heroic expectations of sentimental comedy, daringly continuing the highly theatrical stage setting, reminiscent of Steele and of Sheridan in particular – and then imposing on the traditional stage thunder the silence of the novel. Not a word of direct dialogue is spoken – and yet the effect is of a shared public outpouring of emotion surpassing anything in the earlier drama. In the silence the rising tide of emotion in the characters – and, by sympathy, in the readers – can be heard the more clearly, swelling, in Jeffrey's phrase, to 'the plain consummation'.[15] Thus it is by drawing on and then surprising his audience's expectations, which are derived from the sentimentalist tradition, that Dickens releases their emotions. It is, when seen in its historical and literary context, a supreme example of artistic control and innovation.

When they encountered the sentimentalist heroine in Dickens, particularly Florence, twentieth-century critics were often confused by their tendency, derived from New Criticism, to read Dickens in isolation. It is part of the purpose of the present work to put him back into a context from which his continuances and innovations can be more clearly seen. Julian Moynahan has perhaps been the most influential of these 'a-contextual' critics:

> Remove her pall of quasi-religious mystery and Dombey's daughter is at best a sentimentalist lacking decent self-respect and at worst a masochist.[16]

Moynahan's defensive brusqueness here involves a deep and sensitive perception of the power of this novel followed by an abrupt rejection of that power. Moynahan characterises Dombey acutely: to Dombey, he says, 'the sharing of love seems a death by water', but then adds sharply, 'It seems a dismal conclusion.'[17] Dismal it may be, but it certainly is part of Dickens's unillusioned vision. Dombey's eventual rescue by Florence *is* the death of his old private self, and a victory for the very public values of sentimentalism, embodied in Florence as theatrical sentimental heroine. Here 'public' and 'private' execute a complex *volte face* over their connotations elsewhere in the novel. Dickens, understanding the complexity of the movement, presents it simultaneously in the language of victory and of defeat:

> He dressed himself for going out, with a docile submission to her entreaty; and... passed out with her into the hall. Florence...keeping close to him, with her eyes upon his face, and his arm about her, led him out to a coach that was waiting at the door, and carried him away. (803)

Quite apart from Moynahan's Dombey-like fear of feeling, but equally limiting, is his ahistorical approach. He describes Florence with unconscious tautology as 'a sentimental heroine upon whom angelic powers and attributes have arbitrarily been grafted'.[18] The sentimental heroine of the eighteenth and nineteenth centuries was *by definition* 'love made visible' a blending of human and divine, a type of virtue, a 'gentle Madonna' (in George Eliot's words), an emblematic figure. She was also, by definition, extremely emotionally powerful while physically weak – and it is this that Moynahan misses by treating Florence as a special case. One of the central sentimental paradoxes, which links it with Christianity and which possibly could only have emerged from Christian culture, is that the more passive the heroine is in the plot, the more active is her spiritual power. This contradictory power is already in evidence in Thomas Otway's Belvidera (see Chapter 1) whose influence over her father is described in metaphorical terms of 'hardness' and 'softness' which Dickens very patently inherited. Florence, like her literary predecessors, is a mythical figure whose function it is to 'wake dead nature' in her father, to purge him of thought so that his 'natural' goodness may emerge (sentimentalism in every era being apparently posited on the assumption of *innate* goodness in the human heart). Her power is apparent in the Romantic ability of Goethe's 'das Ewige Weiblich' to 'draw' other characters to her. In *Our Mutual Friend* Headstone exclaims to Lizzie, 'You could draw me to fire, you could draw me to water, you could draw me to the gallows, you could draw me to any death, you could draw me to anything I most avoided, you could draw me to any exposure or disgrace.'[19] This is a moral, not a sexual process: Edith Dombey too is 'drawn' and thus finds release from guilt:

> She started, stopped and looked in.
> A light was burning there, and showed her Florence, in her bloom of innocence and beauty, fast asleep. Edith held her breath, and felt herself drawn on towards her.
> Drawn nearer, nearer, nearer yet; at last, drawn so near, that stooping down, she pressed her lips upon the gentle hand that lay outside the bed, and put it softly to her neck. Its touch was like the prophet's rod of old, upon the rock. Her tears sprung forth beneath it, as she sunk upon her knees, and laid her aching head and streaming hair upon the pillow by its side. (420)

This is the religious use of the sentimentalist mode but, in the succeeding two centuries, it has also acquired a strong political charge. The 'passive resistance' which in our century and the last has become the civilised way of opposing force, is an extension of the sentimental paradox and similarly asserts the moral superiority of the victim over the persecutor. In Dickens, this heroic passivity extends from the heroine to the figure of the 'sentimental child'. Oliver at Fagin's trial is an early example:

> 'Oh God forgive this wretched man!' cried the boy, with a burst of tears. Oliver nearly swooned after this frightful scene, and was so weak that for an hour or more, he had not the strength to walk. (364)

John Carey, also writing in the mid-twentieth century, produced a reading of the scene which supports Moynahan's:

> Dickens could furnish this type of saintly confection in unlimited quantities, but the triumphs of his art stick out of it like islands and there is no difficulty about distinguishing them.[20]

I would argue instead that the scene needs to be read in terms of a long and honourable sentimentalist tradition. It certainly fails miserably as realism but it seems obtuse to read it that way. Moynahan's refusal to accept as legitimate any canons but those of realism leads him to ridiculous lengths in misreading Dombey: 'Dombey does not interest us as a human soul' he asserts. 'We are interested in Dombey as a London business man'[21] – which is the equivalent of saying about Dostoevsky's *The Idiot*, 'We are not interested in Prince Myshkin as a human soul… we are interested in him as a case of epilepsy.'

*Dombey and Son* can only be read fully, fairly and contextually if one accepts the sentimentalist *donnée* (or Bourdieu's habitus) and recognises Florence as a centre of power genuinely matched against Dombey. The whole action of the novel then becomes a titanic and elemental struggle between 'hardness' and 'softness' between industrial materialism and human values, with a hard-won (but, as I shall show, ultimately ambiguous) victory for the latter.

*Dombey and Son* shows other signs of its derivation from eighteenth-century sentimentalist literature. Mr Toots is a wonderfully extravagant parody of sentimental renunciation – of the sort taken seriously in *The Frozen Deep* and *A Tale of Two Cities*. Carker's flight from Dombey and towards death borrows several features from the flight from death in *Tristram Shandy* and in *A Sentimental Journey*. All three novels are very precisely about death – what it is, how to recognise its approach and how to meet it.

> Boulogne! – hah! So we are all got together – debtors and sinners before heaven; a jolly set of us – but I can't stay and quaff it off with you – I'm pursued myself like a hundred devils, and shall be overtaken before I can well change horses: for heaven's sake, make haste… Hollo! Ho! – the whole world's asleep! – bring out the horses – grease the wheels – tie on the mail – and drive a nail into the moulding – I'll not lose a moment – [22]
>
> A vision of change upon change, and still the same monotony of bells and wheels, and horses' feet, and no rest. Of town and country, postyards, horses, drivers, hill and valley, light and darkness, road and pavement, height and hollow, wet weather and dry, and still the same monotony of bells and wheels, and horses' feet and no rest… (738)

Despite its obvious inheritances from the eighteenth century, however, *Dombey and Son* is a monument of nineteenth-century sentimentalism; a comparison between Dickens and his younger contemporary Wilkie Collins reveals the specific features of Dickens's development of the mode. The following extracts represent two climactic moments in their respective novels. Here is Dickens:

> Yes, his daughter! Look at her! Look here! Down upon the ground, clinging to him, calling to him, folding her hands, praying to him.

'Papa! Dearest papa! Pardon me, forgive me! I have come back to ask forgiveness on my knees. I never can be happy more without it!'

Unchanged still. Of all the world unchanged. Raising the same face to his, as on that miserable night. Asking *his* forgiveness. (801)

Here, fourteen years later, is Collins:

He stooped and lifted Magdalen in his arms. Her head rested gently on the sailor's breast; her eyes looked up wonderingly into the sailor's face. She smiled and whispered to him vacantly. Her mind had wandered back to the old days at home; and her few broken words showed that she fancied herself a child again in her father's arms. 'Poor Papa!' she cried softly. 'Why do you look so sorry? Poor papa!'[23]

At these two highly charged moments, the differences between the prose styles of Dickens and Collins emerge sharply. The sentimental register is common to both: the simplified, heavily weighted affective vocabulary: daughter, Papa, child, on my knees, breast, old days at home, in her father's arms. Emotions are evoked by this naming of key words which are full of shared connotations within a secure 'interpretive community'. But beyond a shared register, the Dickensian rhetoric of intensification has little in common with Collins's characteristic rhetoric of exposition. Dickens's tableau demands a response – Mr Dombey himself appeals to a third party, 'Look at her! Look here!' – recalling Lear at the death of Cordelia but also revealing the basic theatricality of the sentimental scene. The present participles function as adjectives – 'clinging...calling...folding... praying' – to create a statuesque sense of 'static movement' so that the figure of Florence is presented like Bernini's Saint Theresa – an object to be explored. Emotions are represented with baroque extravagance. Sentences are monolithic: there are few subjects or verbs, for what is being aimed at is the effect of a tableau.

The art historian Sir Kenneth Clark described baroque architecture as space 'controlled...to work on our emotions'.[24] Dickens manipulates literary affect in similar fashion. Emotion is separated systematically from mental processes and becomes a spontaneous outpouring, analogous to that of sexual release. Ratiocination would destroy the 'here and now' of both processes and must be suppressed. Casting one's mind into past or future hinders the spontaneous movement of emotion (a 'moving out') and of physical climax. Collins's effects are not, on this analysis, sentimental. *His* reader is required to join the narrator in a strenuous exploration of contingent circumstances. One recalls the differences between the two men over the staging of *The Frozen Deep*. Collins distributed the interest of the play widely, including speeches about the heroine's past and from an old nurse with second sight about the future; Dickens pared this down and threw all interest onto the figure of Wardour, to achieve one final powerful moment of emotional release for the audience – and for himself in acting the role.

In the declaration of love between Florence and Walter, Dickens draws again on all his resources of sentimental rhetoric to achieve the emotional climax. The scene needs to be quoted in length for its careful, highly wrought organisation to emerge. This is the acme of Dickensian sentimentalism, reliant on his inheritance from the eighteenth-century sentimentalist tradition, but neatly embodying the changes he had made in evolving that tradition into a recognisably nineteenth-century form.

> She raised her head, and spoke to him with such a solemn sweetness in her eyes; with such a calm, bright, placid smile shining on him through her tears; with such a low, soft tremble in her frame and voice; that the innermost chords of his heart were touched, and his sight was dim as he listened.
>
> 'No, Walter, I cannot forget it. I would not forget it, for the world. Are you – are you very poor?'
>
> 'I am but a wanderer,' said Walter, 'making voyages to live, across the sea. That is my calling now.'
>
> 'Are you soon going away again, Walter?'
>
> 'Very soon.'
>
> She sat looking at him for a moment; then timidly put her trembling hand in his.
>
> 'If you will take me for your wife, Walter, I will love you dearly. If you will let me go with you, Walter, I will go to the world's end without fear. I can give up nothing for you – I have nothing to resign, and no one to forsake; but all my love and life shall be devoted to you, and with my last breath I will breathe your name to God if I have sense and memory left.'
>
> He caught her to his heart, and laid her cheek against his own, and now, no more repulsed, no more forlorn, she wept indeed, upon the breast of her dear lover.
>
> Blessed Sunday Bells, ringing so tranquilly in their entranced and happy ears! Blessed Sunday peace and quiet, harmonising with the calmness in their souls, and making holy air around them! Blessed twilight stealing on, and shading her so soothingly and gravely, as she falls asleep, like a hushed child, upon the bosom she has clung to!
>
> Oh load of love and trustfulness that lies so lightly there! Aye, look down on the closed eyes, Walter, with a proudly tender gaze; for in all the wide wide world they seek but thee now, – only thee! (679)

The denotative content of this passage is easily, baldly and unsentimentally summarised:

WALTER: Florence, please forget what I have said.
FLORENCE: I don't want to forget it. Are you very poor?
WALTER: I am a poor sailor.
FLORENCE: Are you soon going away again?
WALTER: Very soon.
FLORENCE: Will you take me with you as your wife?
WALTER: (implied) Yes.

What the sentimentalist rhetoric does – as, say, in a similar scene in one of Puccini's operas – is to transform this simple, almost banal, exchange into an intense emotional, intentionally non-intellectual experience for the reader. The extract is preceded by the ending of a misunderstanding between the lovers which clears the way for the declaration. It involves the removal of the terms 'brother' and 'sister' which have limited their relationship until that moment, but these terms themselves have considerable emotional charge in nineteenth-century sentimental tradition, from Dickens's 'A Child's Dream of a Star' to Robert Browning's 'Blot on the 'Scutcheon'.[25] The rest of the passage is simply a statement and restatement of the new relationship. Dickens's narrator's interventions into the dialogue are all in the interest of intensification, and borrow the religious connotations of sentimentalism so that Florence is presented as an icon whom Walter as worshipper cannot see clearly ('his sight was dim'). Florence's stillness, her preparatory tears, Walter's catching her to his breast and the final climactic full release ('she wept indeed') suggest sentimentalism's characteristic displacement of sexual rhythms into its own rhetoric. The coda returns to the religious register with the 'Blessed Sunday Bells!' This parallel presentation of religious and sexual feeling is very evidently derived from the eighteenth century – from Sterne and Richardson and also from the earlier sentimental drama of Richard Steele. Paradoxically, the adjective trains ('calm, bright, placid') *blur* rather than sharpen meaning and disarm analysis. The lyrical rhythms of the prose provide an emotional shape allowing for the rise and fall of the reader's emotion, and a final pause for the cleansing tears. Each lengthy period (long, convoluted sentences being crucial to the pacing of emotional arousal and release) has a rising and falling action of its own. Florence is presented as 'artless' (one of Collins's favoured terms of approbation and a standard term of approval in the sentimental register), but her avowal of love is an extremely stylised representation of simplicity, much like Mimi's first aria in Puccini's *La Bohème* and with a similar aim. As so often in Dickens's sentimental *tours de force*, its rhythms are those of poetry and the world is that of theatre or, in this case, opera:

> If you will take me for your wife, Walter,
> I will love you dearly.
> If you will let me go with you, Walter,
> I will go to the world's end without fear.
>
> I can give up nothing for you –
> I have nothing to resign, no-one to forsake.
>
> But all my life and love shall be devoted to you,
> And with my last breath I shall breathe your name to God...

The end of the scene is a moment of sentimental consummation, a climax marked by the release of tears: '...she wept indeed, upon the breast of her dear lover' (679). Thus a new nineteenth-century sentimental paradox is illustrated: a highly stylised rhetoric is employed to *stop* the reader from thinking: after the Romantics, it is assumed that the triumph of 'heart' can only be achieved by the defeat of 'head'.

It is in *Dombey and Son* that Dickens most successfully brings together the sentimental and the humorous registers, as they were brought together by Goldsmith and Sheridan, to achieve a novel which is indeed ultimately about the triumph of heart over head but which achieves complex effects too. Little Paul is a complex figure, potentially a sentimental object, described as 'little' and 'old-fashioned' but one who speaks and acts more often than he is described. He shows promising signs, says the non-sentimental narrator, of growing up to be like his father: 'His temper gave abundant promise of being imperious in after-life; and he had as hopeful an apprehension of his own importance, and the rightful subservience of all things and all persons to it, as heart could desire' (93). Only later does he also fulfil the role of the nineteenth-century sentimental child – the victim of education and of mercantile ambition, being killed by a school system designed to prepare him to take over his father's firm. His death, remarkably, is until the very last moment described through his own eyes and is arguably Dickens's greatest 'sentimental deathbed'.[26] Its complexity shows perhaps more than any other scene in Dickens the astonishing potential of the sentimentalist rhetoric to surprise, to engage, to extend the reader's experience and to release emotion:

> [H]e would lie and watch the many-coloured ring about the candle, and wait patiently for day. His only trouble was, the swift and rapid river. He felt forced,

sometimes, to try to stop it – to stem it with his childish hands – or choke its way with sand – and when he saw it coming on, resistless, he cried out! But a word from Florence, who was always at his side, restored him to himself: and leaning his poor head upon her breast, he told Floy of his dream, and smiled. (221)

The language of the child and of the narrator interweave throughout this scene and only in the final apostrophe, when the first voice of the child focaliser has been silenced by death, does the sentimental narrator add his solo comment, designed as it were, both to give permission for and to accompany the reader's tears:

Oh thank GOD, all who see it, for that older fashion yet, of Immortality! And look upon us, angels of young children, with regards not quite estranged, when the swift river bears us to the ocean! (225)

The power of this scene as a public reading illustrates the theatrical power of the mode, and the strange collapse of the distinction between what is public and what is deeply private. 'The Story of Little Dombey' was in fact the first reading from a major novel, performed in St Martins Hall in London on 10 June 1858, after six weeks in which Dickens had read abridgements of the *Christmas Books*. 'It is our greatest triumph everywhere', he reported on the first tour of the provinces. Interaction with the audience was part of that sentimental 'melting' which closed the gap between author and reader, actor and audience, art and life:

If you saw the mothers, and fathers, and sisters, and brothers in mourning who invariably come to 'Little Dombey', and if you studied the wonderful expression of comfort and reliance with which they hang about me, as if I had been with them, all kindness and delicacy, at their own little death-bed, you would think it one of the strangest things in the world.[27]

The conclusion of the novel as we have it officially perpetuates the polarisation of values upon which the plot has been built, of 'hard' and male versus 'soft' and female, simply reversing the hierarchy so that female values are made to triumph over male: Florence's daughter asks the aged and softened Dombey,

'Dear grandpapa, why do you cry when you kiss me?'
   He only answers, 'Little Florence! Little Florence!' and smoothes away the curls that shade her earnest eyes. (833)

The underlying ambiguity of this resolution is evident, however, in two final paragraphs which Dickens cancelled at proof stage, having overwritten by seven lines. These were obviously intended to recall and to balance the conclusion to chapter 16, quoted above. The number plan explicitly reminded Dickens to 'end with the sea – carrying through what the waves were always saying, and the invisible country far away!' (885). Accordingly, chapter 62 originally ended with:

> Never from the mighty sea may voices rise too late, to come between us and the unseen region on the other shore! Better, far better, that they whispered of that region in our childish ears, and the swift river hurried us away! (833)

There are many negatives and self-contradictions in this passage. The 'voices' (of the waves) are said to 'come between' the living and the dead: however, the previous paragraph (and the whole novel) has shown that in fact their function is to collapse such distinctions, to help us to reach 'that blessed shore'. The last sentence strikes a particularly negative note and threatens to negate the earlier hope suggested by Paul's death: its implication can only be that Paul, had he lived, might have been one of those for whom 'the voices rise too late'. In its uncertainty and self-contradiction, this original conclusion reveals an alternative reading which the official narrative voice of the novel has strenuously suppressed: that Florence and the all-embracing love she represents have more to do with death than with life. Life is connected with the railway, with the new Staggs's Gardens, with the bustle of the city. The sea is connected with a whole series of deathbeds, all presided over by Florence, the siren who soothes people into accepting 'easeful death'. When Moynahan talks of Florence's 'pall of quasi-religious mystery', he is being wilfully unfair to Dickens's seriously held belief in the value of Christian meekness, but he does pick up the link between that sort of love and death: to go 'back to the womb' of boundless maternal love would be to die. Thus meaning dissolves into ambiguity as Dickens reaches into the darkest paradoxes of the sentimentalist vision.

 I would like to end this part of the chapter, and this analysis of the functions of the sentimental mode in *Dombey and Son*, with a reading of the novel's sentimentalism through psychoanalysis, suggesting the depths of its power and significance in society and in the individual psyche. Beneath the configurations of tableaux such as father striking daughter, or father kneeling to daughter, psychoanalytical reading suggests a power quite different from that of the realist novel by which Moynahan and others have tried to define this work – the power of sentimentalism to explore our deepest taboos by transforming them into 'safe' language and familiar plot. The whole novel can be read in this way as being about the desire to return to what Jacques Lacan calls the 'imaginary' stage of unlimited contact with the maternal breast – about the most primitive desire of all, in fact, the desire to be nurtured.[28] It begins as a very literal drama about breast feeding and Paul's desperate need for nourishment after his mother's death ('Couldn't something temporary be done with a teapot?' is Mr Chick's immortal contribution (12)). Motherhood and the maternal are then explored, from Polly Toodle's warm fecundity to Mrs Skewton's unnatural sterility. The last words of the latter are a reminder of that primal relationship as she reminds her daughter Edith: 'For I nursed you' (563). The image of the breast is used as a conventional sentimental metaphor for love and virtue: 'And did that breast of Florence – Florence, so ingenuous and true – hold any other secret?' (241).

When Mr Dombey rejects Florence's love after Paul's death, the connotations become more complex and the flexibility of the sentimental rhetoric, moving easily between the metaphorical and the physical, more valuable. Dombey is refusing to be nurtured, but he is also guilty of something analogous to sexual aggression: 'Florence strove against the cruel wound in her breast, and tried to think of him whose hand had made it only with hope' (311). In the climactic scene after Edith's departure, the breast becomes literal once again. Florence's father physically abuses her by striking her, and *she* – the victim rather than the assailant, just as in real-life cases of physical and sexual abuse – feels shame: 'Then she knew – in a moment, for she shunned it instantly, that on her breast was the darkening mark of an angry hand' (630). In the reconciliation scene, Dombey at last submits and allows himself to be nurtured at the breast he had spurned: 'Upon the breast that he had bruised, against the heart that he had almost broken, she laid his face, now covered with his hands, and said, sobbing: "Papa, love, I am a mother"'(802). Femaleness thus overcomes and absorbs into itself the energies of masculinity. The official narrative voice acclaims this as a triumph, but the novel as a whole reads much more ambiguously.

Even if one does not 'buy into' a thorough-going psychoanalytical reading, it is obvious by any reading that *Dombey and Son* is centrally concerned with the rigid separation of male and female values in society. The energy of the narrative comes from the tension between the public values of a male-dominated mercantile society represented by Mr Dombey and the private values of love and female submissiveness represented by Florence. The whole book is therefore structured on the separation of two sets of value terms: hard, cold, male, linearity, money, the railway, on the one hand and soft, warm, female, boundlessness, the sea, on the other. Mid-Victorian society is presented as privileging the first set of (masculine) values over the other. Polly Toodle is one of three transforming female figures in the novel (the third being Harriet Carker) who show how this hierarchy can be reversed.

She teaches this process to the child Florence by rewriting the narrative of her mother's death:

> '[S]he dies, never to be seen again by anyone on earth, and was buried in the ground where the trees grow.'
> 'The cold ground?' said the child, shuddering again.
> 'No! The warm ground,' returned Polly, seizing her advantage, 'where the ugly little seeds turn into beautiful flowers, and into grass, and corn, and I don't know what all besides. Where good people turn into bright angels, and fly away to Heaven!' (26)

After a long process of suffering, this reversal of values, in which the spiritual triumphs over the material, is made permanent and Dombey's firm (and his firmness) are dissolved in Florence's tears.

There is, however, a paradox at the heart of such a resolution. Florence prevails, not by rewriting society's concept of femaleness but by writing it more strongly. She is more, not less, of a Victorian heroine by the end. Michael Slater puts this clearly in *Dickens and Women*:

> Here is Dickens apparently preoccupied with women as the insulted and injured of mid-Victorian England yet voicing no general condemnation of prevailing patriarchal beliefs and attitudes; rather, he seems to see the social and sexual trials of his heroines as a sort of tragic nurture which serves to bring them to their full 'womanly' potential.[29]

The whole enterprise, in fact, lends itself to a deconstructive reading. As Chapter 5 has illustrated, Dickens's early novels are characteristically structured by the setting up and effortful maintenance of rigid, unbending oppositions. *Oliver Twist* is predicated on what Steven Connor calls the 'unnegotiable antagonisim' of good and evil.[30] *Martin Chuzzlewit* schematically divides the selfish from the generous. Dickens's world in *Dombey*, on the other hand, begins confused and seems to become more black and white as the novel progresses. The 'community of good' identifies itself and moves away from the community of evil. Thus the 'sentimental' characters – Sol Gills, Walter, then Captain Cuttle, Mr Toots, Susan Nipper, eventually Polly Toodle and Miss Tox – are gathered in a community loosely based on the Wooden Midshipman, with Florence as the presiding deity. Rob the Grinder has his chance there, but opts instead for Mr Carker. Mrs McStinger makes an attack, but is repulsed. Meanwhile, Carker, Major Bagstock and Mrs Skewton fawn on Mr Dombey. And yet these binary oppositions cannot hold: they collapse because one of the terms, 'boundlessness', closely linked with sentimental blurring and vagueness, encompasses the others. The whole principle of separation goes against the very 'boundlessness' which the novel is at pains to propound, in the central image of the sea. Dickens makes rational distinctions while his language and imagery work *against* making distinctions.

It is the sentimental scenes which show most radically how the dominant mid-Victorian gender ideology of 'heart versus head' may be healthily dissolved. It is through the deep traditional resources of sentimentalism that Dickens makes his most daring psychological explorations and conveys 'what the waves were always saying'.

\*\*\*

The novels after *Dombey and Son* are not centrally built upon the sentimental vision, although its presence continues to be an essential element of their success. They will be dealt with briefly in the rest of this chapter.

In all the major novels of this later period, Dickens continues to gain from the sentimentalist tradition the power to achieve unforgettable emotional effects. Steerforth, the sentimental hero-turned-villain, is washed up on the beach, and found dead, 'lying with his head upon his arm, as I had so often seen him lie at school' (681). In *David Copperfield* the sentimental child is exposed in Dora as a monster of selfishness, in a continuation of the critiquing of the figure begun with Mercy Pecksniff. In this novel however, Dickens's new achievement is to explore the seductive face of selfishness. Just as Mr Micawber's irresponsibility never ceases to be engaging (and is all the more dangerous for that), so Dora Spenlow never fails to charm, while being systematically and unflinchingly exposed as a beautiful parasite. There is even a parallelism suggested between her father's public displacing of personal responsibility onto his business partner, Jorkins, and Dora's private displacing of all responsibility for her life and financial security on to David. The conventions of the sentimental deathbed are exploited here in a new way, to produce poignancy, an emotional release in tears which is not, on this occasion, separated from moral judgement. The move from unthinking grief at the death of Nell to the complicated sharpness of poignancy at the death of David Copperfield's 'child-wife' suggests the range of Dickens's exploitation of 'sentimental release' in these later works.

The shift in sensibility in the second half of the nineteenth century led to a strong reaction against Dickens's sentimental effects. Jeffrey's tearful eulogy, even as he uttered it in the late 1840s, was beginning to sound rather old-fashioned. The rise of realism as the dominant aesthetic in the latter part of the century led to increasing criticism of Dickens's 'exaggerated style' and to Ruskin's double-edged defence that 'we must not lose the use of Dickens's wit and insight, because he chooses to speak in a circle of stage fire'.[31] Thus when, in the preface to *Bleak House* (1853), Dickens talks of his delineation in that novel of 'the romantic side of familiar things', he may well be attempting to signal a move away from his earlier, overtly sentimental concerns towards a more contemporary social outlook.

## Bleak House

*Bleak House* initially *might* seem to be centrally concerned in its narrative structure with the sentimental heroine. It embodies the 'divided style' in the two narrators, setting up a systolic relationship between the public, witty, emotionally detached, male narrative voice and Esther's private, earnest, emotionally involved, female tones. Much has been written on the dual narrators; for my argument, it is enough to recognise that the purpose of the two narrators is a complementary, not an antagonistic, one. They share the task of exploring the web of connections which make up English society and which is the novel's real focus of attention. The male narrator hovers about Esther's narrative, occasionally reaching out almost tenderly towards her: 'while Esther sleeps, and while Esther wakes, it is still wet weather down at the place in Lincolnshire'.[32] Dickens is not, therefore, critiquing Esther's way of looking at the world, but he is delimiting it as her own, rather than society's, vision. Esther's construction of Ada as the sentimental heroine – 'such a beautiful girl! With such rich golden hair, such soft blue eyes…'[33] – as has often been noted, is part of Esther's, not the novel's, sentimentalism. The fact that Esther is obviously transferring her feelings about her old doll with its 'beautiful complexion and rosy lips'[34] onto a living breathing human being is part of Dickens's successful presentation of the psychology which results from a particular sort of abusive upbringing – a characterisation rather than an uncritical presentation of the sentimental vision. This contrasts sharply with the earlier presentation of Rose Maylie in *Oliver Twist*, into which the narrative voice is completely subsumed:

> She was not past seventeen. Cast into so slight and exquisite a mould; so mild and gentle; so pure and beautiful; that the earth seemed not her element, nor its rough creatures her fit companions.[35]

An examination of what Wolfgang Herrlinger calls the 'underlying virtue pattern'[36] of sentimentalism reveals in *Bleak House* complicated changes rung upon the traditional mode. Self-denial, a crucial sentimental term which was evident in eighteenth-century sentimentalism in *The Good-Natured Man* and in nineteenth-century drama in *The Frozen Deep*, is examined minutely in Esther's behaviour and found, after all, to be of limited value. Some readers feel that it is actually parodied (as in Goldsmith) in the excesses of Esther's heroic unselfishness. At the end of the novel, in trying to deny herself the love of Alan Woodcourt, Esther makes both herself and, ultimately, her benefactor, John Jarndyce, unhappy: she ends the novel with husband and children, happy through the exercise of a healthy selfishness. Benevolence too is critiqued in John Jarndyce, whose inability to recognise the venality of Skimpole is presented as a flaw which his disarming 'the wind is in the east' collocation does not excuse. His moral passivity, his inability to resolve the problem of his Chancery suit inheritance, is evident in his inertia within the plot. The 'Good-Natured Man' is not adequate in the world of this novel, any more than he was in Goldsmith's play. The frank and generous hero figure too succumbs, in the person of Richard Carstone, to the lure of wealth. Frankness, openness, generosity are not enough. In contrast, Alan Woodcourt's unshowy medical activity is presented as wholly beneficial – but he hardly qualifies as the sentimental hero. The novel's happy ending is therefore not an uncritical endorsement of but a demystification of sentimentalism.

In Harold Skimpole, Dickens continues the attack on the 'false child' begun in *Martin Chuzzlewit* with Mercy Pecksniff. Skimpole's exaltation of himself as the Romantic child is as outrageous as Mr Pecksniff's exaltation of himself as the 'sentimental man'. It is possibly even more alarming, as Dickens here moves beyond the sentimental tradition's exposure of hypocrisy: Pecksniff memorably ends as 'a drunken, begging, squalid-letter-writing man' (832); the emotional release for the reader of witnessing the exposure of Skimpole, on the other hand, is never achieved: instead, much more sinisterly, he is presented on the edge of the picture, as the figure who quietly sends Jo on his last journey, away from his sanctuary to his death (chapter 57). The exposure of the sentimental hypocrite is thus turned into something much bleaker and darker, as Dickens develops his later version of the sentimentalist vision. Once again he is at pains to critique the sentimental response by showing its potentiality for self-indulgence. Skimpole's selfishness is textually exposed in the juxtaposition of his cruelty to Jo and his singing of a blatantly sentimental ballad about a peasant boy, 'Thrown on the wide world, doomed to wander and roam, / Bereft of his parents, bereft of a home', a song, he says, which 'always made him cry'.[37] Thus Dickens critiques the sentimental tears he elsewhere works so successfully to elicit. It is a powerfully self-reflexive even deconstructive moment, part of the complexity of Dickens's sentimentalist strategy in this novel.[38]

The key moment though, in which the resources of sentimentalism are exploited to the full, is the scene of Jo's death. This sentimental deathbed is not a tableau, as in the death of Little Nell. It is not paralleled, as is the death of Nell, by the outrageousness of a Quilp, but by the sinister exploitativeness of a Skimpole. In the moral structure of the novel it is Skimpole who is Jo's double, false child set against real but denied child. Jo, unlike Nell, is not passive or static; indeed, he dies precisely because of movement, of having forever to 'move on'. The image of the heaving cart in the deathbed scene is a supreme example of Dickens's dazzling linguistic shifts between the physical and the metaphorical in his presentation of the human heart – or, more accurately in this case, human lungs:

> 'Draw breath, Jo!' 'It draws,' says Jo, 'as heavy as a cart.' He might add, 'and rattles like it', but he only mutters, 'I'm a-moving on, sir.' ... [T]he cart so hard to draw, is near its journey's end, and drags over stony ground. All round the clock it labours up the broken steps, shattered and worn... The cart is shaken all to pieces, and the rugged road is very near its end.[39]

Dickens draws on all the resources of the 'child's deathbed scene' and rings changes upon them to achieve something new for the nineteenth-century novel. At *this* child's deathbed there is no grieving family or adoring circle of friends – but simply a new literary figure, the professional man, the doctor, administering what help he can. The Lord's Prayer exerts for Jo the pull of a rival narrative to the terrible industrial narrative of poverty and neglect in which he has been trapped. For twenty-first century readers unmoved by the religious connotations, there is still the power of the Word. Jo is in death literally given, by Woodcourt, the empowerment of words, allowed for the first time to share the linguistic inheritance of the rest of society. The security of the sentimental tradition, steeped as it is in drama and theatricality, is the enabling factor in that terrifying ending, as the expected sentimental narrator is transformed into a Carlylean figure who turns to snarl at the audience, in the boxes, in the stalls, in the circle:

> Dead, your Majesty. Dead, my lords and gentlemen. Dead, Right Reverends and Wrong Reverends of every order. Dead, men and women, born with heavenly compassion in your hearts. And dying thus around us every day.[40]

## *Hard Times*

*Hard Times* is atypical in its uses of the sentimentalist tradition, as in so much else, which is why it is so often dealt with apart from the rest of the Dickensian oeuvre. As the title suggests, this satirical attack on the social horrors of industrialisation is built on the 'hardness/softness' opposition upon which *Dombey and Son* was so successfully constructed, and the rival positions are embodied in the successors to Dombey and Florence, Thomas Gradgrind and Sissy Jupe. The novel's focus is weakened, however, by the accompanying industrial plot of the confrontation between Josiah Bounderby and Stephen Blackpool. The artistic failure of that plot reveals just how dependent sentimentalism is upon narrative structure. Bounderby is a monster, but not of hardness so much as of hypocrisy. Dickens as it were defaults into the sentimentalist plot, with Mrs Pegler as the rejected mother. Stephen Blackpool and Rachael are not clearly enough defined, in literary terms, to represent any metaphorical counterweight, nor clearly enough defined in moral terms to embody innocent victimhood. They are unselfish, thinking only of their duty to others, but this sentimental virtue is complicated and weakened in the juxtaposed and ambiguous presentation of Slackbridge and the Union: thinking of the collective good can be venal, can result indeed in bullying. More importantly, as embodiments of unselfishness, Stephen and Rachael are not sufficiently clearly the *opposite* of Bounderby for any powerful rhetorical opposition to be set up. Bounderby is a continuation of Dickens's study of sentimental hypocrisy (as in *A School for Scandal*); Stephen and Rachael are from a different plot, that of sentimental selfishness (as in *The Good-Natured Man*). The emotional failure of *Hard Times*, in fact, suggests precisely the point made in the previous chapter about two emotionally successful novels: Quilp *needs* Nell just as Pecksniff *needs* Tom Pinch. The paired characters are very literally made for each other. Dickens achieves this pairing, of course, in Gradgrind and Sissy, but again the focus is blurred by the presence of Louisa, which weakens the sentimental catharsis.

Dickens knew Herbert Spencer's *Principles of Psychology* (1855) whose central point was the necessary merging of the cognitive and the affective. H. P. Sucksmith, an early and perceptive critic of the sentimentalist tradition, goes on from this to argue that *Hard Times* anticipates such a concept, and that its central assertion is, like Spencer's, that 'in a state of health, "head" and "heart", the rational and the affective sides of man, co-operate as complementary functions'.[41] These two sides Sucksmith sees as being embodied in two quite different modes, the rhetoric of sympathy and the rhetoric of irony. From this he builds his own central argument, that Dickens's supreme achievement comes whenever he can *unite* these two characteristic modes into a single 'rhetoric of sympathy and irony'. His definition of the action of this rhetoric seems to me to provide some useful critical terms for analysing Dickens's sentimentalism:

> Through the identification which sympathy makes possible, the reader becomes as intimately involved in the experience of the novel as if he were living within its world while, through irony, he remains detached and able to make an objective and critical assessment of the experience he is living through. In this way, both

intellect and emotion are invited to respond to the vision of the novel and what may seem contradictory attitudes in author and reader are united in the paradox of a complex art.[42]

At the same time, I suspect that such a rational account cannot adequately convey the effect of Dickens's novels on the reader. *Hard Times*'s argument may be that healthy life involves the co-operation of head and heart – but *Hard Times* as a reading experience is a dramatisation of a desperate opposition, not co-operation, ending with the triumph of Sissy's world view over Gradgrind's. It ends, untypically, with failure – the failure of Louisa to achieve full womanhood, by implication because of the early stunting of her heart by her utilitarian education. Louisa, like Tom Pinch or the narrator of Charles Lamb's 'Dream Children', is presented as failing to have children. Whereas this lack of issue is incorporated into Tom Pinch's unworldly saintliness, in Louisa it is very obviously a punishment for incomplete maturation. In its lack of idealisation, this novel contains perhaps Dickens's least 'sentimental' ending – but few would argue that this makes it particularly successful. In throwing out the sentimental bathwater, he may well have sluiced away too the essential final catharsis.

## *Little Dorrit*

In *Little Dorrit*, Dickens returns to the figure of the 'Romantic child', complicating it on this occasion by reversing the variation he had created in Mercy Pecksniff. Amy Dorrit *looks* like a child but has put away 'all childish things' in order to mother her motherless family. She is dangerously close to the many stunted children in earlier novels, though the word 'stunted' is kept away from descriptions of her 'small' 'meagre' figure. Dickens guards against any tendency towards parody by adding an obviously parodic child, Maggie, who accompanies Little Dorrit, notably in her night of homelessness in 'Little Dorrit's Party' (chapter 14), so that Amy may safely enter and take possession of Little Nell's domain. The erotic charge of the words 'sister' and 'daughter' (as seen in the discussion of *Dombey and Son*) is a peculiar nineteenth-century development of sentimentalism, dependent on its force upon stricter linguistic and sexual taboos than those pertaining to eighteenth-century literature. Clennam's confusion about the appropriate emotional role for Little Dorrit results in a denouement very close to that in *Dombey and Son*, the reinscribing of a relationship resulting in the sentimental release into tears, of both characters and readers:

> Never to part, my dearest Arthur; never any more until the last! I never was rich before, I never was proud before, I never was happy before. I am rich in being

taken by you, I am proud in having been resigned by you, I am happy in being
with you in this prison... (792)

The final paragraphs bring sentimentalism into the industrial age in a
marvellously modern twist, as the lovers shrink from centrality and become
part of something larger – the alienating urban world. It was this anti-
sentimental world which so threatened the Nicklebys that they were forced to
retreat into the rural past in order to keep their values intact. In *Little Dorrit*,
Dickens daringly sends his lovers out into that very alien heart of the great city,
into 'the roaring streets, [but] inseparable and blessed' (802), trusting to the
power of the sentimental vision to survive even there.

It is tempting to make a narrative of progress in Dickens's use of
sentimentalism, from the nostalgic, backward-looking ending of *Nicholas
Nickleby*, at Smike's grave, to this bold embracing of the industrial city:
sentimentalism comes of age and enters the urban world. However, such
narratives of progress may themselves be 'sentimental', in the sense of their
being over-simplified. Dickens's engagement with the mode and with society
fluctuates, as do our readings of his novels. Sentimentalism's ontological and
ethical certainties, as has been shown, are actually circumscribed in all the
novels and variously critiqued at every stage.

## *A Tale of Two Cities*

*A Tale of Two Cities* (1859) continues the theme and the dramatic structure
of *The Frozen Deep* (1856) for its study of what Herrlinger identifies as one
of the key 'sentimental virtues', self-denial.[43] Sidney Carton's dissolute lawyer
finally emerges in his true colours as the sentimental hero as he goes to his
death in order to send his surrogate, Charles Darnay, back to the woman they
both love. Dickens's achievement here is to use the power of this traditional
mode to approach horrific material. The *tricoteuses*, the casual murder in the
streets, the brutal deaths of men, women and children by the cruel knife
of the guillotine, the sheer horrors of the Revolution, could not have been
conveyed to a mid-Victorian audience except through the familiar rhetoric
of sentimentalism. The dramatic schema of *The Frozen Deep* proves adaptable,
therefore, to a much more serious purpose. Dickens's rhetoric in the opening
and closing paragraphs of the novel is recognisably sentimental rhetoric,
built on anaphora, repetition, opposition and intensification. It has the added
power, in retrospect, and in the light of Dickens's performance as Richard
Wardour, of suggesting a shared identity between Carton and the narrative
voice: only Carton, one realises, could have formulated that initial dry, witty,

cynical assessment of 'the times'. He and his narrator are and have always been one:

> It was the best of times, it was the worst of times, it was the age of wisdom, it was the age of foolishness, it was the epoch of belief, it was the epoch of incredulity, it was the season of Light, it was the season of Darkness, it was the spring of hope, it was the winter of despair, we had everything before us, we had nothing before us, we were all going direct to Heaven, we were all going direct the other way…[44]

Once again, as in *The Frozen Deep*, Dickens steals the limelight. In disguising his 'good', that is, socially acceptable, alter ego as Frank Aldersley or (more cleverly) as Charles Darnay, he liberates his darker self to take centre-stage and reveals that darker self in the final moments to be the sentimental hero, upon whom the sentimental tears of the audience rain down:

> It is a far, far better thing that I do, than I have ever done; it is a far, far better rest that I go to, than I have ever known.[45]

The preface, already cited briefly in earlier chapters, is worth quoting at this point at greater length. Dickens writes of having conceived the germ of the novel while acting in *The Frozen Deep* and goes on:

> A *strong desire was upon me then, to embody it in my own person*; and I traced out in my fancy, the state of mind of which it would necessitate the presentation to an observant *spectator*, with particular care and interest.
>
> As the idea became familiar to me, it gradually shaped itself into its present form. Throughout its execution, it has *had the complete possession of me*; I have so far verified what is done and suffered on theses pages, as *to have certainly done and suffered it myself*.[46]

This remarkably theatrical explanation of the creative process is that of an actor rather than of a novelist: it is impossible to imagine, say, George Eliot giving a similar account of the composition of *Middlemarch*. Sentimentalism, as revealed here, is a public mode, only masquerading as a private one: the tears shed are shed in company; they spring from shared human experience rather than from the pain of isolation or uniqueness.

### *Great Expectations*

In *Great Expectations* sentimentalism comes under harsh scrutiny, unexpectedly, in the figure of Joe Gargery, the 'Good-Natured Man' descended into the labouring classes, whose sweetness of temper is expressed physically in his eye colour:

> Joe was a fair man, with curls of flaxen hair on each side of his smooth face, and with eyes of such an undecided blue that they seemed to have somehow got mixed with their own whites.[47]

Joe cannot protect Pip from abuse – and this is uncompromisingly presented as a limitation, a fault. Mark Tapley's optimism in *Martin Chuzzlewit* is never ironised (although, as a 'humour' figure, he does not bear too much thematic weight); Jarndyce's benevolence in *Bleak House* is examined more critically; and in *Great Expectations*, fantastical changes are rung on the notion of benevolence and specifically on the figure of the 'benevolent benefactor' – in Magwitch and Miss Havisham, of course, but also, more subtly, in Mr Jaggers, who is much closer to the traditional figure of power, Sheridan's Sir Oliver Surface or Goldsmith's Mr Burchell, and whose ambiguous presence utterly estranges the notion of sentimental benevolence.

## *Our Mutual Friend*

In *Our Mutual Friend* Dickens again returns, in perhaps his darkest and most socially daring novel, to the security of sentimental conventions. The Boffins recall Mr Hardcastle in *She Stoops to Conquer* in their bucolic domesticity. More revealingly, Mr Boffin's adoption of miserly disguise in order to test and to educate Bella Wilfer, is borrowed from the familiar plots of Goldsmith and Sheridan and once again raises the notion of 'character as performance'. The key difference, of course, is that Boffin is both the authority figure who tests the hero/heroine (like Sheridan's Sir Oliver) and a sentimental figure in his own right – the figure of innocence: he is implicated therefore in two different and contradictory parts of the sentimental plot, which might explain the awkwardness of the parts of the novel in which he appears. Jenny Wren is a complex version of the 'child as victim', a sophisticated variation on the strong but simple effect achieved by Little Nell. She is obviously vulnerable, but also a businesswoman in her own right, sharp, shrewish and able to articulate and to focus the key question in the novel: what is it to be alive, what is it to be dead? 'Come Up and Be Dead!' uncannily reverses conventional life/death, heaven/hell polarities and questions conventional definitions. It was from *Our Mutual Friend* that Gilles Deleuze took a key moment to illustrate his own new definition of what it is to be alive, as I shall discuss in the Conclusion.

Finally, Eugene Wrayburn ends Dickens's lifelong exploration of the sentimental 'reformed rake' figure, a figure blended in the nineteenth century with that of the urban *flâneur*. Sir Mulberry Hawk in *Nicholas Nickleby* was the wicked aristocrat from melodrama; Dick Swiveller was another earlier, more impoverished, *flâneur*, whose play with language was, at the beginning of the novel, equated with irresponsibility in human emotions. Dick's reclamation by the Marchioness anticipates Eugene's by Lizzie. In Eugene's case, the reclamation is signalled by a shift from the language of wit to the language of sentiment. In a key passage which was written, according to Dickens's *Book of Memoranda*,[48] long before the rest of the novel (and which was briefly quoted in the discussion of Goldsmith in Chapter 4), Eugene adopts the heroic register of Richard Wardour, but for dramatically different and richer ends as he overturns the English class system:

> I will fight it out to the last gasp, with her and for her, here, in the open field. When I hide her, or strike for her, faintheartedly, in a hole or corner, do you whom I love next best on earth, tell me what I shall righteously deserve to be told: – that she would have done well to turn me over with her foot that night when I lay bleeding to death, and spat upon my dastard face. (813)

The emotional crescendo, via parallelisms, anaphora and repetitions ('with her and for her', 'hide her and strike for her') is delayed, with consequent increase of tension, by the colon, and reaches its climax with the stress on 'spat'. The intensity comes from the complete rejection of Eugene's former register of wit, the substitution of idealism for cynicism and in the prose, of crescendos for the dying falls, the bathos of the comic mode. It is a powerful, simple effect. Dickens embraces the full resources of sentimentalism to achieve an extreme resolution: Eugene is marrying a girl, not even from the respectable working class but from the underclass: Gaffer Hexam was a scavenger for dead bodies on the River Thames. The question of whether sentimentalism can be subversive is here triumphantly answered: both the sentimental mode and extreme sentimentalist rhetoric are needed at this point to proclaim the possibility of a new sort of English society. Only through that traditional mode and its familiar rhetoric of absolutes can Dickens convey his passionate vision of a new world.

Thus from the safety of the shared 'interpretive community' of the sentimental audience, Dickens can risk his most alarming and original effects. In *Our Mutual Friend* death occurs, not on the sentimental deathbed, where Little Paul watched the golden light as he floated down a river of sentiment towards his dead mother, but in the slime of the great River Thames where bodies rot and merge back into the slime. The later novels might be seen indeed as evolving a 'sentimentalism after Darwin': an optimistic mode, arguably more necessary than ever, is unarguably very much harder – both in literature and in society – to maintain.[49]

Wolfgang Herrlinger has argued that the last great Victorian novel built on the sentimentalist tradition was Thackeray's *Vanity Fair*, a novel in which, he says, 'Thackeray evokes the whole repertoire of sentimental strategies in order to defamiliarise them and to make his readers aware of the clichés of sentimental philosophy and literature. After Thackeray' he concludes, 'sentimental literature stands outside the mainstream of English literature.'[50] Barbara Hardy constructs a similar linear narrative of development in *Forms of Feeling in Victorian Fiction*.[51] The neatness of these conclusions, however, suggests their limits. As the previous chapter has shown, Dickens himself was *always* aware of the problematics of sentimentalism and even in his early novels critiqued the mode in various ways.

Herrlinger's conclusion about the watershed significance of *Vanity Fair* is suggestive though, particularly in its pointing to the 1840s as the period in which the power of sentimentalism as a cultural and literary force seems to have peaked. Paul Schlicke reminds us that 'by the time of [Dickens's] death in 1870 obituarists routinely expressed bafflement over the enthusiasm which the previous generation had described as its response to Dickens's sentiment'.[52] From the 1850s onwards, though the sentimental bond between Dickens and his readers persisted, those readers were aware of larger, darker concerns, in novels whose moral heart was elsewhere.

# Conclusion

# THE AFTERLIFE OF SENTIMENTALISM

### 'Who will write the history of tears?'[1]

In *Dombey and Son* Dickens makes a virtue of the restrictions imposed by nineteenth-century sentimentalism, modulating them into a monument to the sentimentalist vision. This vision had evolved, as has been shown, from eighteenth-century rationalism and 'sentiment' as sententiousness, via the epistolary novel and the anarchic experimentations of Sterne, through sentimental comedy into the complexities of Goldsmith and Sheridan. In the move from these two dramatists to early nineteenth-century drama, dramatic complexity was lost in the rise of the 'divided style' of the great Victorians, involving a newly judgemental voice. It became impossible, in Charles Lamb's words, to imagine 'a state of things for which there is neither reward not punishment'.[2] Dickens's generation of early Victorians misread or ignored the rich ambiguities of Sterne, Goldsmith, Sheridan and even Fielding, measuring them narrowly in terms of their own 'coxcombry of moral judgment'.[3] This was linked with a move from many 'implied readers' in the audiences of Goldsmith and Sheridan, to the single, united, judgemental voice of the Victorian public, a public which Dickens went on to seduce and make his own. Thackeray – always drawn to but always suspicious of sentimentalism – exposes its artistic limits in *Vanity Fair*. The final revelation of Amelia's inadequacy and Dobbin's cynicism, according to Wolfgang Herrlinger, constitutes Thackeray's attempted *coup de grace* for sentimentalism.[4] Dickens's *Dombey and Son* was serialised in 1847, at the same time as *Vanity Fair*, having been prompted, bizarrely, by his reading of *Tristram Shandy*. Unlike Thackeray, Dickens accepts the constraints of the sentimentalist mode and turns them to advantage. His experience of acting sentimental heroes such as Lord Wilmot and Richard Wardour ('embodying' them 'in my own person') developed the intensely emotional but public relationship with his audience which he translated to the page in the evolution of the voice of the sentimental narrator (and to the stage, towards the end of his life, in the public readings).[5] The very restrictions upon the sentimental narrator's vision and vocabulary further encouraged the development of that warmly affectionate, genially knowing, public (but experienced on both sides as deeply private) relationship with the reader which is perhaps the most recognisable characteristic of Dickens's prose.

## Nineteenth-Century Anti-sentimentalism

Anti-sentimentalism was always present in the response to the novels, just as humour has been found to be always inseparable from the writing itself. An anonymous *Athenaeum* reviewer as early as 1836 famously described the Dickensian formula as 'two pounds of Smollett, three ounces of Sterne, a handful of hook, a dash of a grammatical Pierce Egan'.[6] Critical attacks on Dickens's 'sentimentality' increased and became more focused in the second half of the century, as the tenets of novelistic realism took hold. John Stuart Mill, George Eliot, George Henry Lewes and others complained that Dickens's idealisations hindered social reform. George Henry Lewes found his characters 'unreal and impossible...speaking a language never heard in life' and, while acknowledging his astonishing power, concluded that 'his was merely an animal intelligence, i.e. restricted to perceptions'.[7]

John Stuart Mill, loathing what he took to be misogyny in the creation of Mrs Jellyby and Mrs Pardiggle, wrote to his wife of '[t]hat creature Dickens, whose *Bleak House*, I found accidentally at the London Library the other day and took home and read, much the worst of his things and the only one of them I altogether dislike...'[8] George Eliot also objected to Dickens's 'preternaturally virtuous poor children and artisans' on the grounds that they encouraged 'the miserable fallacy that high morality and refined sentiment can grow out of harsh social relations, ignorance and want'.[9]

Other critics were less concerned with political ideals than with Dickens's perceived emotionalism per se. Walter Bagehot identifies unfavourably, as weaknesses, several stylistic characteristics that I have suggested are central to the sentimental vision. First he notes Dickens's anti-intellectualism. Dickens, he says,

> is utterly deficient in the faculty of reasoning...he is often troubled by the idea that he must reflect, and his reflections are perhaps the worst reading in the world. There is a sentimental confusion about them; we never find the consecutive precision of mature theory, or the cold distinctness of clear thought.[10]

Bagehot is also perceptive on the differences between Dickens and Sheridan in the presentation of their heroes and heroines:

> One of Sheridan's best comedies is remarkable for having no scene in which the hero and heroine are on stage together... Mr Dickens would have done

well to imitate so astute a policy; but he has none of [Sheridan's] managing shrewdness... Mr Dickens, on the contrary, pours out painful sentiments as if he wished abundance should make up for the inferior quality. The excruciating writing which is expended on Ruth Pinch passes belief... (134)

The reason, surmises Bagehot, is Dickens's peculiar innocence, evident in a comparison with Thackeray:

No one can read Mr Thackeray's writings without feeling that he is perpetually treading as close as he dare to the border-line that separates the world that may be described in books from the world which it is prohibited so to describe... Everyone may perceive what is passing in his fancy. Mr Dickens is chargeable with no such defect: he does not seem to feel the temptation... [He is never disposed to] 'make capital' out of the most commonly tempting part of human sentiment... (135)

An anonymous review of the library edition of Dickens's works, in the *Saturday Review* in 1858, launches a more serious attack, a full-blown Scroogeian assault on an artistic vision which is seen as 'humbug'. There is an evident contempt for the eighteenth-century optimism which appears to have survived, inappropriately, in Dickens's novels. Already much in evidence is the strain which became prominent in twentieth-century attacks on Dickensian sentimentalism: a mixture of social elitism and misogyny — exactly the misogyny, ironically, that Mill had found in Dickens himself:

From first to last, [Mr Dickens] has tried about as much to make his readers cry as to make them laugh; and there is a very large section of the British public — especially of the younger, weaker and more ignorant part of it — which considers these two functions as comprising the whole duty of novelists...if anyone can get a pretty little girl to go to heaven prattling of her dolls, and her little brothers and sisters, and quoting texts of Scripture with appropriate gasps, dashes and broken sentences, he may send half the women in London, with tears in their eyes, to Mr Mudie's or Mr Booth's. This kind of taste has not only been flattered but prodigiously developed, by Mr Dickens... No man can offer the public so large a stock of death-beds adapted for either sex and for any age from five-and-twenty downwards... This union of banter and sentiment appears to us to form the very essence of Mr Dickens's view of life. In the main, it is a very lovely world, a very good and happy world, in which we live. We ought all to be particularly fond of each other and infinitely pleased with our position.[11]

Hippolyte Taine too recognised the ideas ridiculed by the anonymous *Saturday Review* writer and showed a dry awareness of the dangers of that vision, notably its potential to encourage self-indulgent emotionalism:

> In reality, the novels of Dickens can be reduced to one phrase, to wit: Be good, and love; there is genuine joy only in the emotions of the heart; sensibility is the whole man... Believe that humanity, pity, forgiveness, are the finest things in man; believe that intimacy, expansion, tenderness, tears, are the sweetest things in the world. To live is nothing; to be powerful, learned, illustrious, is little; to be useful is not enough. He alone has lived and is a man who has wept at the remembrance of a kind action which he himself has performed or received.[12]

It is revealing that the first half of Taine's account acutely characterises the Christian virtues ('humanity, pity, forgiveness') to which not only Dickens but Western Christian culture more generally would surely subscribe, while only the second half ('intimacy, expansion, tenderness') shows the over-balancing of those qualities into excess: Taine in other words enacts in his prose the move from sentimentalism to what came to be seen as its excessive and increasingly unacceptable form, 'sentimentality'.

## Twentieth-Century Anti-sentimentalism

The prevailing attitude to sentimentalism in the 1920s is usefully glossed by Stanley T. Williams in the *Sewanee Review* of 1925. The cynical tone of Virginia Woolf and Aldous Huxley is struck early. 'One aspect of sentimental comedy' he says, 'is its dullness':

> It is only when we read a hundred plays by these dramatists [that we perceive] their weatherbeaten plots, their reminiscent characters, their denouements of ghastly make-believe, their grandiose preachments, their thin laughter and their triumphant unoriginality.[13]

It seems impossible that Williams could ever overcome this characteristic 1920–30s tone. He does however, and after reviewing the period, he admits refreshingly that 'it is difficult in the twentieth century to comprehend the subversive character of this belief' in virtue and goes on to show how much twentieth-century political and social assumptions incorporate the sentimentalist philosophy of the eighteenth century.[14] Williams ends, with unusual sympathy and insight for the decade in which he wrote, that, whatever their failings, the sentimentalists were 'wistful after the mysteries of human emotion' (426). The modernist writers were less perceptive and were pungent in their condemnation of anything they construed as 'sentimentality'. Aldous Huxley's response to *The Old Curiosity Shop* focused on his dislike of Dickens's rhythmic prose at moments of heightened emotion: he attacked this 'atrocious blank verse [which] is meant to be poetical...and succeeds in being the worst kind of fustian'.[15] 'Fustian' is a revealing term of abuse: it suggests workaday lower class garb, as opposed (presumably) to the elite and aristocratic dress in which blank verse was conventionally supposed to appear. Very often, in every century, attacks on sentimentalism are implicitly attacks on a popular response from which the writer wants to separate him/herself. Judging from the vituperative attacks on Dickens by Virginia Woolf and Aldous Huxley, modernist elitism seems to have felt particularly threatened by what Eric Bentley dubs the 'poor man's catharsis' of sentimental tears.[16]

## Later Twentieth Century: The Rehabilitation of Sentimentalism?

What eventually prompted the critical rereading of sentimentalism was, unexpectedly, the rise of critical theory, which involved a turning away from the author towards a more nuanced textuality concerned not with authorial intent but with the complexities of textual effects on the reader. Roland Barthes, for example, in 'In Praise of Tears'[17] cites Goethe's *The Sorrows of Young Werther* as his key text, explaining rhapsodically the erotic significance of lovers weeping together:

> The slightest amorous emotion, whether of happiness or of disappointment, brings Werther to tears. Werther weeps often, very often, and in floods... By releasing his tears without constraint, he follows the orders of the amorous body, which is a body in liquid expansion, a bathed body: to weep together, to flow together: delicious tears finish off the reading of Klopstock which Charlotte and Werther perform together. Where does the lover obtain the right to cry, if not in a reversal of values, of which the body is the first target? He accepts rediscovering the *infant body*.

Barthes' elision here of the infant and the sexualised body seems particularly relevant to a study of nineteenth-century sentimental writing, in which the child itself can become an intensely emotional, even sexualised, object and in which the question of childlikeness is central, particularly, to the construction of the heroine. Dickens may be guilty of this himself in his immolation of Little Nell and his presentation of Little Dorrit, but he can also recognise and satirise the process, notably in *Martin Chuzzlewit*, in Mercy Pecksniff's deliberate sexualising of herself by acting and dressing as a child:

> Miss Pecksniff sat upon a stool because of her simplicity and innocence, which were very great: very great. Miss Pecksniff sat upon a stool because she was all girlishness and playfulness, and wildness, and kittenish buoyancy. She was the most arch and the same time, the most artless creature, was the youngest Miss Pecksniff, that you can possibly imagine. It was her great charm. She was too fresh and guileless, and too full of childlike vivacity, was the youngest Miss Pecksniff, to wear combs in her hair… She wore it in a crop, a loosely flowing drop, which had so many rows of curls in it, that the top row was only one curl. Moderately buxom was her shape, and quite womanly too; but sometimes – yes, sometimes – she even wore a pinafore; and how charming that was![18]

## Twenty-first Century: The 'Affective Turn' and the Rehabilitation of Sentimentalism

The fresh interest in the literary construction of emotion in current critical thinking has already been outlined in the Introduction. Much has been written in the first decade of the twenty-first century on the physicalising of emotion, on the literary presentation of the body. However, perhaps the most impressive criticism has been that which has approached emotional writing through cultural politics. Juliet John's influential *Dickens's Villains: Melodrama, Character, Popular Culture* argues that 'Dickens's most consistent political aim was to counter cultural elitism'[19] and that this aim was best served by a theatrical aesthetic which externalises emotion. He is, she says, always suspicious of 'interiority' (as in the repressed passion of Bradley Headstone) and she links this with his love of popular entertainments like the music hall and therefore with anti-elitism: 'his populism is…inextricable from his anti-intellectualism'.[20] This chimes in with the argument of the present work that Dickens uses the sentimentalist tradition to disable thinking in his readers, in order to prompt in them the healthy overflow of tears noted in Francis Jeffrey's response recorded at the beginning of this book.[21] I am less convinced than John that Dickens's aims are consistently 'anti-elitist' or that he is unremittingly radical. However, just as John is concerned to promote a new and richer understanding of melodrama, so my aim has been to develop a similar understanding of sentimentalism. What is public and populist (sentimentalism or melodrama) needs to be recognised as having a cultural, if not an aesthetic, value equal to that of the individual and private (the Romantic).

Sentimentalism's links with popular culture have resulted in the first decades of the twenty-first century in a rush of books which contribute to cultural studies, rather than to literary criticism more narrowly defined.

## CONCLUSION

In 2010 Michele Byers and David Lavery edited a collection of essays entitled *On the Verge of Tears: Why the Movies, Television, Music, Art, Popular Culture, Literature and the Real World Make Us Cry*.[22] The *ad hominem* approach indicated by the title was part of the point: that sentimentalism is generally regarded as not intellectually respectable precisely because it works by getting under the radar of the intellect. The dedications the two editors chose to make, blatantly, but presumably inadvertently, highlighted the issue of gender and sentimentalism as well as epitomising the double nature of the mode: Byers dedicates her part of the book to her children: 'Mommy loves you forever with her whole heart'; Lavery dedicates his to his new granddaughter, 'whose knowledge of crying puts us all to shame'. The effusion of the first (female) co-editor is balanced by the more wry wording of the second (male), who draws on the insulating resources of humour which so often (as I have shown in earlier chapters) is necessary to complete, rather than to negate, the sentimental response.

Cecilia Feilla's chapter in the Byers/Lavery volume attempts to bring the heavy guns of twentieth-century critical theory to bear on sentimentalism. She quotes (as I have done) from Roland Barthes' 'A Lover's Discourse', arguing with Barthes that tears 'are always social, directed towards another'. They

> follow conventions and codes, adhere to particular literary and social functions, and thus, though felt to be intensely personal, are socially and historically determined. 'Who will write the history of tears?' Barthes asks. 'In which societies, in which periods, have we wept? Since when is it that men (and Women) no longer cry?'[23]

Feilla's comments, and her enlisting of Barthes to her cause, are helpful in readdressing the issue of Dickens and sentimentalism in twenty-first century terms. Certainly the paradoxical link between the 'intensely personal' and the 'socially and historically determined' is central to understanding Dickens's sentimental rhetoric. Crying in public, or being the cause of public weeping, as in the impersonation of Richard Wardour in *The Frozen Deep*, mattered enormously to him, as did the powerful effect of the public readings. If eighteenth-century sentimentalism was very obviously a public mode, then so was its very different successor in the nineteenth century. The rise of psychology as a discipline in the nineteenth century encouraged a new interest in the physical nature of the sentimental response and of its possibly beneficial effects – hence Jeffrey's tearful thanks to Dickens for having made him weep. In 1872, Charles Darwin noted in puzzlement that:

> The feelings which we call tender are difficult to analyse; they seem to be compounded of affection, joy, and especially of sympathy. These feelings are in themselves of a pleasurable nature... They are remarkable...from so readily

exciting the secretion of tears... Sympathy with the distress of others, even with the imaginary distresses of a heroine in a pathetic story, for whom we feel no affection, readily excites tears.[24]

In the twentieth century, emotion continued to be explored as part of a physical rather than a spiritual economy. There are signs, however, that, in the twenty-first century, the physical and the spiritual are once more being linked. Gilles Deleuze, in his 2001 volume of three essays, *Pure Immanence*,[25] moves into what seems to me to be something close to the impersonal experience of sentimental 'melting'. He examines in the first essay, 'Immanence: A Life' a concept which he later capitalises, 'A LIFE' (27), and which one reviewer paraphrased as: 'a paradoxical experience/duration in which individuality fades and becomes "a singular essence" [and in which] what is common is impersonal and what is impersonal is common'.[26] Deleuze gives two striking examples to illustrate this ambiguous state of space/time, the first from Rogue Riderhood's return to life from near-drowning in Dickens's *Our Mutual Friend*:

> What is immanence? A life... No one has described what a life is better than Charles Dickens, if we take the indefinite article as an index of the transcendental. A disagreeable man, a rogue, held in contempt by everyone, is found as he lies dying. Suddenly, those taking care of him manifest an eagerness, respect, even love, for his slightest sign of life. Everybody bustles about to save him, to the point where, in his deepest coma, this wicked man himself senses something soft and sweet penetrating him. But to the degree that he comes back to life, his saviours turn colder, and he becomes once again mean and crude. Between his life and his death, there is a moment that is only that of a life playing with death. (28)

In another example, Deleuze calls attention to very small children, who are yet unformed as individuals and all tend to resemble one another. The passage recalls Dickens's childlike need to pull faces as he created his written characters:

> It even seems that a singular life might do without any individuality, without any other concomitant that individualizes it. For example, small children all resemble one another and have hardly any individuality, but they have singularities: a smile, a gesture, a funny face – not subjective qualities. Small children, through all their sufferings and weaknesses, are infused with an immanent life that is pure power and even bliss. (30)

This impersonality, this bliss, is linked to the sentimental response: what is experienced as subjective, private and personal turns out to be part of what is an essentially shared, impersonalising, non-intellectual human experience. Jeffrey's experience of 'blessedness' when he wept over the death of Little Nell, Dickens's experience of being wept over as he died on stage as Richard Wardour, is part of the mystery of sentimental tears. They are not to be dismissed as unintelligent simply because they do not involve the intellect: perhaps when we cry in a crowd or when reading Dickens we are losing our identity but experiencing the ecstasy of being purely, merely, irrationally, human; perhaps this is what Deleuze means by the infusion of 'pure power and bliss'.

\*\*\*

## Summary

It was by a process of selective rereading and possibly misreading that Dickens assimilated the work of his predecessors and evolved his own peculiarly nineteenth-century version of sentimentalism – the version so often branded (and dismissed) as sentimentality. This book has examined the eighteenth-century sentimentalisms he inherited, both directly and indirectly, from his influential predecessors in the novel, Fielding, Richardson and Sterne, and in the drama, Goldsmith and Sheridan. Four of these obvious influences on Dickens were sentimentalists with a difference, who were often classed as its discontents. Their own complexity and ambivalence may be part of the reason for Dickens's selective reading and occasionally, as in the case of Sterne, *mis*-reading, of the eighteenth-century tradition.

In the eighteenth century, the Lockean assumption of a continuum of mental, emotional and physical stimuli allowed writers such as Sterne to achieve bewilderingly complex effects within the sentimentalist mode, as I have hoped to show in close readings of passages from *Tristram Shandy* and *A Sentimental Journey*. However, as the semantic shift of the term 'sentimental' from 'thoughtful feeling' to 'feeling *as opposed* to thought' took place during the Romantic period, so nineteenth-century sentimental writing, in writers as different as Dickens and George Eliot, developed into a rhetoric of intensification which functioned to disable thought and to build up an emotional climax in the audience/reader. Thus a new sentimental paradox emerged in nineteenth-century literature: a highly stylised and thoughtful rhetoric was developed in order to disarm and disable thought.

Nineteenth-century sentimental writing, like the 'separate spheres' of mid-Victorian society, usually relies for its effects on the separation of sentiment and humour or wit. Some of Dickens's early novels, notably *Nicholas Nickleby*, illustrate this. It is possible to make a case for a narrative of progression in which, in the later novels, in particular in *Dombey and Son*, a more complex and integrated sentimental rhetoric emerges. However, this is to ignore the variety of 'sentimentalisms' evident in Dickens's novels at every stage and the range of uses to which they are put. New features entering Dickens's nineteenth century sentimentalist vocabulary include the dying child, the loveable grotesque and the anti-industrial community of the good, all of which were exploited to a lesser extent by his contemporaries and successors.

In order to ensure the 'fuller, fairer reading of Dickens' which was my original aim, I have attempted to show that nineteenth-century sentimentalism evolved a strong tradition of its own, worthy of serious study. I have further argued that, just as Dickens, consciously or unconsciously, misread Goldsmith and Sheridan, so he has been misread, or read too narrowly, by later readers. The Victorians' 'divided feeling about emotion' could, in a further study, be shown to be present in Dickens's contemporaries such as Thackeray, Eliot, Ruskin and Collins and to continue in twenty-first century writers in ever more fractured forms.[27] A fuller fairer reading of Dickens will probably only be possible if, moving beyond postmodernism, we can learn to accept and to analyse, rather than simply dismissing out of hand our own capacity for sentimental tears.

# NOTES

## Introduction

1 A. A. Gill, *The Sunday Times Magazine*, 30 April 2011, 17.
2 The critic, Francis, Lord Jeffrey on the death of Little Paul in *Dombey and Son* (31 January 1847), quoted in *Dickens: The Critical Heritage*, ed. Philip Collins (London: Routledge and Kegan Paul, 1971), 217.
3 Preface to *The Conscious Lovers*, in Richard Steele, *The Plays of Richard Steele*, ed. Shirley Strum Kenny (Oxford: Clarendon Press, 1971), 5.
4 Gabriel Pearson, 'The Old Curiosity Shop', in *Dickens and the Twentieth Century*, ed. John Gross and Gabriel Pearson (London: Routledge and Kegan Paul, 1962), 77.
5 *Oxford English Dictionary*, 20 vols, 2nd ed. (Oxford: Clarendon Press, 1991).
6 Paul Parnell, 'The Sentimental Mask', *PMLA* 78 (1963): 529.
7 Juliet John, *Dickens's Villains* (Oxford: Oxford University Press, 2001), 81.
8 Alison Case and Harry E. Shaw, *Reading the Nineteenth-Century Novel* (Oxford: Blackwell, 2008), 10.
9 Wolfgang Herrlinger, *Sentimentalismus und Post-Sentimentalismus* (Tubingen: Max Niemeyer, 1987), 'Einführung', 1–9 and 'Summary', 363.
10 Herrlinger, ibid., unpublished translation by Jane Barry (2011), 1.
11 Herrlinger, ibid., trans. Barry, v.
12 Gillian Beer, *Darwin's Plots*, 3rd ed. (Cambridge: Cambridge University Press), 4.
13 Fred Kaplan, *Sacred Tears* (Princeton: Princeton University Press, 1987), blurb from dust jacket.
14 See in particular: Gilles Deleuze, *Pure Immanence* (New York: Zone Books, 2001); Félix Guattari, *Chaosmosis: An Ethico-Aesthetic Paradigm* (Bloomington and Indianapolis: Indiana University Press, 1995); Patricia Ticineto Clough, ed., *The Affective Turn* (Durham, NC: Duke University Press, 2007).
15 'Mr Popular Sentiment: Dickens and Feeling', 16 October 2010, organised by Birkbeck, University of London, and the University of Leicester.
16 Pierre Bourdieu, *Outline of a Theory of Practice*, translated by Richard Nice (Cambridge: Cambridge University Press, 1977); cited in Gesa Stedman, *Stemming the Torrent* (Aldershot: Ashgate, 2002), 3.
17 Kirstie Blair, *Victorian Poetry and the Culture of the Heart* (Oxford: Oxford University Press, 2006); Blair points out, for example, that the scientist John Elliotson, whose early research was on the heart, was a friend of Dickens.
18 Roy Porter, 'History of the Body', in *New Perspectives on Historical Writing*, ed. Peter Burke (Cambridge: Polity Press, 1991), 207.
19 Fred Kaplan, *Sacred Tears* (Princeton: Princeton University Press, 1987), 5.

20  Frank Ellis, *Sentimental Comedy: Theory and Practice* (Cambridge: Cambridge University Press, 1991), 123.
21  Monika Fludernik, 'The Eighteenth-Century Legacy' in *A Companion to Charles Dickens*, ed. David Paroissien (Oxford: Blackwell, 2008), 65–80.
22  Ellis, *Sentimental Comedy*, 4.
23  Cited in Ellis, *Sentimental Comedy*, 122.
24  Quoted in John, *Dickens's Villains*, 73.
25  Samuel Taylor Coleridge, *Biographia Literaria or Biographical Sketches of My Literary Life and Opinions*, 2nd ed. (London: William Pickering, 1847) I, 13, 297–8.
26  Charles Bray, *The Education of the Feelings* (London: Taylor and Watson, 1838), 3.
27  Gesa Stedman, *Stemming the Torrent: Expression and Control in the Victorian Discourses on Emotion 1830–1872* (Aldershot: Ashgate, 2002), 75.
28  W. Cooke (1852), quoted in Stedman, *Stemming the Torrent*, 78.
29  Valentine Cunningham, 'Dickens and Christianity', in Paroissien, *A Companion to Charles Dickens*, 255–6.
30  Laurence Sterne, *The Life and Opinions of Tristram Shandy, Gentleman*, ed. Ian Watt (Boston: Houghton Mifflin, 1965), 179.
31  Steele, Preface to *The Conscious Lovers*, 5.
32  Jean-Jacques Rousseau, *Emile: or, On Education*, trans. Allan Bloom (New York: HarperCollins, 1979), 79.
33  Friedrich Schiller, *Uber Naive und Sentimentalische Dichtung*, translated by Julius A. Elias (New York: Frederick Ungar Publishing Co., 1966), 87.
34  Peter Coveney, *The Image of Childhood* (Harmondsworth: Penguin, 1967). First published as *Poor Monkey* (London: Rockliff, 1957).
35  See Anne-Louise Russell, 'The Iconic Function of the Child in Mid-Victorian Literature', unpublished Anglia Ruskin University undergraduate dissertation, 2011.
36  Samuel Richardson, *Clarissa or The History of a Young Lady* (Boston: Houghton Mifflin, 1962), 263.
37  Laurence Sterne, *The Life and Opinions of Tristram Shandy, Gentleman* (London: Penguin, 2003), 140.
38  Marcus Wood, *Slavery, Empathy and Pornography* (Oxford: Oxford University Press, 2002), 18.
39  Blair, *Victorian Poetry and the Culture of the Heart*, 14.
40  Stedman, *Stemming the Torrent*, 148.
41  John Keats, 'Ode to a Nightingale', *The Poems of Keats*, ed. Miriam Allott (London: Longman, 1970), 529.
42  Andrew Sanders, *Charles Dickens Resurrectionist* (London: Palgrave Macmillan, 1982). As Sanders suggests, Dickens frequently uses death in his novels as part of an overarching narrative pattern of sin, repentance and 'rebirth'.
43  Stanley T. Williams, 'The English Sentimental Drama from Steele to Cumberland', *Sewanee Review* 33, no. 4 (October 1925): 408.
44  Marcus Wood, *Slavery, Empathy and Pornography* (Oxford: Oxford University Press, 2002), 18.
45  See, for example, George Taylor, '"The Just Delineation of the Passions": Theories of Acting in the Age of Garrick', in *Essays on the Eighteenth-Century English Stage*, ed. Kenneth Richards and Peter Thomson (London: Methuen, 1972), 51–73, and Bertram Joseph, *The Tragic Actor* (London: Routledge and Kegan Paul, 1959). Charles Bell in *The Anatomy and Philosophy of Expression, as Connected with the Fine Arts*, 7th ed. (London: John

Murray, 1877) – first published as *Essays on the Anatomy of Expression in Painting* (London: Longman, 1806) – discusses in detail this notion of the 'performative' (see below, Chapter 1).

46 The underlying question of whether this visceral, physical response is a universal one or, as Roland Barthes, Pierre Bourdieu and others would argue, culturally conditioned, is beyond the scope of the present work. Dickens himself would undoubtedly have believed in its universality.

## Chapter 1   Dickens and the Sentimentalist Tradition

1 Peter Happé, ed., *English Mystery Plays* (London: Penguin, 1975), 145. Spelling modernised.
2 Happé, ed., *English Mystery Plays*, 293. Spelling modernised.
3 Thomas Otway, *Venice Preserved* (London: Edward Arnold, 1969), 77. All subsequent references are to act, scene and line in this edition.
4 Allardyce Nicoll, *A History of English Drama 1660–1900*, 6 vols (Cambridge: Cambridge University Press 1923–59), passim.
5 Julia Swindells explores the political implications of these later plays in *Glorious Causes: The Grand Theatre of Political Change 1789–1833* (Oxford: Oxford University Press, 2001).
6 William Hazlitt, *Essays*, ed. Charles Whibley (London: Blackie, 1906), 399–400.
7 Mario Praz, *The Hero in Eclipse in Victorian Fiction*, trans. A. Davidson (London: Oxford University Press, 1956).
8 Erik Erämetsä, *A Study of the Word 'Sentimental'* (Helsinki: Suomalainen Tiedeakatemia, 1951), 14.
9 Erämetsä, *A Study of the Word 'Sentimental'*, 36, citing Henry Home, Lord Kames, *The Elements of Criticism* (Edinburgh, 1762):

> It is beyond the power of music to raise a passion or sentiment: but it is in the power of music to raise emotions similar to what are raised by sentiments expressed in words pronounced with propriety and grace; and such music may justly be termed *sentimental*.

Erämetsä comments: 'The words of definition remain the same, but the source of virtue and moral conduct was being transferred from the Head to the Heart' (36).

10 Oliver Goldsmith, Letter VI, quoted in Erämetsä, *A Study of the Word 'Sentimental'*, 34.
11 Wolfgang Herrlinger, *Sentimentalismus und Post-Sentimentalismus* (Tubingen: Max Niemeyer, 1987), unpublished trans. Jane Barry (2011), 3.
12 Isobel Armstrong, 'The Role and Treatment of Emotion in Victorian Criticism of Poetry', *Victorian Periodicals Newsletter* 10, no. 1 (March 1977): 3.
13 John Stuart Mill, 'What is Poetry?' and 'Two Kinds of Poetry', cited in Armstrong, 'The Role and Treatment of Emotion', 15. These articles originally appeared in the *Monthly Repository*, n.s. 7 (Jan. and Oct. 1833): 60–70, 714–24, and were reprinted in *English Critical Essays (Nineteenth Century)*, ed. E. D. Jones (Oxford: Oxford University Press 1916, reprinted 1950).
14 George Henry Lewes, 'Hegel's Aesthetics', *British and Foreign Review* 13 (1842): 9, quoted in Armstrong, 'The Role and Treatment of Emotion', 3.

15 Arthur Henry Hallam, unsigned review of Alfred Tennyson's *Poems, Chiefly Lyrical* (London: Effingham Wilson, 1830), *Englishman's Magazine* 1 (August 1831): 616–28. Reprinted in *Tennyson: The Critical Heritage*, ed. John Jump (London: Routledge and Kegan Paul, 1967), 34–49.
16 Jason R. Rudy, *Electric Meters: Victorian Physiological Poetics* (Athens, OH: Ohio University Press, 2009), 58.
17 Claude A. Prance, *A Companion to Charles Lamb: A Guide to People and Places 1760–1847* (Anne Arbor, MI: University of Michigan Press, 1983), 225; *The Diaries of W. C. Macready 1833–1851*, ed. W. Toynbee (London: Chapman and Hall, 1912).
18 Johann Wolfgang von Goethe, *The Sorrows of Young Werther*, trans. Victor Lange (New York: Holt, Rinehart and Winston, 1949), 34.
19 The echoes of Paolo and Francesca in Dante's *Divine Comedy* enhance the suggestion of the erotic potential of tears.
20 Nahum Tate, *King Lear*, in *Shakespeare Adaptations*, ed. Montague Summers (New York: Blom), 177.
21 Alexander Welsh, *From Copyright to Copperfield: The Identity of Dickens* (Cambridge, MA: Harvard University Press, 1987), 104.
22 'Wandering Feelings: The Transmission of Emotion in the Long Nineteenth Century', one-day research colloquium held at Queen Mary, University of London, November 2011, organised by Carolyn Burdett and Tiffany Watt-Smith, Queen Mary. Online 'Call for Proposals': http://www.qmul.ac.uk/emotions/docs/50522.pdf (accessed 11 September 2011).
23 John Keble, *Keble's Lectures on Poetry, 1832–41*, trans. Edward Kershaw Francis, 2 vols (Oxford: Clarendon Press 1912), I, lecture 1, 19, quoted in Gesa Stedman, *Stemming the Torrent: Expression and Control in the Victorian Discourses on Emotion, 1830–1872* (Aldershot: Ashgate, 2002), 51. My discussion of Keble, Bell and Bray owes a great deal to Stedman, *Stemming the Torrent*, chapter 3, '"I Could not Speak the Feeling": Emotions and the Body'.
24 Keble, *Lectures on Poetry*, I, lecture 16, 327, in Stedman, *Stemming the Torrent*, 51–2.
25 Quoted in Stedman, *Stemming the Torrent*, 138.
26 Charles Bray, *The Education of the Feelings* (London: Taylor and Watson, 1838), 3.
27 Valentine Cunningham, 'Dickens and Christianity', in *A Companion to Charles Dickens*, ed. David Paroissien (Oxford: Blackwell, 2008), 258.
28 Charles Bell, *The Anatomy and Philosophy of Expression, as Connected with the Fine Arts*, 3rd ed. (London: John Murray, 1844).
29 Peter Ackroyd, *Dickens* (London: Sinclair-Stevenson, 1990), 664.
30 Michael Slater, *Charles Dickens: A Life Defined by Writing* (London: Yale University Press, 2009), 277.
31 Horace Dobell, *On Affections of the Heart and in its Neighbourhood* (London: H. K. Lewis, 1872).
32 Dobell, *On the Affections of the Heart*, dedication page, no pagination.
33 Samuel Richardson, *Pamela: Or Virtue Rewarded* (Oxford: Oxford University Press, 2001), 74.
34 R. L. Brannan, *Under the Management of Mr Charles Dickens: His Production of 'The Frozen Deep'* (Ithaca, NY: Cornell University Press, 2004), 132.
35 Roland Barthes, from 'A Lover's Discourse' in *A Roland Barthes Reader*, ed. Susan Sontag (London: Vintage, 1982), 426–7.
36 Dylan Evans, *Emotion: The Science of Sentiment* (Oxford: Oxford University Press, 2001), 85, 81, 83.

37 See William S. Sahakian, *History and Systems of Psychology* (New York: John Wiley and Sons, 1975), 44–70.
38 '"It seems to me hard," said Little Dorrit, "that he should have lost so many years and suffered so much, and at last pay all the debts as well... Yes, I know I am wrong," she pleaded timidly, "don't think any worse of me; it has grown up with me here"... [I]t was the first speck Clennam had ever seen, it was the last speck Clennam ever saw, of the prison atmosphere upon her.' *Little Dorrit*, 409.
39 Josephine Miles, *Wordsworth and the Vocabulary of Emotion* (New York: Octagon, 1965), 87.
40 Bertram Joseph, *The Tragic Actor* (London: Routledge and Kegan Paul, 1959).
41 William Shakespeare, *Hamlet*, Arden Edition, ed. Ann Thompson and Neil Taylor (London: Thomson Learning, 2002), 353.
42 Allan S. Downer, '"Nature to Advantage Dress'd": Eighteenth-Century Acting', *PMLA* 58, no. 4 (1943): 1030.
43 Richard Wollheim, *Art and its Objects: An Introduction to Aesthetics* (New York and London: Harper and Row, 1968).
44 Ludwig Wittgenstein, *Philosophical Investigations*, trans. G. E. M. Anscombe, 2nd ed. (Oxford: Basil Blackwell, 1963), part 1, sections 66 and 67: 31–2.
45 Northrop Frye, 'Dickens and the Comedy of Humours, in *The Stubborn Structure* (London: Methuen, 1970), 221.

## Chapter 2  Sentimentalism and its Discontents in the Eighteenth-Century Novel: Fielding, Richardson and Sterne

1 Laurence Sterne, *The Life and Opinions of Tristram Shandy, Gentleman*, ed. Ian Watt (Boston: Houghton Mifflin, 1965), 449.
2 From *David Copperfield*, chapter 4, quoted in John Forster, *The Life of Charles Dickens*, 2 vols (London: J. M. Dent, 1966), I, 7–8.
3 Wilhelm Dibelius, *Charles Dickens* (Leipzig: B. Teubner, 1916), 429.
4 I have not dealt in this chapter with Dickens's considerable debt to Tobias Smollett. In Smollett, Dickens found a range of wildly grotesque characters and a stylistic dash, energy and violence which he developed in his own work, notably in *Barnaby Rudge*. The influence is undoubtedly important, but is not central to a discussion of sentimentalism, nor to the complicated misreadings with which this chapter engages.
5 Monika Fludernik, 'The Eighteenth-Century Legacy', in *A Companion to Charles Dickens*, ed. David Paroissien (Oxford: Blackwell, 2008), 65–80; Fludernik, 'The Eighteenth-Century Legacy', 68.
6 Henry MacKenzie's *The Man of Feeling* (1771), still popular at the beginning of the nineteenth century and a novel Dickens cites in his own account of his literary forebears, presents a gentle hero in a series of moving scenes. MacKenzie's sentimental narrator, Harley, 'a child in the drama of the world', can be compared with Goldsmith's Dr Primrose in his idealism, and there is a similar uncertainty, for later readers, as to whether that idealism is always held up for admiration. Although Dickens includes Mackenzie in the 1841 reface to *Oliver Twist*, in which he lists his literary predecessors, it seems unlikely that this fragmentary novel is a major influence. There is a quixotic quality to the reference in any case, since Dickens adds Mackenzie to a list of 'the noblest range of

English literature' as an author who 'brought upon the scene the very scum and refuse of the land' (*Oliver Twist* (London: Penguin, 1986), 35). He must here be referring to Mackenzie's second novel, *The Man of the World*, since *The Man of Feeling* is a tear-soaked tale in idealised settings which deliberately eschews contact with social realism.

7 Martin Battestin, 'Introduction to Henry Fielding', *Joseph Andrews; and, Shamela* (Boston: Houghton Mifflin, 1961), v.
8 Fludernik, 'The Eighteenth-Century Legacy', 68.
9 Henry Fielding, *The History of Tom Jones, a Foundling* (London: Wordsworth Classics, 1999), 95.
10 Ibid., 96.
11 Ibid., 97.
12 Fludernik, 'The Eighteenth-Century Legacy', 70.
13 Fielding, *Tom Jones*, 9.
14 Ibid.
15 *Nicholas Nickleby* (London: Dent, 1994), 7.
16 Fielding, *Tom Jones*, 708.
17 Ibid., 711.
18 *Nicholas Nickleby*, 762.
19 *Little Dorrit*, 778.
20 Helen Small, 'Dickens and Fielding', in F. O'Gorman and K. Turner, eds, *The Victorians and the Eighteenth Century: Reassessing the Tradition* (Aldershot: Ashgate, 2004), 16.
21 Fludernik, 'The Eighteenth-Century Legacy', 73.
22 Quoted in George Sherburn, 'Introduction to Samuel Richardson', *Clarissa or The History of a Young Lady* (Boston: Houghton Mifflin, 1962), xiv.
23 Anthony Kearney, *Samuel Richardson, Clarissa*, Studies in English Literature, no. 55 (London: Edward Arnold, 1975), 59–60. My emphasis.
24 Chapter 6 contains a fuller study of this aspect of *Dombey and Son*.
25 Richardson, *Clarissa*, 302.
26 Ibid., 323.
27 Ibid., 285.
28 *The Mystery of Edwin Drood*, 169–73.
29 Juliet John, *Dickens's Villains* (Oxford: Oxford University Press, 2001), 236.
30 Richardson, *Clarissa*, 469.
31 Frank H. Ellis, *Sentimental Comedy: Theory and Practice* (Cambridge: Cambridge University Press, 1991), 119.
32 *Oliver Twist* (London: Penguin, 1986), 35.
33 *Letters*, IV, 574.
34 Harold Bloom, *The Anxiety of Influence*, 2nd ed. (Oxford: OUP, 1997).
35 *Letters*, IV, 646.
36 Laurence Sterne, *Letters of Laurence Sterne*, ed. L. P. Curtis (Oxford: Oxford University Press, 1935), 411.
37 Richard Cumberland, *The West Indian*, in *The British Theatre: or, A Collection of Plays*, ed. Elizabeth Inchbald, vol. 18 (London: Longman, 1808), 26.
38 W. M. Thackeray, *The English Humorists* (London: Smith Elder, 1889), 318.
39 Thomas Jefferson quoted by Ian Watt, 'Introduction to Sterne', *Tristram Shandy*, xxxii.
40 See: John Bayley *The Uses of Division: Unity and Disharmony in Literature* (London: Chatto and Windus, 1976); Frank Kermode, *The Sense of an Ending: Studies in the Theory of*

Fiction (London: Oxford University Press, 1967); Bloom, *The Anxiety of Influence*; Roland Barthes, 'The Death of the Author' in David Lodge, ed., *Modern Criticism and Theory* (Harlow: Longman, 1988), 167–72.
41  Mikhail Bakhtin, 'From the prehistory of novelistic discourse' in David Lodge, ed., *Modern Criticism and Theory* (Harlow: Longman, 1988), 125–56.
42  *The Beauties of Sterne; including all his Pathetic Tales, and most distinguished OBSERVATIONS on LIFE. Selected for the Heart of Sensibility*, compiled by Mr. W. H., cited in Q. D. Leavis, *Fiction and the Reading Public* (London: Chatto and Windus, 1965), 134–5.
43  A. D. Nuttall, *A Common Sky: Philosophy and the Literary Imagination* (London: Chatto and Windus, 1974), 91.
44  Laurence Sterne, *Tristram Shandy* (Boston: Houghton Mifflin, 1965), 414.
45  Ibid., 354.
46  *Dombey and Son*, 787.
47  Kirstie Blair, 'Introduction', *Victorian Poetry and the Culture of the Heart* (Oxford: Oxford University Press, 2006).
48  *Tristram Shandy*, 174.
49  Ibid., 55.
50  Laurence Sterne, *A Sentimental Journey Through France and Italy by Mr Yorick* (London: Penguin, 2005).
51  *Tristram Shandy*, 449.
52  Ibid., 601.
53  Ibid., 598.
54  Ibid., 559.
55  Samuel Johnson, *Johnson's Dictionary: A Modern Selection* by E. L. MacAdam, Jr and George Milne (London: Victor Gollancz, 1963), 331.
56  *Tristram Shandy*, 600. All subsequent quotations from this scene (volume IX, chapter 24), are from pages 600–602.
57  See the 'Introduction to Laurence Sterne', *A Sentimental Journey*, ed. Gardner D. Stout (Berkeley, CA: University of California Press, 1967).
58  Letter to Hannah quoted by A. Alvarez, 'Introduction to Laurence Sterne', *A Sentimental Journey Through France and Italy by Mr. Yorick*, ed. Graham Petrie (Harmondsworth: Penguin, 1967), 11.
59  *Dombey and Son*, 375.
60  *A Sentimental Journey*, 136.
61  Ibid., 137–8.
62  Letter from Mrs Greville quoted by Fanny Burney in *Memoirs of Dr Burney* (London: Edward Moxon, 1832), 201.
63  *A Sentimental Journey*, 139.
64  Ibid., 140.
65  25 May 1858, *Letters*, V, 74, the 'Violated Letter', quoted from *Mr and Mrs Charles Dickens: His Letters to Her*, ed. Walter Dexter (London: Constable, 1935), 275.
66  See 'Sentimentalism and Christianity' section in the Introduction.
67  Sigmund Freud, *The Interpretation of Dreams*, 3rd ed., trans. A. A. Brill (London: George Allen, 1913), 683.
68  *The Old Curiosity Shop*, 539.
69  *Bleak House*, 705.
70  Ellis, *Sentimental Comedy*, 120.
71  *Tristram Shandy*, 344.

72 George Meredith, *Diana of the Crossways* (London: Virago, 1980), 14. More than any of his contemporaries, Meredith seems to have grasped the erotic potential of the mode. He continues: 'sentimentalism springs from the former [the grossly material], merely badly aping the latter [the spiritual]; – fire flower, or pinnacle flame-spire, of sensualism that it is, how could it do other?

73 Thackeray, *The English Humorists*, 318.

74 Ibid.

75 *Tristram Shandy*, 278.

## Chapter 3  Sentimentalism and its Discontents in Eighteenth-Century Drama: Goldsmith and Sheridan

1 Oliver Goldsmith, *The Good-Natured Man*, in *Poems and Plays*, ed. Tom Davis (London: J. M. Dent, 1990), Act III, line 21 (29).

2 Oliver Goldsmith, 'An Essay on the Theatre', *Westminster Magazine* (1773), quoted in *A Goldsmith Selection*, ed. A. Norman Jeffares (London: Macmillan, 1963), 42.

3 Richard Brinsley Sheridan, prologue to *The Rivals*, in *The School for Scandal and Other Plays* (Oxford: Oxford University Press, 2008 ), 11.

4 John Forster, *The Life of Charles Dickens*, 2 vols, Everyman's Library (London: J. M. Dent, 1966), I, 11.

5 I shall look more closely at *The Vicar of Wakefield* at the beginning of Chapter 5. See Philip Collins, 'Dickens's Reading', *Dickensian* 60 (1964): 136–42. Dickens signed himself 'Tibbs', after Goldsmith's Beau Tibbs, when writing for the *Evening Chronicle* in 1835.

6 Collins, 'Dickens's Reading', *Dickensian* 60 (1964): 136.

7 Graham Storey and Kathleen Tillotson, eds, *Letters*, VIII, 523.

8 12 December 1840, *Letters*, II, 163.

9 5 August 1841, *Letters*, II, 363.

10 7 May 1842, *Letters*, III, 234.

11 To W. C. Macready, 3 January 1844, *Letters*, IV, 10.

12 29 November 1849, *Letters*, V, 660.

13 See Mary Boyle, *Mary Boyle, Her Book*, ed. Courtenay Boyle and Muriel S. Boyle (London: J. Murray, 1901), 229–43. This (wholly literary) flirtation seems also to have continued the roles the two acted in *Used Up* on 15 January 1851. Edgar Johnson (in *Charles Dickens: His Tragedy and His Triumph*, 2 vols (New York: Simon and Schuster, 1952), II, 865) quotes a Morgan manuscript dated 21 July 1856 which contains the phrases 'Beloved Mary... O breezes waft...my Mary to my arms. Ever to distraction Joseph.' On his first North American trip, Dickens wrote to Forster (12 May 1842, *Letters*, III, 237) about some planned theatricals: 'If they had done *Love, Law and Physick*, as at first proposed, I was already "up" in Flexible, having played it of old, before my authorship days.'

14 See Robert Hopkins, *The True Genius of Oliver Goldsmith* (Baltimore: Johns Hopkins University Press, 1969), 5 and Ricardo Quintana, *Oliver Goldsmith: A Georgian Study* (London: Wiedenfeld and Nicholson, 1967), 12.

15 Quoted in *Goldsmith: The Critical Heritage*, ed. G. S. Rousseau (London: Routledge and Kegan Paul, 1974), 277. My emphasis.

16 Cleanth Brooks, *Modern Poetry and the Tradition* (Chapel Hill: University of North Carolina Press, 1948), 46.

17 See Frank Kermode, *The Sense of an Ending: Studies in the Theory of Fiction* (London: Oxford University Press, 1967) and John Bayley *The Uses of Division: Unity and Disharmony in Literature* (London: Chatto and Windus, 1976).
18 W. M. Thackeray, *The English Humorists of the Eighteenth Century* (London: Smith Elder, 1853), 248–71. Quoted in *Goldsmith: The Critical Heritage*, ed. Rousseau, 338.
19 Goldsmith, *Poems and Plays*, 141.
20 Quoted in *Goldsmith: The Critical Heritage*, 348–9. My emphasis.
21 Shirley Strum Kenny, introduction to *The Conscious Lovers*, in Richard Steele, *The Plays of Richard Steele* (Oxford: Clarendon Press, 1971), xii.
22 Goldsmith, *Poems and Plays* (1990), 5–6. All subsequent page references in the text are to this edition.
23 *Martin Chuzzlewit*, 36.
24 *Bleak House*, 289.
25 Hopkins, *The True Genius*, 18. My emphasis.
26 F. R. Leavis, *The Common Pursuit* (London: Chatto and Windus 1972), 75.
27 Oliver Goldsmith, *She Stoops the Conquer* in *Poems and Plays* (1990), 69. All subsequent page references in the text are to this edition.
28 The speaker, of course, is the dangerous rake, Lovelace, and it could well be argued that Richardson is actually presenting the sentimental vision here as an ideal, a response to the new, debauched urban values of his villain. What is interesting is its link already with nostalgia for old ways under threat from new – another aspect of sentimentalism which Dickens was to develop in the following century.
29 *Our Mutual Friend*, 56. My emphasis.
30 Quoted in R. B. Sheridan, *The Plays and Poems*, ed. R. Crompton Rhodes, 3 vols (Oxford: Blackwell, 1928), III, 12.
31 R. B. Sheridan, *The Rivals*, Act IV Scene ii, in *The School for Scandal and Other Plays*, ed. Michael Cordner (Oxford: Oxford University Press 2008), 58.
32 *The Rivals*, I.i.29.
33 Charles Lamb, 'On the Artificial Comedy of the Last Century', *Essays of Elia* (London: Hesperus Press, 2009), 162.
34 Mark Auburn, *Sheridan's Comedies: Their Contexts and Achievements* (Lincoln, NE: University of Nebraska Press, 1977), 179.
35 Sheridan, *The School for Scandal and Other Plays*, ed. Cordner, 286.
36 W. A. Darlington, *Sheridan*. Writers and Their Work, no. 18 (London: Longmans, Green & Co., 1966).

## Chapter 4  Dickens and Nineteenth-Century Drama

1 Charles Lamb, 'On the Artificial Comedy of the Last Century', in *Essays of Elia* (London: Hesperus Press, 2009), 161.
2 Ibid., 165–6.
3 John Bayley makes a similar point in 'Things as they Really Are', *Dickens and the Twentieth Century*, ed. John Gross and Gabriel Pearson (London: Routledge and Kegan Paul, 1962), 49, but without mentioning the drama:

> No novelist has profited more richly than Dickens from not examining what went on in his own mind. His genius avoids itself like a sleep-walker avoiding an open window. Chesterton says what a good thing it is we are not shown Pecksniff's thoughts – they would be too horrible – but the point about Pecksniff is that

he has no thoughts: he is as much a sleep-walker as Dickens: he is the perfect hypocrite because he does not know what he is like. Dickens recoiled from what he called 'dissective' art, and if he had been able and willing to analyse the relation between our inner and outer selves, he could never have created the rhetoric that so marvellously ignores the distinction between them. Unlike us, he had no diagrammatic view of the mind, no constricting terminology for the psyche. The being of Bumble, Pecksniff and Mrs Gamp is not compartmented: their inner being is their outer self.

4. Michael Slater, *Charles Dickens* (New York and London: Yale University Press, 2009), 481.
5. S. T. Coleridge, 'This Lime Tree Bower My Prison', *Poems of S. T. Coleridge*, ed. John Beer (London: Dent, 1996), 9–12.
6. 6 August 1800, *Letters of Charles and Mary Anne Lamb*, ed. Edwin W. Marrs Jr, 3 vols (Ithaca, NY and London: Cornell University Press, 1976), II, 217–18.
7. William Wordsworth, 'Extemporary Effusion on the Death of James Hogg', [1835], in *William Wordsworth: The Poems*, ed. John O. Hayden, 2 vols (London: Penguin, 1977; repr. 1989), II, 800.
8. NNDB. Online: http://www.nndb.com/people/943/000095658/ (accessed 31 August 2011).
9. Lamb, *Essays of Elia*, 110–14.
10. *Master Humphrey's Clock*, New Oxford Illustrated Dickens (London: Oxford University Press, 1963), 110–13.
11. Ibid., 113
12. Ibid. Michael Slater develops this comparison in *Charles Dickens*, 173.
13. Slater, *Charles Dickens*, 353.
14. Andrew Bennett and Nicholas Royle, *An Introduction to Literary Theory and Criticism* (Harlow: Pearson, Longman, 2009), 40.
15. Lamb, 'Dream Children', *Essays of Elia*, 114.
16. Charles Dickens, *Hard Times*, New Oxford Illustrated Dickens (London: Oxford University Press, 1959), 298.
17. See Michael Slater, *Charles Dickens*, 357.
18. Lamb, 'On the Artificial Comedy of the Last Century', *Essays of Elia*, 161, 162.
19. Paul Schlicke, *Dickens and Popular Entertainment* (London: Unwin Hyman, 1988), 236–41.
20. Mark Auburn, *Sheridan's Comedies: Their Contexts and Achievements* (Lincoln, NE: University of Nebraska Press, 1977), 179.
21. Julia Swindells, *Glorious Causes: The Grand Theatre of Political Change 1789–1833* (Oxford: Oxford University Press, 2001), 154. Swindells identifies in the theatres a 'spirit or ideology representing humanitarian sensibility in the theatres', she argues, involved and indeed necessitated 'the open acknowledgement of class conflict and diversity of class interest.' According to this account, sentimental drama in the Georgian period, despite or more probably because of its overt moralism, its confusion of art and life, embodied values which encouraged rather than hindered political reform.
22. Samuel Johnson, 'Preface to Shakespeare' in *English Critical Texts*, ed. D. J. Enright and Ernst de Chickera (Oxford: Oxford University Press, 1962), 140.
23. W. M. Thackeray, from 'Catherine', *Fraser's Magazine*, vol. 21, February 1840, 211, reprint. In Stephen Wall, *Penguin Critical Anthologies: Charles Dickens* (London: Penguin, 1970), 53.

24 Elizabeth Inchbald's plays act as 'bridging passages' between eighteenth- and nineteenth-century sentimentalism. Mr Harmony, in *Everyone Has His Fault*, for example, is a recognisable 'humour' figure descended from Jonson, but his humour is to show 'hearts cold and closed to each other, warmed and expanded, as every human creature's ought to be.' (Reprinted in Davis, *Sentimental Comedy*, 179.) The central action of much eighteenth-century sentimental drama is the conversion of the central character from misapprehension to true values; the central action here, expressed in a significantly different metaphor, is the softening of the powerful Lord Norland's heart. Earlier 'conversions' involved a change of sentiments, that is, ideas, while later nineteenth century 'softenings' involve an accumulation of emotion until the hard character becomes soft and sympathetic. This typical and popular sentimental plot reaches its apogee in *Dombey and Son*.
25 Preface to *A Tale of Two Cities* (London: Dent 1994), no page number. My emphasis.
26 Adrian Poole, Introduction to *Our Mutual Friend* (London: Penguin, 1997), xv–xvi. James Sheridan Knowles's second Christian name itself might also suggest the transmission of theatrical tradition.
27 Juliet John, *Dickens's Villains* (2001); Sally Ledger, *Dickens and the Popular Radical Imagination* (2008); Paul Schlicke, *Dickens and Popular Entertainment* (1988). See Bibliography for full details.
28 For details, see Michael Slater, *Charles Dickens*, 236–8.
29 See, for example, Paul Schlicke, *Oxford Reader's Companion to Dickens* (Oxford: Oxford University Press, 1999), 304.
30 8 and 10 August 1845, *Letters*, IV, 350 and 351.
31 To Head, 13 August 1845, *Letters*, IV, 253.
32 *Letters*, VI, 256–8.
33 See, for example, Judith Butler, *Gender Trouble: Feminism and the Subversion of Identity* (London: Routledge 1990).
34 Ben Jonson, *Every Man in His Humour* (London: A&C Black, 1998), I.iv.30. All
35 Letter to George Cattermole, 3 September 1845, cited in Slater, *Charles Dickens*, 237.
36 *Letters*, VI, 256–8.
37 Edward Bulwer, Lord Lytton, *Dramatic Works* (London: George Routledge, n.d.) 413–78.
38 John Forster, *The Life of Charles Dickens*, 2 vols. (London: J. M. Dent, 1966), II, 71.
39 Lytton, *Dramatic Works*, 478. All subsequent page references are to act, scene and line in this edition.
40 Eve Kosofsky Sedgwick, *Between Men* (New York: Columbia University Press, 1985).
41 Forster, *Life of Dickens*, II, 73.
42 R. H. Horne, 'Bygone Celebrities', *Gentleman's Magazine* 231 (1871): 256.
43 Dickens, Our Mutual Friend (Oxford: New Oxford Illustrated Dickens, 1964), 396.
44 R. L. Brannan, *Under the Management of Mr Charles Dickens* (Ithaca, NY: Cornell University Press, 1966), 12–24.
45 *Household Words* (9 December 1854): 392–3.
46 Juliet John, *Dickens's Villains* (Oxford: Oxford University Press, 2001), 7.
47 Charles Dickens, *Bleak House*, Oxford Illustrated Dickens (London: Oxford University Press, 1991), 269.
48 Fred Kaplan discusses the different stresses of Romanticism and sentimentalism in *Sacred Tears: Sentimentality in Victorian Literature* (Princeton: Princeton University Press, 1987), 9.

49 Wilkie Collins, *The Frozen Deep*, reproduced in R. L. Brannan, *Under the Management of Mr Charles Dickens* (Ithaca, NY: Cornell University Press, 1966), 160.
50 'All that she saw was new and wonderful, but it was not real; it seemed to her as if those visions of mountains and picturesque countries might melt away at any moment, and the carriage, turning some abrupt corner, bring up with a jolt at the old Marshalsea gate.' *Little Dorrit*, 463.
51 Brannan, *Under the Management of Mr Charles Dickens*, 23.
52 Eve Kosofsky Sedgwick, *Between Men* (New York: Columbia University Press, 1985), 162.
53 Barbara Hardy, *Forms of Feeling in Victorian Fiction* (London: Methuen 1985), 12f.
54 *Our Mutual Friend*, 812.
55 Cited in Brannan, 75–6.
56 *The Examiner* (17 January 1857): 38–9.
57 Brannan, *Under the Management of Mr Charles Dickens*, 77.
58 Johann Wolfgang von Goethe, *The Sorrows of Young Werther* (1774). See my Introduction.
59 *Dickensian*, 38 (1942), 189–91, quoted in Brannan, *Under the Management of Mr Charles Dickens*, 72. My emphasis.
60 To Mrs Richard Watson, *Letters*, VIII, 488.
61 To Collins, 21 March 1858, *Letters*, VIII, 536.
62 Gesa Stedman, *Stemming the Torrent* (Aldershot: Ashgate, 2002), 42.
63 *Letters*, VIII, 441–2.
64 *Letters*, VIII, 624.
65 George Meredith, *Diana of the Crossways* (London: Virago, 1980), 14.

# Chapter 5   The Early Novels and *The Vicar of Wakefield*

1 *The Old Curiosity Shop*, 412.
2 *A Christmas Carol* is obviously relevant to any argument about Dickens's sentimentalism, and I deal with it more extensively elsewhere (in *Sentimentalism in the Nineteenth-Century Novel*, forthcoming). Like *Barnaby Rudge* (1841) one of Dickens's two excursions into the genre of historical novel, it deserves much fuller consideration than the brief note I have been able to accord it here. *Barnaby Rudge* contains the figure of Dolly Varden, one of Dickens's few coquettish sentimental heroines, while *A Christmas Carol* builds on the figure of the crippled child as a locus of sentimental and reforming emotion.
3 Michael Slater, *Charles Dickens* (New York and London: Yale University Press, 2009), 262.
4 Philip Collins, 'Dickens's Reading', *Dickensian* 60 (1964): 136–42.
5 Clive T. Probyn, *English Fiction of the Eighteenth Century* (London: Longman, 1987), 157.
6 Oliver Goldsmith, *The Vicar of Wakefield* (Oxford: Oxford University Press, 2008), 90. All subsequent page references in the text are to this edition.
7 Roland Barthes, 'The Death of the Author', from *Image-Music-Text*, translated by Stephen Heath, 1977. Reprinted in David Lodge, ed., *Modern Criticism and Theory* (Harlow: Longman, 1987), 167–72.
8 Wolfgang Iser, *The Implied Reader: Patterns of Communication in Prose Fiction from Bunyan to Beckett* (Baltimore: Johns Hopkins Press, 1974), passim.
9 Quoted in A. Alvarez's introduction to Laurence Sterne, *A Sentimental Journey through France and Italy by Mr Yorick*, ed. Graham Petrie, with an introduction by A. Alvarez (Harmondsworth: Penguin, 1967), 11.

10 Q. D. Leavis, *Fiction and the Reading Public* (London: Chatto and Windus, 1965), passim, for example 233, 266.
11 R. Robison, 'Dickens and the Sentimental Tradition: Mr Pickwick and Uncle Toby', *University of Toronto Quarterly* 39 (1970): 258–73; David Parker '*The Pickwick Papers*', *A Companion to Charles Dickens*, ed. David Paroissien (Oxford: Blackwell, 2008): 297–308.
12 Quoted in John Forster, *The Life of Charles Dickens*, 2 vols, Everyman's Library (London: J. M. Dent, 1966), I, 59.
13 David Parker, '*The Pickwick Papers*', in David Paroissien, *A Companion to Charles Dickens* (Oxford: Blackwell, 2008), 301.
14 Barbara Hardy, *Forms of Feeling in Victorian Fiction* (London: Methuen, 1985), 5.
15 Steven Connor, Introduction to *Oliver Twist* (London: Dent, 1994), xxx.
16 Brian Cheadle, '*Oliver Twist*', in *A Companion to Charles Dickens*, ed. Paroissien, 312.
17 Kirstie Blair, *Victorian Poetry and the Culture of the Heart* (Oxford: Oxford University Press, 2006), 24, 1, 11.
18 Ibid., 1.
19 Ibid., 11.
20 Charles Bell, *Essays on the Anatomy and Philosophy of Expression, as Connected with the Fine Arts*. (London: John Murray, 1834), 84ff.
21 Charles Bray, *The Education of the Feelings* (London: Taylor and Watson, 1838), 13.
22 Marcus Wood, *Slavery, Empathy and Pornography* (Oxford: Oxford University Press, 2002), 129.
23 Goldsmith, *The Vicar of Wakefield*, 80.
24 *Bleak House* (London: Penguin, 1971), 696.
25 *Nicholas Nickleby* (London: Dent, 1994), 408.
26 Ibid., 518.
27 Ibid., 762.
28 *The Old Curiosity Shop*, 33.
29 Charles Darwin, *On the Expression of Emotion in Man and Animals* (London: The Folio Society, 1990), 111.
30 Norman Page, Introduction to *The Old Curiosity Shop* (London: Penguin, 2000), xii; *The Old Curiosity Shop* (London: Penguin, 2000), 401.
31 Bray, *The Education of the Feelings*, 153.
32 See, for example, Tzvetan Todorov, *The Poetics of Prose*, trans. Richard Howard (Oxford: Wiley-Blackwell, 1977), passim.
33 *The Old Curiosity Shop*, 377.
34 Ibid., 557.
35 Gabriel Pearson, '*The Old Curiosity Shop*', in *Dickens and the Twentieth Century*, ed. John Gross and Gabriel Pearson (London: Routledge and Kegan Paul 1962), 85.
36 Algernon Swinburne, 'Charles Dickens', *Quarterly Review* 196 (1902): 196.
37 Gabriel Pearson in *Dickens and the Twentieth Century*, 84.
38 Gill Ballinger, '*The Old Curiosity Shop*', in *A Companion to Charles Dickens*, ed. Paroissien, 330.
39 Ibid., 330.
40 Matthew Arnold, 'The Future', in *Poems of Matthew Arnold*, ed. Kenneth Allott (London: Longman, 1965), 263–7.
41 Matthew Arnold, 'The Study of Poetry', in *English Critical Texts*, ed. D. J. Enright and Ernst de Chickera (Oxford: Oxford University Press, 1962), 260.
42 Dickens's presentation of Betsy Trotwood's protégé, Mr Dick, in *David Copperfield* is a similarly radical treatment of insanity, making mental disturbance acceptable to the reading public through the use of sentimentalist techniques.

43 George Gissing, *Critical Studies of the Works of Charles Dickens* (New York: Greenberg, 1924), 122.
44 This discussion owes a great deal to Juliet Binns's unpublished Anglia Ruskin University undergraduate dissertation, 'Dickens's Christmases: A New Historicist Approach' (2011), 10–11.
45 In *Sentimentalism in the Nineteenth-Century Novel* (forthcoming).
46 Richard Brinsley Sheridan, *The School for Scandal and Other Plays* (Oxford: Oxford University Press, 2008), 211.
47 Richard Brinsley Sheridan, *The School for Scandal*, ed. F. W. Bateson (London: Ernest Benn, 1979), 13.
48 Ibid., 13.
49 From the Everyman edition, ed. Michael Slater (London: Dent, 1994), 786. The version used in the Clarendon edition (below) is in this case less appropriate to the point being made:

> As it resounds within thee and without…the noble music, rolling round her in a cloud of melody, shuts out the grosser prospect of an earthly parting, and uplifts her, Tom, to Heaven!

50 Preface to the first Cheap Edition of *Martin Chuzzlewit* (London: Chapman and Hall, 1849), reprinted in Slater's 1994 edition, xlii.
51 Charles Bray, *The Education of the Feelings*, 25.
52 Steven Marcus, *Dickens from Pickwick to Dombey* (New York: Norton, 1985), 213.
53 Dylan Evans, *Emotion: The Science of Sentiment* (Oxford: Oxford University Press, 2001), 85.
54 *Martin Chuzzlewit*, ed. Slater, xxviii.
55 *Letters*, III, 590.
56 Mamie Dickens's account is quoted in Philip Collins, ed., *Dickens: The Critical Heritage* (London: Routledge and Kegan Paul, 1971), 121.
57 Goldie Morgenthaler, 'Martin Chuzzlewit', in *A Companion to Charles Dickens*, ed. Paroissien, 349.
58 'Thee' was still a powerful term of intimacy until late in the nineteenth century. Alfred, Lord Tennyson and his wife Emily used it in their letters to each other throughout their lives.
59 Oliver Goldsmith, *The Vicar of Wakefield*, ed. Arthur Friedman and Robert L. Mack (Oxford: Oxford University Press, 2006), 9.
60 Charles Lamb, 'Dream Children', *Essays of Elia* (London: Hesperus Press, 2009), 113.

## Chapter 6   The Later Novels

1 *Dombey and Son*, title of chapter 16, describing Paul's death.
2 Virginia Woolf, 'David Copperfield', *Nation*, 22 August 1925 (collected in *The Moment and Other Essays*, 1947) reprinted in Stephen Wall, ed., *Charles Dickens* (Harmondsworth: Penguin, 1970), 274.
3 Robert Garis, *The Dickens Theatre: A Reassessment of the Novels* (Oxford: Clarendon Press, 1965), 98.
4 Reprinted in *Charles Dickens: A Critical Anthology*, ed. Stephen Wall (Harmondsworth: Penguin, 1970), 176.
5 The 'interview' takes place at the end of chapter 24 in Peter Ackroyd, *Dickens* (London: Sinclair-Stevenson, 1990), 753–55.

6 Bradley Deane, *The Making of the Victorian Novelist* (New York: Routledge, 2003).
7 Samuel Johnson, 'Preface to Shakespeare' in *English Critical Texts*, ed. D. J. Enright and Ernst de Chickera (Oxford: Oxford University Press, 1962), 140.
8 Master Humphrey is a character in the action (intradiegetic); he gives way to a more anonymous extradiegetic narrator when the novel changes and becomes *The Old Curiosity Shop*. The terms were established by narratologist Gerard Genette in *Narrative Discourse* (Ithaca, NY: Cornell University Press, 1980; originally *Figures III*, Paris: Seuil, 1972) and are most accessibly used by Shlomith Rimmon-Kenan in *Narrative Fiction: Contemporary Poetics* (London: Methuen, 1983), 91–4.
9 John Forster, *The Life of Charles Dickens*, 2 vols (London: J. M. Dent, 1966), II, 23.
10 Ibid., II, 29.
11 Ibid., I, 31.
12 Colley Cibber, *The Careless Husband* [1704] (London: British Library Historical Collection, n.d.), 51.
13 Fanny Burney, *Evelina or the History of a Young Lady's Entrance into the World* (Stroud: Nonesuch, 2007), 423–4.
14 All subsequent quotations from this scene are from 483–4.
15 31 January 1847, quoted by Philip Collins, ed., in *Dickens: The Critical Heritage* (London: Routledge and Kegan Paul, 1971), 217. The moral and the aesthetic blend in Jeffrey's account, just as they did in the sentimental scene itself: 'Since the divine Nelly was found dead on her humble couch, beneath the snow and the ivy, there has been nothing like the actual dying of that sweet Paul, in the summer sunshine of that lofty room. And the long vista, that leads us so gently and sadly, and yet so gracefully and winningly, to the plain consummation!'
16 Julian Moynahan, 'Dealings with the Firm of Dombey and Son: Firmness v. Wetness', in *Dickens and the Twentieth Century*, ed. John Gross and Gabriel Pearson (London: Routledge and Kegan Paul, 1962), 121–31.
17 Ibid., 124–5.
18 Ibid., 130.
19 *Our Mutual Friend*, New Oxford Illustrated Dickens (1964), 397.
20 John Carey, *The Violent Effigy: A Study of Dickens' Imagination* (London: Faber, 1973), 20.
21 Moynahan in *Dickens and the Twentieth Century*, 127.
22 Laurence Sterne, *The Life and Opinions of Tristram Shandy, Gentleman* (London: Penguin, 2003), 438, 444.
23 Wilkie Collins, *No Name* (Oxford: Oxford University Press, 2008), 699.
24 Kenneth Clark, *Civilisation: A Personal View* (London: British Broadcasting Corporation, 1971), 226.
25 Dickens's extraordinarily strong response to Browning's play is recorded in Forster, *Life* (1966) I, 274–5: it threw him, Dickens confesses, 'into a perfect passion of sorrow… I know nothing that is so affecting, nothing in any book I have read… I know no love like it, no passion like it…'
26 Q. D. Leavis recognised the complexity of Dickens's presentation of Paul in *Dickens the Novelist* (London: Chatto and Windus, 1970), 14–23, but her argument, which has been extremely influential on all later readings, is that the success indicated a triumph over the sentimental. Juliet John gives an energising rereading of the *melodramatic* as opposed to the sentimental aspects of the novel in *Dickens's Villains* (Oxford: Oxford University Press 2001), 215–23.

27 *Letters*, VIII, 676.
28 Jacques Lacan's triadic system of the symbolic, imaginary and the real is most clearly explained by Malcolm Bowie in *Lacan* (London: Fontana Press, 1991), 91–106.
29 Michael Slater, *Dickens and Women* (London: Dent, 1983), 144.
30 Steven Connor, Introduction to *Oliver Twist* (London: Dent, 1994), xxvii.
31 John Ruskin, 'Unto This Last' (1862) in *Works*, ed. E. T. Cook and Alexander Wedderburn, 39 vols (London: George Allen, 1903–1912), XXXVII, 91n.
32 *Bleak House* (London: Penguin, 1971), 131.
33 Ibid., 77.
34 Ibid., 62.
35 *Oliver Twist* (London: Dent, 1994), 206.
36 Wolfgang Herrlinger, *Sentimentalismus und Postsentimentalismus: Studien zum englischen Roman bis zur Mitte des 19. Jahrhunderts* (Tubingen: Max Niemeyer, 1987), 364.
37 Ibid., 492.
38 A similar point is made in Alison Case and Harry E. Shaw, *Reading the Nineteenth-Century Novel: Austen to Eliot* (Oxford: Blackwell, 2008), 134.
39 *Bleak House*, 692, 703, 705.
40 Ibid., 705.
41 Harvey Peter Sucksmith, *The Narrative Art of Charles Dickens* (Oxford: Clarendon Press, 1970), 172.
42 Ibid., 173.
43 Herrlinger, *Sentimentalismus*, 365.
44 *A Tale of Two Cities* (London: Dent, 1994), 3.
45 Ibid., 377.
46 Ibid., no page number. My emphases.
47 *Great Expectations* (London: Penguin 1994), 9.
48 *Charles Dickens' Book of Memoranda*, ed. Fred Kaplan (New York: New York Public Library, 1981); cited in Adrian Poole, introduction to *Our Mutual Friend* (London: Penguin, 1997), xi.
49 In Dickens's final, unfinished novel, *The Mystery of Edwin Drood*, Dickens turns back in a key scene between John Jasper and Rosa Bud, to the simple sentimental rhetoric of *Oliver Twist*. Arguably he needs to do so, as he does in Oliver, to balance the power of the 'dark' scenes in the novel. The novel after all begins with a central character in a drugged stupor in a London opium den. However, it seems unlikely that the Jasper/Rosa confrontation would have appealed to the reading public in the 1870s as it would have done in the 1830s.
50 Herrlinger, *Sentimentalismus*, 365.
51 Barbara Hardy, *Forms of Feeling in Victorian Fiction* (London: Methuen 1985), 63–76.
52 Paul Schlicke, ed., *The Oxford Reader's Companion to Charles Dickens* (Oxford: Oxford University Press, 1999), 513.

## Conclusion   The Afterlife of Sentimentalism

1 Roland Barthes, 'A Lover's Discourse', reprinted in *A Barthes Reader*, ed. Susan Sontag (London: Jonathan Cape, 1982), 427.
2 Charles Lamb, 'On the Artificial Comedy of the Last Century', *Essays of Elia* (London: Hesperus Press, 2009), 161.

3 Ibid., 162.
4 Wolfgang Herrlinger, *Sentimentalismus und Postsentimentalismus: Studien zum englischen Roman bis zur Mitte des 19. Jahrhunderts* (Tubingen: Max Niemeyer, 1987), 365.
5 I am well aware that Dickens has a range of complex narrative voices – as David Parker has explored in relation to *A Christmas Carol* and as I suggest in Chapter 5 in exploring the move from didactic guide to sympathetic friend – but my point is that one clearly recognisable and recurring tone is that of the familiar and reassuring sentimental narrator.
6 *Athenaeum* (3 December 1836): 841–3, reprinted in *Dickens: The Critical Heritage*, ed. Philip Collins (London: Routledge and Kegan Paul, 1971), 32.
7 George Henry Lewes, 'Dickens in Relation to Criticism', *Fortnightly Review*, 27 (1872): 143–51; quoted in *Charles Dickens: A Critical Anthology*, ed. Stephen Wall (Harmondsworth: Penguin, 1970), 195, 202.
8 John Stuart Mill, letter to Harriet Mill, March 1854, quoted in *Charles Dickens: A Critical Anthology*, ed. Wall, 95.
9 From 'The Natural History of German Life', *Westminster Review* 66 (July 1856), quoted in *Charles Dickens: A Critical Anthology*, ed. Wall, 98.
10 Walter Bagehot, from 'Charles Dickens', a review of the library edition of Dickens's *Works*, *National Review* 7 (October 1858), reprinted in *Literary Studies* 2 (1911), quoted in *Charles Dickens: A Critical Anthology*, ed. Wall, 124–5.
11 *Saturday Review* 5 (8 May 1858): 474–5.
12 From Hippolyte Taine, 'Charles Dickens, son talent et ses œuvres', *Revue des Deux Mondes* (February 1856), later incorporated into his *History of English Literature*, trans. H. Van Laun, 2 vols (Edinburgh: Edmonston and Douglas, 1871), book 5, chapter 1, quoted in *Charles Dickens: A Critical Anthology*, ed. Wall, 99.
13 Stanley T. Williams, 'The English Sentimental Drama from Steele to Cumberland', *Sewanee Review* 33, no. 4 (October 1925): 408.
14 Ibid., 410.
15 Aldous Huxley, *Vulgarity in Literature* (London: Chatto and Windus, 1930), 56, quoted in *A Companion to Charles Dickens*, ed. David Paroissien (Oxford: Blackwell, 2008), 331.
16 Eric Bentley, *The Life of the Drama* (New York: Athenaeum, 1964), 198, quoted in Juliet John, *Dickens's Villains* (Oxford: Oxford University Press, 2001), 42.
17 Roland Barthes, 'In Praise of Tears', in *A Lover's Discourse*, trans. Richard Howard (New York: Hill and Wang, 1978), 426–7.
18 *Martin Chuzzlewit*, 10.
19 Juliet Johns, *Dickens's Villains* (Oxford: Oxford University Press, 2001), 16.
20 Ibid., 6.
21 It is certainly true that sentimentalism works by disarming an intellectual response, but that rhetorical process requires considerable technical skill and is not to be confused for lack of intelligence – on the part of writer or reader.
22 Michele Byers and David Lavery, eds, *On the Verge of Tears: Why the Movies, Television, Music, Art, Popular Culture, Literature and the Real World Make Us Cry* (2010).
23 Roland Barthes, 'In Praise of Tears', in *A Lover's Discourse*, translated by Richard Howard (New York: Hill and Wang, 1978), 426–7.
24 Charles Darwin, *On the Expression of the Emotions in Man and in Animals* [1872] (London: Folio Society, 1990), 147.
25 Gilles Deleuze, *Pure Immanence*, trans. Anne Boyman (New York: Zone Books, 2001), reviewed by Ellen E. Berry: http://www.reconstruction.eserver.org/BRreviews/revPure.

htm (accessed 10 October 2011). I would like to thank Jason Wakefield for drawing my attention to this volume.
26 Ellen E. Berry, ibid.
27 Isobel Armstrong, 'The Role and Treatment of Emotion in Victorian Criticism of Poetry', *Victorian Periodicals Newsletter* 10, no. 1 (1977): 2.

# BIBLIOGRAPHY

## Primary Sources

Abercrombie, John. *The Philosophy of the Moral Feelings*. London: John Murray, 1833.
Bell, Charles. *Essays on the Anatomy and Philosophy of Expression, as Connected with the Fine Arts*. London: John Murray, 1834.
Bray, Charles. *The Education of the Feelings*. London: Taylor and Watson, 1838.
Burney, Fanny. *Evelina or the History of a Young Lady's Entrance into the World*. London: J. M. Dent, 1960.
———. *Memoirs of Dr. Burney*. London: Edward Moxon, 1832.
Collins, Wilkie. *The Frozen Deep and Other Tales*. London: Chatto and Windus, 1905.
———. *No Name*. London: Anthony Blond, 1966.
Cumberland, Richard. *The West Indian*. In *The British Theatre: or, A Collection of Plays*, edited by Elizabeth Inchbald, vol. 18. London: Longman, 1808.
Darwin, Charles. *On the Origin of Species*. London: John Murray 1859.
[Dickens, Charles]. 'A Child's Dream of a Star'. *Household Words* 1 (6 April 1850): 25–6. In *Dickens' Journalism, Volume 2 – The Amusements of the People and Other Papers: Reports, Essays and Reviews 1834–51*, edited by Michael Slater, 185–88. London: J. M. Dent, 1996.
Dobell, Horace. *On Affections of the Heart and in Its Neighbourhood*. London: H. K. Lewis, 1872.
Fielding, Henry. *The History of Tom Jones, A Foundling*. London: Wordsworth Classics, 1999.
———. *Joseph Andrews; and, Shamela*. Edited by Martin Battestin. Boston: Houghton Mifflin, 1961.
Forster, John. *The Life of Charles Dickens*. 2 vols. Everyman's Library. London: J. M. Dent, 1966.
Furnivall, J. J. *The Diagnosis, Prevention and Treatment of Disease of the Heart*. London: John Churchill, 1845.
Goethe, Johann Wolfgang von. *The Sorrows of Young Werther; The New Melusina; Novelle*. Translated by Victor Lange. New York: Holt, Rinehart and Winston, 1949.
Goldsmith, Oliver. *Poems and Plays*. Edited by Tom Davis. London: J. M. Dent, 1990.
———. 'A Comparison between Laughing and Sentimental Comedy'. *The Westminster Magazine* (1773) reprinted in *Goldsmith: The Critical Heritage*, edited by G. S. Rousseau. London: Routledge and Kegan Paul, 1974.
———. *The Vicar of Wakefield*. Edited by Arthur Friedman and Robert L. Mack. Oxford: Oxford University Press, 2006.
Inchbald, Elizabeth. *Every One has His Fault: A Comedy*. In *Sentimental Comedy: Theory and Practice*, edited by Frank H. Ellis, 176–221. Cambridge: Cambridge University Press, 1991.

———, ed. *Werter*. In *The Modern Theatre: A Collection of Modern Plays*, vol. 3, 292–319. London: Longman, Hurst, Rees, Orme and Brown, 1811.
Jonson, Ben, *Every Man in His Humour*. London: A&C Black, 1998.
Keble, John. *Keble's Lectures on Poetry, 1832–41*. Translated by Edward Kershaw Francis. 2 vols. Oxford: Clarendon Press, 1912.
Lamb, Charles. 'On the Artificial Comedy of the Last Century'. In *Essays of Elia*. London: Hesperus Press, 2009.
Lytton, Edward Bulwer Lytton, Baron. *Dramatic Works*. London: George Routledge, n.d.
Mackenzie, Henry. *The Man of Feeling* 2nd ed. London: printed for T. Cadell, 1771.
———. *The Man of the World*. In two parts. London: printed for W. Strahan and T. Cadell, 1773.
Otway, Thomas. *Venice Preserved*. Edited by Malcolm Kelsall. London: Edward Arnold, 1969.
Richardson, Samuel. *Clarissa or The History of a Young Lady*. Abridged by George Sherburn. Boston: Houghton Mifflin, 1962.
———. *Pamela: Or Virtue Rewarded*. Oxford: Oxford University Press, 2001.
Shaftesbury, Anthony Ashley Cooper, Earl of. *Characteristics of Men, Manners, Opinions, Times*. Edited by John M. Robertson. New York: Bobbs-Merrill, 1964.
Sheridan, Richard Brinsley. *The Plays and Poems*. Edited by R. Crompton-Rhodes. Oxford: Basil Blackwell, 1928.
———. *The School for Scandal and Other Plays*. Oxford: Oxford University Press, 1998.
Schiller, Friedrich. *Uber Naive und Sentimentalische Dichtung*. Translated by Julius A. Elias. New York: Frederick Ungar Publishing Co., 1966.
Steele, Richard. *The Plays of Richard Steele*. Edited by Shirley Strum Kenny. Oxford: Clarendon Press, 1971.
Sterne, Laurence. *The Life and Opinions of Tristram Shandy, Gentleman*. Edited by Ian Watt. Boston: Houghton Mifflin, 1965.
———. *Letters of Laurence Sterne*. Edited by L. P. Curtis. Oxford: Oxford University Press, 1935.
———. *A Sentimental Journey through France and Italy by Mr. Yorick*. Edited by Graham Petrie, with an Introduction by A. Alvarez. Harmondsworth: Penguin, 1967.
Tate, Nahum. *King Lear*. In *Shakespeare Adaptations: The Tempest, the Mock Tempest, and King Lear*, edited by Montague Summers. New York: Blom, 1966.
Thackeray, W. M. *The English Humorists*. London: Smith Elder, 1889.

## Secondary Sources

Ackroyd, Peter. *Dickens*. London: Sinclair-Stevenson, 1990.
Armstrong, Isobel. 'The Role and Treatment of Emotion in Victorian Criticism of Poetry'. *Victorian Periodicals Newsletter* 10, no. 1 (March 1977): 13–16.
———. *Victorian Poetry: Poetry, Poetics and Politics*. London: Routledge, 1993.
Auburn, Mark S. *Sheridan's Comedies: Their Contexts and Achievements*. Lincoln, NE: University of Nebraska Press, 1977.
Axton, William. *Circle of Fire: Dickens' Vision and Style and the Popular Victorian Theatre*. Lexington: University of Kentucky Press, 1966.
Bakhtin, Mikhail. *The Dialogic Imagination*. Edited by Michael Holquist, translated by Caryl Emerson and Michael Holquist. Austin: University of Texas Press, 1981.

Barthes, Roland. *A Lover's Discourse*. Translated by Richard Howard. New York: Hill and Wang, 1978.
Bayley, John. *The Uses of Division: Unity and Disharmony in Literature*. London: Chatto and Windus, 1976.
Beer, Gillian. *Darwin's Plots: Evolutionary Narrative in Darwin, George Eliot and Nineteenth-Century Fiction*. 3rd ed. Cambridge: Cambridge University Press, 2009.
Bentley, Eric. *The Life of the Drama*. New York: Atheneum, 1964.
Bernbaum, Ernest. *The Drama of Sensibility*. Boston: Ginn, 1915.
Bevis, Matthew. 'Temporising Dickens'. *Review of English Studies* 52 (2001): 171–91.
Blair, Kirstie. *Victorian Poetry and the Culture of the Heart*. Oxford: Oxford University Press, 2006.
Bloom, Harold. *The Anxiety of Influence*. 2nd ed. Oxford: Oxford University Press. 1997.
Bourdieu, Pierre. *Outline of a Theory of Practice*. Translated by Richard Nice. Cambridge: Cambridge University Press, 1977.
Brannan, R. L. *Under the Management of Mr Charles Dickens: His Production of "The Frozen Deep"*. Ithaca, NY: Cornell University Press, 1966.
Brennan, Teresa. *The Transmission of Affect*. Ithaca, NY: Cornell University Press, 2004.
Brooks, Cleanth. *Modern Poetry and the Tradition*. Chapel Hill: University of North Carolina Press, 1948.
Butler, Judith. *Gender Trouble: Feminism and the Subversion of Identity*. London: Routledge, 1990.
Carey, John. *The Violent Effigy: A Study of Dickens' Imagination*. London: Faber, 1973.
Churchill, R. C. 'Dickens, Drama and Tradition'. *Scrutiny* 10 (April 1942): 358–75.
Collins, Philip, ed. *Dickens: The Critical Heritage*. London: Routledge and Kegan Paul, 1971.
———. *From Manly Tear to Stiff Upper Lip: The Victorians and Pathos*. Wellington: Victoria University Press, 1975.
Cornelius, Randolph. *The Science of Emotion*. Upper Saddle River, NJ: Prentice-Hall, 1995.
Cunningham, Valentine. 'Dickens and Christianity'. In *A Companion to Charles Dickens*, edited by David Paroissien, 255–76. Oxford: Blackwell, 2008.
Darlington, W. A. *Sheridan: Writers and Their Work*, no. 18. London: Longmans, Green, & Co.1966.
Davis, Earle R. *The Flint and the Flame: The Artistry of Charles Dickens*. Columbia: University of Missouri Press, 1963.
Deane, Bradley. *The Making of the Victorian Novelist*. New York: Routledge, 2003.
Dibelius, Wilhelm. *Charles Dickens*. Leipzig: B. Teubner, 1916.
Downer, Alan S. 'Nature to Advantage Dressed: Eighteenth-Century Acting'. *PMLA* 58, no. 4 (1943): 1002–37.
Ellis, Frank H. *Sentimental Comedy: Theory and Practice*. Cambridge: Cambridge University Press, 1991.
Erämetsä, Eric. *A Study of the Word 'Sentimental' and of Other Linguistic Characteristics of Eighteenth-Century Sentimentalism in England*. Helsinki: Suomalainen Tiedeakatemia, 1951.
Evans, Dylan. *Emotion: The Science of Sentiment*. Oxford: Oxford University Press, 2001.
Flint, Kate. *Dickens*. Brighton: Harvester Press, 1986.
Fludernik, Monika. 'The Eighteenth-Century Legacy'. In *A Companion to Charles Dickens*, edited by David Paroissien, 65–80. Oxford: Blackwell, 2008.
Freud, Sigmund. 'On Dreams'. In *The Essentials of Psychoanalysis*, 81–125. London: Penguin, 1986.
Frey, William. *Crying: The Mystery of Tears*. Minneapolis: Winston Press, 1985.

Genette, Gerard, *Narrative Discourse: An Essay on Method*. Translated by Janet E. Lewin (Ithaca, NY: Cornell University Press, 1983).
Gissing, George. *Critical Studies of the Works of Charles Dickens*. New York: Greenberg, 1924.
Gummer, Ellis N. *Dickens' Works in Germany*. New York: Octagon Books, 1976.
Hardy, Barbara. *Forms of Feeling in Victorian Fiction*. London: Methuen, 1985.
Herrlinger, Wolfgang. *Sentimentalismus und Postsentimentalismus: Studien zum englischen Roman bis zur Mitte des 19. Jahrhunderts*. Tubingen: Max Niemeyer, 1987.
Hopkins, Robert H. *The True Genius of Oliver Goldsmith*. Baltimore: Johns Hopkins University Press, 1969.
Jeffares, A. Norman. *A Goldsmith Selection*. Basingstoke: Macmillan, 1963.
John, Juliet. *Dickens's Villains*. Oxford: Oxford University Press, 2001.
John, Juliet and Alice Jenkins, eds. *Rethinking Victorian Culture*. Basingstoke: Macmillan, 2000.
Johnson, Edgar. *Charles Dickens: His Tragedy and His Triumph*. Rev. and abbr. ed. Harmondsworth: Penguin, 1979.
Joseph, Bertram. *The Tragic Actor*. London: Routledge and Kegan Paul, 1959.
Kaplan, Fred. *Sacred Tears: Sentimentality in Victorian Literature*. Princeton: Princeton University Press, 1987.
Kearney, Anthony M. *Samuel Richardson, Clarissa*. Studies in English Literature, no. 55. London: Edward Arnold, 1975.
Kermode, Frank. *The Sense of an Ending: with a new Epilogue*. Oxford: Oxford University Press 2000.
Ledger, Sally. *Dickens and the Popular Radical Imagination*. Cambridge: Cambridge University Press, 2007.
Leavis, F. R. and Q. D. Leavis. *Dickens the Novelist*. London: Chatto and Windus, 1970.
Leavis, F. R. *The Common Pursuit*. London: Chatto and Windus, 1972.
Leavis, Q. D. *Fiction and the Reading Public*. London: Chatto and Windus, 1965.
Marcus, Steven. *Dickens, from Pickwick to Dombey*. New York: W. W. Norton, 1985.
Miles, Josephine. *Wordsworth and the Vocabulary of Emotion*. New York: Octagon, 1965.
Nicoll, Allardyce. *A History of English Drama 1660–1900*. 6 vols. Cambridge: Cambridge University Press, 1923–59.
Nuttall, A. D. *A Common Sky: Philosophy and the Literary Imagination*. London: Chatto and Windus, 1974.
O'Gorman, F. and K. Turner, eds. *The Victorians and the Eighteenth Century: Reassessing the Tradition*. Aldershot: Ashgate, 2004.
Page, Norman. 'A language fit for heroes: Speech in *Oliver Twist* and *Our Mutual Friend*'. *Dickensian* 65 (May 1969): 100–10.
———. *Speech in the English Novel*. London: Longman, 1973.
Parker, David. 'Dickens's Archness'. *Dickensian* 67 (September 1971): 149–58.
———. '*The Pickwick Papers*'. In *A Companion to Charles Dickens*, edited by David Paroissien, 297–308. Oxford: Blackwell, 2008.
Patten, Robert L. '"I thought of Mr Pickwick and Wrote the First Number": Dickens and the Evolution of Character'. *Dickens Quarterly* 3 (1986): 18–25.
Perkins, David. *Wordsworth and the Poetry of Sincerity*. Cambridge, MA: Belknap Press, 1964.
Porter, Roy. 'History of the Body'. In *New Perspectives on Historical Writing*, edited by Peter Burke, 206–32. Cambridge: Polity Press, 1991.
Praz, Mario. *The Hero in Eclipse in Victorian Fiction*. Translated by A. Davidson. London: Oxford University Press, 1956.

Probyn, Clive T. *English Fiction of the Eighteenth Century*. London: Longman, 1987.
Probyn, Elspeth. *Blush: Faces of Shame*. Sydney: University of New South Wales Press, 2005.
Quintana, Ricardo. *Oliver Goldsmith: A Georgian Study*. London: Weidenfeld and Nicholson, 1967.
Quirk, Randolph. *Charles Dickens and Appropriate Language*. Durham: University of Durham, 1969.
Rimmon-Kenan, Shlomith. *Narrative Fiction: Contemporary Poetics*. London: Methuen, 1983.
Robison, R. 'Dickens and the Sentimental Tradition: Mr Pickwick and Uncle Toby'. *University of Toronto Quarterly* 39 (1970): 258–73.
Rousseau, G. S., ed. *Goldsmith: The Critical Heritage*. London: Routledge and Kegan Paul, 1974.
Schad, John, ed. *Dickens Refigured: Bodies, Desires and Other Histories*. Manchester: Manchester University Press, 1996.
Schlicke, Paul. *Dickens and Popular Entertainment*. London: Unwin Hyman, 1988.
———, ed. *The Oxford Reader's Companion to Dickens*. Oxford: Oxford University Press, 1999.
Sedgwick, Eve Kosofsky. *Between Men: English Literature and Male Homosocial Desire*. New York: Columbia University Press, 1985.
Sherbo, Arthur. *English Sentimental Drama*. East Lansing: Michigan State University Press, 1957.
Slater, Michael. *Dickens and Women*. London: Dent, 1983.
———. *Charles Dickens*. New York and London: Yale University Press, 2009.
Small, Helen. 'The Debt to Society: Dickens, Fielding and the Genealogy of Independence'. In *The Victorians and the Eighteenth Century: Reassessing the Tradition*, edited by F. O'Gorman and K. Turner, 14–40. Aldershot: Ashgate, 2004.
Stedman, Gesa. *Stemming the Torrent: Expression and Control in the Victorian Discourses on Emotion, 1830–1872*. Aldershot: Ashgate, 2002.
Stone, Harry. *The Night Side of Dickens: Cannibalism, Passion, Necessity*. Columbus: Ohio State University Press, 1994.
Sucksmith, Harvey Peter. *The Narrative Art of Charles Dickens*. Oxford: Clarendon Press, 1970.
Sussman, Herbert L. *Victorian Masculinities: Manhood and Masculine Poetics in Early Victorian Literature and Art*. Cambridge: Cambridge University Press, 1995.
Swindells, Julia. *Glorious Causes: The Grand Theatre of Political Change 1789–1833*. Oxford: Oxford University Press, 2001.
Tambling, Jeremy. *Dickens, Violence and the Modern State: Dreams of the Scaffold*. Basingstoke: Macmillan, 1995.
Taylor, George. '"The Just Delineation of the Passions": Theories of Acting in the Age of Garrick'. In *Essays on the Eighteenth-Century English Stage*, edited by Kenneth Richards and Peter Thomson, 51–73. London: Methuen, 1972.
Todd, Janet. *Sensibility: An Introduction*. London: Methuen, 1976.
Wall, Stephen, ed. *Charles Dickens: A Critical Anthology*. Harmondsworth: Penguin, 1970.
Waters, Catherine. *Dickens and the Politics of the Family*. Cambridge: Cambridge University Press, 1997.
Watt, Ian. *The Rise of the Novel: Studies in Defoe, Richardson and Fielding*. 2nd American ed. Berkeley and Los Angeles: University of California Press, 2001.
Williams, Stanley T. 'The English Sentimental Drama from Steele to Cumberland'. *Sewanee Review* 33, no. 4 (October 1925): 405–26.

Wilson, Angus. 'The Heroes and Heroines of Dickens'. In *Dickens and the Twentieth Century*, edited by John Gross and Gabriel Pearson. London: Routledge and Kegan Paul 1962.

Wilson, Edmund. 'Dickens: The Two Scrooges'. In *The Wound and the Bow: Seven Studies in Literature*, 1–93. London: Methuen, 1941.

Wollheim, Richard. *Art and its Objects: An Introduction to Aesthetics*. New York and London: Harper and Row, 1968.

Wood, Marcus. *Slavery, Empathy and Pornography*. Oxford: Oxford University Press, 2002.

# INDEX

Addison, Joseph xx, 2
Arnold, Matthew 108
associationism xxii, 15–16, 32, 103, 113
Austen, Jane 3, 22, 96; *Northanger Abbey* 64; *Sense and Sensibility* 3

Bagehot, Walter 152–3
Bagstock, Major (*Dombey and Son*) 47
Bakhtin, Mikhail 31, 38
Barthes, Roland 14–15, 31, 94, 155–7
*Battle of Life, The* 11, 91
Bell, Charles 11, 99–101
benevolence 10, 21, 23, 34, 50, 54, 59–61, 66, 91, 95–6, 101, 113, 141, 147
Bentham, Jeremy xviii
*Beowulf* xx
Bernini, Gian Lorenzo 131
Blackpool, Stephen (*Hard Times*) 143
Blake, William 25
*Bleak House* 59–61, 140–42, 152
body, the xvii–xviii, xxii, xiv, 8, 11–13, 94, 99–101
Boffin, Nicodemus (*Our Mutual Friend*) 55, 58, 147
Bourdieu, Pierre 130
Boswell, James 21
Bounderby, Josiah (*Hard Times*) 77, 123
Boyle, Mary 47–8
Bray, Charles xx, 9–10, 103, 113; *The Anatomy and Philosophy of Expression* 11; *The Education of the Feelings* xx, 9–10
Brecht, Bertolt 70
*British and Foreign Review, The* 5
Brownlow, Mr (*Oliver Twist*) 61
Browning, Robert 36; 'A Blot in the 'Scutcheon' 133

Bunyan, John 102
Burney, Frances 92; *Evelina* 125

Carlyle, Thomas 142
Carroll, Lewis 116
Carstone, Richard (*Bleak House*) 141
Carton, Sydney (*A Tale of Two Cities*) 61, 90
catharsis xxiv, 7, 41, 15, 88, 106, 155
Cattermole, George 77
Chadband, Reverend (*Bleak House*) 59, 82–3
Chambers, Robert: *Vestiges of the Natural History of Creation* 12
Cheeryble brothers (*Nicholas Nickleby*) 21, 61
children xv, xviii, xxii–xxiii, 4, 108, 155–6, 158; death of xv, xviii, xxvi, 13, 41, 124, 134–6, 141–2; education of 10, 103, 113; Romantic xxii–xxiii, 59, 64, 105–6, 141, 144; sentimental xxiii, 129, 134, 139; as victims xxiii, 101–2, 147
'Child's Dream of a Star, A' 72, 133
'Child's Story, The' 71
Christianity xxi–xxii, 9–11, 25, 40–41, 81, 85, 128, 142, 154
*Christmas Carol, A* 110
Chuzzlewit, Martin (*Martin Chuzzlewit*) 23
Cibber, Colley 2–3, 42, 46, 74; *The Careless Husband* 125–6
Clare, Ada (*Bleak House*) 140
Clark, Kenneth, Sir 131
Clennam, Arthur (*Little Dorrit*) 16, 81, 144
Coavinses (*Bleak House*) 59–60
Coleridge, Samuel Taylor xx, 70
Collins, Wilkie 78, 80, 130–33, 160; *The Frozen Deep* 14, 74–90, 103, 106,

130–32, 141, 145–6, 157, 159;
  *No Name* 81, 130–31; *No
  Thoroughfare* 84
Colman, George 2
comedy, sentimental 45–6, 86
costume 76, 117–18
Cratchit, Bob (*A Christmas Carol*) 73
*Cricket on the Hearth, The* 74, 77
Cruikshank, George 73, 81
Crummles troupe (*Nicholas Nickleby*) 67, 75
culture, popular xiv, 7, 75, 156–7
Cumberland, Richard 3, 30–31, 38
cynicism xiii, 22

Darnay, Charles (*A Tale of Two
  Cities*) 61, 90
Darwin, Charles xvii, 11–12, 15, 33,
  103, 157–8; *On the Expression of the
  Emotions in Man and Animals* 11–12,
  103; *On the Origin of Species* 11–12
*David Copperfield* 124, 139
death xiv, xxiv–xxv, 71, 83, 98, 107–8,
  130, 136, 139, 147–8; of children
  xv, xviii, xxvi, 13, 41, 124; of
  mothers xx, 30, 124; and sex 83;
  Victorian attitudes to xxv;
  *see also* graves
Dedlock, Lady (*Bleak House*) 9, 78
Descartes, René xx
Dick, Mr (*David Copperfield*) xxiii, 20
Dickens, Catherine 81
Dickens, Charles: as actor xxvi, 14, 47–8,
  50, 59, 73–90, 118, 146, 151; as
  Boz 46; childhood reading of 19,
  70; Christianity of xxi–xxii, 18, 22,
  136; 'divided style' of xix, 21, 29,
  31 – 3, 42, 67, 94, 105; ethics of
  xxi, 10, 18; influence of Goldsmith
  and Sheridan on 46–8, 55, 91–2,
  108, 119, 159; influence of Charles
  Lamb on 70–73, 108, 119; letters
  of, quoted 30, 46–7, 76–7, 80, 84,
  88–9, 115, 124, 135; misreading of
  authors by 30–31, 61, 67, 91–2,
  94, 159; narrative voices of xxvi,
  18, 22, 34, 59, 97, 109, 114, 122,
  124–7, 135, 140, 142, 146, 151;
  physical appearance of 81; private
  life of 81, 88, 123–4; readers of
  30, 94–5, 116, 121–3, 149, 151–2;
  public readings by 89, 123, 135; *see
  also under individual names/titles*
Dickens, Frances (Fanny) 124
Dickens, Mary (Mamie) 89, 118, 123
Dobell, Horace 12–14; *On Affections of the
  Heart* 12–14
*Dombey and Son* xxvi, 8, 25, 30, 32–3, 43,
  83, 103–4, 111, 114, 123–39, 143,
  151, 160
Dombey family (*Dombey and Son*) 1
Dombey, Florence (*Dombey and Son*) 1,
  25–6, 124–34, 136– 8
Dombey, Paul (Little) (*Dombey and Son*)
  xxiii, 106–7, 122, 134–6, 149
Dombey, Paul (Mr) (*Dombey and Son*)
  124–31, 135, 137
Dorrit, Amy (*Little Dorrit*) 1, 6, 144–5, 155
Dostoevsky, Fyodor 33; *The Idiot* 130
drama xxvi–xxvii; eighteenth-century
  2–3, 18, 45–67, 74, 86, 110;
  nineteenth-century 16–18, 69–90;
  Restoration 2, 56, 69, 79; *see also*
  mystery plays, medieval
Drood, Edwin (*The Mystery of Edwin
  Drood*) 61

Eliot, George 127–8, 146, 152, 159–60
emotions xiv, xvi–xviii, xx–xxi, xxiv–xxvi,
  4–5, 8–9, 11–12, 15–18, 23, 35,
  38–9, 42–3, 81, 83, 88–9, 115–17,
  131–3, 152, 156–8
*Englishman's Magazine, The* 5
eroticism xviii, xxii–xxiv, 6–7, 14–15,
  24–7, 33, 36, 83, 88, 90
Estella (*Great Expectations*) 16
evil 91–3, 97, 102, 111

femininity 28
Fezziwigs, The (*A Christmas Carol*) 55
Fielding, Henry xix, 20–24, 28–9, 36,
  151, 159; *Shamela Andrews* 29; *Tom
  Jones* 19–23
Finching, Flora (*Little Dorrit*) 61–2
FitzGerald, Edward xii, 105
Forster, John 71, 78, 80, 83, 115, 124
Franklin, John, Sir 82–9

## INDEX

Freud, Sigmund 41, 90
Frye, Northrop 18

Gargery, Joe (*Great Expectations*) xxiv, 13, 16, 146–7
Gay, Walter (*Dombey and Son*) 132–3
Gill, A. A. xiii
Goethe, Johann Wolfgang von 48–9, 91–2, 129; *The Sorrows of Young Werther* 3, 6–7, 14–15, 48, 83, 87 155
Goldsmith, Oliver xv, xix, 2, 4, 6, 21, 45–61, 66, 73–4, 91, 105, 108, 119–20, 134, 151, 159–60; *The Bee* 46, 102; *The Citizen of the World* 46; *Essays* 52; *The Good-Natured Man* 21, 46–7, 49–54, 56–7, 59, 64, 78–9, 95, 140, 143, 146; *She Stoops to Conquer* 49–50, 54–58, 64–5, 79, 147; *The Vicar of Wakefield* 46, 55, 91–5, 98–100, 147
Gradgrind, Thomas (*Hard Times*) 5
Gradgrind, Louisa (*Hard Times*) 72
Graham, Mary (*Martin Chuzzlewit*) 9, 117
Grainger, Edith (*Dombey and Son*) 9, 127, 129, 137
graves xxv, 23, 94, 102, 107–8, 145; *see also* death
*Great Expectations* xvii, 15–16, 146–7

Hallam, Arthur 5
*Hard Times* xvii, 8, 10, 72, 142–4
Havisham, Miss (*Great Expectations*) 147
Hawk, Mulberry, Sir (*Nicholas Nickleby*) 148
Headstone, Bradley (*Our Mutual Friend*) 7, 17, 61, 78–80, 123, 129, 156
heart, the 12–13, 18, 39, 83, 99–102, 110, 118, 142
heart and head xv, xix–xxi, 5, 34, 82–3, 134, 139, 143–4
hero, sentimental xxv, 10, 23, 45, 53–4, 83, 86, 118, 141, 145
heroine, sentimental xviii, xxii, xxiv–xxv, 9, 13, 24–9, 42, 45, 53–4, 57, 60, 63, 85–6, 105–6, 117, 126–34, 138, 140
Hexam, Lizzie (*Our Mutual Friend*) 58

Holcroft, Thomas 3
*Household Words* xx, 71, 84
humour xix, 31–3, 42, 53, 67, 157; definition of 35
Huxley, Aldous 154–5
hypocrisy xv, xxiii, 39–40, 56–7, 64, 73, 92, 117–18, 141, 143

imagination xx, 5, 71, 109
Inchbald, Elizabeth 3, 6–7, 74; *Animal Magnetism* 74–5; *Every One Has His Fault* 74
industrialisation xxiii, 5, 23, 55, 97, 102–3, 106, 130, 142–3, 145, 160
irony xiii–xiv, xxvi, 21, 31–3, 48–50, 52, 56–9, 66–7, 92–4, 100

Jaggers, Mr (*Great Expectations*) 147
Jarndyce, John (*Bleak House*) 21, 59, 79, 147
Jasper, John (*The Mystery of Edwin Drood*) 7, 26, 61
Jefferson, Thomas 31
Jeffrey, Francis, Lord Jeffrey xiii, xxiv, 127, 139, 156–7, 159
Jellyby, Mrs (*Bleak House*) 59
Jo (*Bleak House*) xviii, 41, 101, 141–2
Johnson, Samuel 36, 74, 96
Jonson, Ben: *Every Man in His Humour* 7 4–7
Jowett, Benjamin 121
Joyce, James 114
Jupe, Sissy (*Hard Times*) 5

Keats, John xxv, 83
Keble, John 9
*King Lear* (Shakespeare/Tate/Macready) 7–8, 24, 33, 131
Knowles, James Sheridan 75

Lacan, Jacques 136–7
Lamb, Charles 6, 65–6, 69–74, 101, 119–20, 151; 'Dream Children' 71–2, 108, 144; *Essays of Elia* 70, 72; 'On the Artificial Comedy of the Last Century' 66, 69
Lamb, Mary 71
Lewes, George Henry 5, 152

Lightwood, Mortimer (*Our Mutual Friend*) 78, 84–5
*Little Dorrit* 16, 81, 83, 93, 144–5
Little Nell (Trent) (*The Old Curiosity Shop*) xiii, xxiii, xxv–xxvii, 16, 27, 41–3, 103–9, 118, 139, 147, 155
Locke, John xxii, 15, 32–3, 35–6, 43, 103, 113, 159
London xv, 71, 103, 114, 145, 148, 155
Lytton, Edward Bulwer Lytton, Baron 47, 65; *Money* 47; *Not So Bad As We Seem* 74, 77–81, 90

Macaulay, Thomas Babington 49–50
Mackenzie, Henry 3, 29; *The Man of Feeling* 3
Macready, William Charles 6–8, 16, 18, 30, 47
Magwitch (*Great Expectations*) 13, 16, 114
male friendship 83–5
Manette, Lucie (*A Tale of Two Cities*) 78
Marchioness, The (*The Old Curiosity Shop*) 105
*Martin Chuzzlewit* 94, 110–19, 143
Martineau, Harriet xxv
masculinity 20, 23, 70, 79–80, 82, 137
*Master Humphrey's Clock* 71–2, 122
Mathews, Charles 6, 73, 116; *Used Up* 75
mawk xiv
Maylie, Rose (*Oliver Twist*) 140
melodrama xv, xviii, 2, 26, 118, 156
Meredith, George 42–3, 90; *The Egoist* 64
mesmerism 74–5
Mill, John Stuart 4–5, 15, 152
*Monthly Repository, The* 4–5, 9
Morley, Henry: 'The Lost English Sailors' 84
Morton, Thomas 2: *Speed the Plough* 2
*Mystery of Edwin Drood, The* 26, 95
mystery plays, medieval xix–xx, 1

narrator, sentimental 21–3, 31–6
Nell, Little: *see* Little Nell
*Nicholas Nickleby* xviii, 22–3, 64–5, 92–4, 98–102, 111, 145, 159
Nickleby, Kate (*Nicholas Nickleby*) 67
Nickleby, Mrs (*Nicholas Nickleby*) 61–2
Nickleby, Nicholas (*Nicholas Nickleby*) 5, 23, 84, 123

Nickleby, Ralph (*Nocholas Nickleby*) 5, 42, 92–3, 118
*No Thoroughfare* (Collins/Dickens) 84
novels xvi; eighteenth-century xvi, 4, 19–43; nineteenth-century 91–149
Nubbles, Kit (*The Old Curiosity Shop*) xxiv, 13

*Old Curiosity Shop, The* xiii, 8, 18, 27, 47, 102–9, 111, 122, 143, 155
*Oliver Twist* xxiii, 20, 28–9, 43, 97–8
optimism 18, 23, 153
Otway, Thomas 1–2, 128; *The Orphan* 2; *Venice Preserved* 1–2
*Our Mutual Friend* 43, 58, 75, 78–80, 83–5, 158

Palmer, William (the Rugeley poisoner) xx
Pardiggle, Mrs (*Bleak House*) 152
pathos 1–3, 8, 32
Pecksniff, Mercy (*Martin Chuzzlewit*) xxiii, 117, 139, 141, 156
Pecksniff, Mr (*Martin Chuzzlewit*) xv, 52, 61, 67, 73, 76, 95, 111–17, 141
Pegler, Mrs (*Hard Times*) 143
*Pickwick Papers, The* 95–6, 122
Pickwick, Samuel (*The Pickwick Papers*) 20, 34, 61, 95–6
Pinch, Ruth (*Martin Chuzzlewit*) 114–15, 117–18
Pinch, Tom (*Martin Chuzzlewit*) xxiii, 70, 73, 94, 111–19, 144
Pip (*Great Expectations*) xxiv–xxv, 23, 81, 106
Pipchin, Mrs (*Dombey and Son*) 124
Podsnap, Mr (*Our Mutual Friend*) 81
poetry, Victorian 4–5
'Poor Relation's Story, The' 71
Pope, Alexander 3; *Essay on Criticism* 3
Puccini, Giacomo 133

Quilp, Daniel (*The Old Curiosity Shop*) 27, 104–7

Rabelais, François 37–8
Rachael (*Hard Times*) 143
rationalism, eighteenth-century xvi, 3
realism xv, xix – xx, 28, 101, 130, 139–40
Reynolds, Frederick 2

# INDEX

Richardson, Samuel xxiii–xxiv, 4, 14, 18, 20–21, 24–9, 133, 159; *Clarissa* xxiii–xxv, 4, 18, 24–9; *Pamela* 14
Riderhood, Rogue (*Our Mutual Friend*) 158
Rockingham Castle 47
Romanticism xv, xix–xx, 83, 86–7, 95, 134
Rousseau, Jean-Jacques xviii, xxii, xxv
Ruskin, John 140, 160

*Saturday Review, The* 153
Schiller, Friedrich xxii
sensibility 3–4
sentiment xx, 3, 5, 65–7, 70, 110–11
sentimentalism xiv–xxvii, 1–18; criticism of xiii–xiv, 24, 152–5; definition of 18; 'divided style' of 21, 29, 140, 151, 159; history of xx, 1, 111, 152–60; and irony 50, 94, 105; and nostalgia xxvi, 71–2; and sex xxiii–xxiv, 21, 70, 85–7, 136–7; and utilitarianism 82
sentimentality xiii–xiv, xvii, xx, xxiii–xxiv, 3, 4, 21, 111, 154, 159
Shaftesbury, Anthony Ashley Cooper, Earl of xx, 2–4
Shakespeare, William xxvi, 7–8, 42; *Hamlet* 17, 42; *King Lear* 7–8, 24, 33, 131; *The Winter's Tale* 1
Sheridan, Richard Brinsley xv, xix, 2, 6, 45, 61–7, 73–4, 101, 105, 127, 134, 147, 151–3, 159–60; *The Critic* 47; *The Duenna* 47; *Pizarro* 47; *The Rivals* 47, 61–5; *The School for Scandal* 47–8, 50, 65–6, 69, 73–4, 78, 92, 110–11, 143, 147
Sheridan, Thomas 61
Sikes, Bill (*Oliver Twist*) 118
*Sketches by Boz* 46
Skewton, Mrs (*Dombey and Son*) 39–40, 137
Skimpole, Harold (*Bleak House*) xxiii, 59–61, 67, 141–2
slavery xxv–xxvi
Smallweed, Grandfather (*Bleak House*) 52
Smike (*Nicholas Nickleby*) xxv, 84, 118
Smith, Adam: *The Theory of Moral Sentiments* xx, 2
Smollett, Tobias 19, 118, 152
soap operas ii

social reform xviii, xxv, 108, 152
space, sentimental 98, 102–3
*Spectator, The* 2
Spencer, Herbert 15; *Principles of Psychology* 143
Squeers, Fanny (*Nicholas Nickleby*) 62, 67
Squeers, Wackford (*Nicholas Nickleby*) 62
Steele, Richard xiii, xx, 2, 40, 42, 46, 50, 74, 127, 133; *The Conscious Lovers* 50, 52–3, 63; *The Tender Husband* 24
Sterne, Laurence xix, xxii–xxv, 2, 4, 14, 17, 20, 29–43, 48, 57, 100–101, 114, 126, 133, 151–2, 159; *The Beauties of Sterne* 31, 38; *Letters* 40; *A Sentimental Journey* 34–40, 94, 130; *Tristram Shandy* xxiv, 29–40, 42, 130
Summerson, Esther (*Bleak House*) 57, 59
Swinburne, Algernon 106
Swiveller, Dick (*The Old Curiosity Shop*) 104, 106, 148

Taine, Hippolyte 154
*Tale of Two Cities, A* 75, 90, 122, 130, 145–6
Talfourd, Thomas 71
Tapley, Mark (*Martin Chuzzlewit*) 147
Tate, Nahum 7–8, 24
*Tatler, The* 2
tears xiii, xvi–xvii, xxii, xxiv, xxvi–xxvii, 1, 4, 7, 9, 14–15, 24, 27–8, 87–8, 92–3, 98, 100, 102–3, 115, 123, 134, 138, 141, 146, 151, 155–7, 159
Ternan, Ellen 81, 88
Ternan, Maria 88
Thackeray, William Makepeace xxiv, 30–31, 43, 49, 74, 92, 105, 127, 151, 153, 160; *Vanity Fair* 149
Toodle, Polly (*Dombey and Son*) 137–8
Toots, Mr (*Dombey and Son*) 130
Twist, Oliver (*Oliver Twist*) 16, 129

*Uncommercial Traveller, The* 73
utilitarianism xxiii, 10, 15, 82

Varden, Dolly (*Barnaby Rudge*) 57
Voltaire, François-Marie Arouet 41–2

weeping: *see* tears
Weller, Sam (*The Pickwick Papers*) 76

Wemmick, Mr (*Great Expectations*) 73
*Westminster Review, The* 9–10
Wickfield, Agnes (*David Copperfield*) 9
Wilberforce, William xxv
Wilde, Oscar xiii, 13; *The Picture of Dorian Gray* 13
Wilfer, Bella (*Our Mutual Friend*) 58
wit 20, 58–8, 67, 79, 145–6, 148
Wittgenstein, Ludwig 18

Woodcourt, Alan (*Bleak House*) 141–2
Woolf, Virginia 121, 154–5
Wopsle, Mr (*Great Expectations*) 75
Wordsworth, William xxii, 70–71, 105
Wrayburn, Eugene (*Our Mutual Friend*) 58, 61, 75, 78–80, 84–5, 147–8
Wren, Jenny (*Our Mutual Friend*) 147
Wright, Thomas: *The Passions of the Mind in General* 17

www.ingramcontent.com/pod-product-compliance
Lightning Source LLC
Chambersburg PA
CBHW021827300426
44114CB00009BA/354